AFTER SUNDAY

"Focused on the everyday life of the laity, this engaging, well-written book fills a surprising but real gap on the theological spectrum. Pointing out that faith is exercised not only on Sunday morning or in clerical councils, it promotes secular work as a Christian vocation just as important as ecclesiastical ministry. Mining a religious vein that sees such work as a godly activity, it recognizes and valorizes as religiously significant the daily work that most people do—mechanics, dieticians, plumbers, homemakers, etc. The author has a wonderful way of describing the nitty-gritty of various professions. And his argument delves deeper than ethics and spirituality in the workplace to the foundation stone of creating and the ongoing presence of the Trinitarian God in the world. Original, refreshing, and encouraging in this hour of the laity."

—Elizabeth A. Johnson, author of *Truly Our Sister:*
A Theology of Mary in the Communion of Saints

After Sunday

A THEOLOGY OF WORK

Armand Larive

continuum
NEW YORK • LONDON

2004

The Continuum International Publishing Group Inc
15 East 26th Street, New York NY 10010

The Continuum International Publishing Group Ltd
The Tower Building, 11 York Road, London SE1 7NX

Library of Congress Cataloging-in-Publication Data

Larive, Armand.
    After Sunday : a theology of work / by Armand Larive.
      p. cm.
    Includes bibliographical references.
    ISBN 0-8264-1585-7 (alk. paper) — ISBN 0-8264-1591-1 (pbk. : alk. paper)
    1. Work—Religious aspects—Christianity. I. Title.
BT738.5.L29 2004
261.8'5--dc22
                                    2003024103

for
David

Contents

Acknowledgments

SOMETIMES LIFE'S THEATER CURTAIN goes down and when it comes back up again, everything looks different. That's what happened to me when I read Charles Y. Glock's *To Comfort or to Challenge*. I began to think much more widely about the great variety of working people, the importance of what they do, and how poorly it is honored by the church. After stealing time where I could over a number of years, I was able to make this book a reality.

Along the way I have become indebted to many people, whom I now wish to thank. Chief among them are the various folk who have shared work experiences with me in ordinary laboring contexts of a railway switchyard, wheat harvest, food processing, construction, teaching, and the like. Even more important was the support given me during an extended stint in graduate school by my wife, Ruby, and sons, Brett and Andrew. I am also grateful to my parish of St. James, in Pullman, Washington, for giving me extra time on this project. Especially encouraging were secretaries Catherine Ritchie, Alison Mixter, and fellow writer, Kirsten Peters. I thank my seminary, Bexley Hall, for a Rossiter scholarship, and for library assistance from Vancouver School of Theology and Washington State University. Other thanks go to Professor Douglas Meeks of Vanderbilt, who plowed through an earlier version, and editor Jeff Gainey, for persuading me to make considerable revisions. Finer corrections came with help from John Kevern, Dean of Bexley Hall, and the hard work of Continuum editor Frank Oveis, and copyeditors Maurya Horgan and Paul Kobelski of the Scriptorium in Denver.

Introduction

GETTING OUT OF BED is a religious act. A homemaker in Cleveland gets up to fix breakfast for her husband and two daughters. A utility district lineman in Yakima is called out of bed to locate a downed power line. In Phoenix, a company of firemen rise to a 3:00 A.M. alarm. Somewhere in the Dakotas, a truck driver rouses himself from a rest stop and starts back down the interstate. A neurologist in Birmingham is up by 5:00 A.M. so she can be at the hospital to assist in surgery by 7:00.

Getting up can be the most important de facto religious act because it betrays a primary meaning people give themselves for facing the day, a commitment to family, a manifold of obligations, but particularly to work. It is a religious act because losing a job brings not only a severe spiritual crisis of having a big part of one's raison d'être jerked away but also a feeling of being torn from ordinary human transactions, of not being needed, of deflated self-worth. People out of work find it difficult to rise and shine.

Of course many jobs are, in Studs Terkel's words, "too small for the human spirit"; they can provide only a marginally living wage and come with a tyrannical boss, excessive hours, or a glass ceiling. Furthermore, there is hardly any occupation that doesn't have its toilsome aspects. No one is blamed for finding some features of an occupation irksome or boring. Despite all this, many people approach their work sincerely, with commitment, as if to gain "honors" rather than just a "pass" by their efforts.[1]

Because people's occupations often center life's meaning so powerfully, does that mean they are bending the knee in de facto obeisance to secular gods, kingdoms, and morals of a workaday world, saving only Sundays for Christian activity? What does the church say to someone who is out in the world of commerce and industry, someone whose Christian vocation seems challenged by service to idols of mammon? Typically, the church's response is a palliative suggestion that one's job can be a springboard for kindness toward others, a platform for keeping the Ten Commandments, an opportunity to

1

make a witness, a location for a ministry of presence, or a context from which arrow prayers may be shot. This message implies that, while so-called secular careers have some value as a service to others, they possess no inherent value in their own right.

But what about the welder who believes welding per se is his Christian activity? What about the homemaker who believes she shares a personal delight with God in a good cheese soufflé? Would it be possible that God motivates the engineer who works on fuel cells or sustains a man who collects garbage? Could it be that the knack for finding good teaching methods is not just hard work but also the prompting and gift giving of the Holy Spirit? Could the promise of Christ be part of what motivates the designer who wants to improve sewage disposal?

Mother Teresa's followers are deservedly lauded for their ministry to the dying. Should there be equal praise for the marginal life of migrant workers who thin our carrots and sugar beets? George Herbert is renowned as a country parson and poet. Might not George Sturt be of equal standing as a village wagon maker, expositor, and tradesman? Are not all of these equally cases of godly work?[2]

It is the thesis of this book that these questions should have an affirmative answer. There are many Christians in the working world who either believe, or *should believe,* that the Holy Trinity is involved with them primarily in their work itself. If this is the case, then there is a rich theological vein to be mined in the way God is present with workaday activity.

Unfortunately, the Christian church has a voracious appetite to keep itself going as an institution, creating a myopia that makes it difficult to see and consider a theology outside its gates. There are, however, many Christians in the "secular" world who strongly believe that they are indeed engaged in godly activity. They make vigorous complaints about the institutional church's[3] blithe way of ignoring whatever connections might be made between the Christian faith and the workaday world where these same laypeople devote most of their lives.[4] Indeed, when pronouncements are made regarding some secular state of affairs, the church often leaps over the wisdom and expertise of an already involved laity or else gives only negative guidance on what not to do. Quoting Roman Catholic historian David O'Brien:

> . . . in their working lives the laity find themselves detached from [the church]. This detachment results no more from their ignoring the church than from the Church ignoring them. Until the Church leaders learn—or care to learn—to affirm the secular lives of the laity . . . the church will not assist the political culture to face matters of war, abortion and injustice, nor contribute anything more to the nation than resounding *no's.*[5]

On the other hand, some related topics have been pursued. Liberation theology, for example, with its emphasis on work as praxis, is certainly a yeomanly applied understanding of the faith.[6] There is also an increasing amount of attention given by Christians to specialized fields of ethics, such as medical, business, environmental, and legal ethics. European Catholic countries have experience with Christian labor and political movements. In the history of the Catholic tradition, there is the Benedictine attempt to bridge soulful transcendence with manual labor under the teaching *ora et labora,* "pray and work," describing an inherent harmony between work and prayer.[7] And from the Protestant side, there is Max Weber's thesis crediting Calvinistic strains within Protestantism as the impetus for those workers who founded modern capitalism and the efficiency of mechanized industry.[8]

Nevertheless, today's Christians—who are homemakers, sell insurance, service automobiles, work on assembly lines, devise computer programs, find themselves in the echelons of middle management or at some other station in the weekday working world—have little idea or guidance as to whether their work constitutes a genuine Christian ministry. Indeed, many believers would find such a suggestion quite strange. A public school teacher, for example, might think she has a "ministry" if she were teaching church school, but she sees the purpose of her daily job as outside the purview of the church and therefore not part of her ministry. Barbara Brown Zikmund has summed up the confusion this way:

> The four ways we tell serious Christians to live out their vocation are either simplistic and shallow, or they are so demanding that people pale at the task. At the risk of caricature, we insist that an authentic understanding of Christian vocation: (1) has little to do with our jobs, (2) has something to do with all jobs, (3) has more to do with certain jobs, (4) or has everything to do with on-the-job and off-the-job existence. No wonder good Christians get confused.[9]

Zikmund's observation betrays a lack of commitment toward instruction in theology of work at the level where pastoral church leaders get their training. One can search seminary academic catalogues in vain for any such course offerings. There is also an inherent difficulty in spanning the chasm between theologically articulate and academically credentialed church people, on the one side, and, on the other side, those who have jobs in the "secular" world where the church has no credentials and little expertise. Consequently, professional preaching and instruction at the congregational level tend to focus on private personal piety and morals, institutional church needs, biblical texts, sacred traditions, and infrequent forays into broad social issues. Of course, when asked, clergy will say that bringing one's faith to the workplace is a necessary part of Christian living, and there are a number of mostly "lite" popular books with suggestions about how this should be done,[10] some of them sincere efforts of the laity. But there is little in the way of a systematic theological assault on the topic.

The purpose of this book is to explore the question more deeply. I assume that there is godly activity within the secular working world that is of equal, or even more, merit than that of the ecclesiastical world. This work is considered *cocreative* with God. It assumes that good work is often animated with a holy vigor well known to working people, a vigor that can be called out of working people just as Socrates called principles of geometry out of a slave boy in the *Meno*. This innately known vigor of working people centers on what God is like, and what responsibilities are given to the creativity of humans. This knowledge, which working people seem to possess innately, can be articulated in the way work is served by the Trinity. There is, in other words, a very familiar aspect to work that can be related respectively to the Father/Mother, the Son, and the Holy Spirit.

There are, however, some firewalls in ecclesiastical and theological tradition that obstruct the theological honor work ought to have. There are also some theological categories that must be changed in order to give a theology of work its necessary logical space. These are the tasks this book will undertake.

It is not, however, the case that this book navigates wholly uncharted waters. There are other useful efforts in this theological path. From the ecclesiastical side, the papal encyclical *Laborem exercens* uses the doctrine of creation and cocreativity as a framework. This book will use the same premise. *Laborem* owes quite a bit to preceding works by the French personalists Jacques Maritain and Emmanuel Mounier.[11] Beginning in the 1930s, Robert Calhoun made an important effort to connect the faith with common life from a Protestant perspective.[12] A small blossoming of effort appeared in the 1950s and 1960s, and other significant work in the late 1980s and early 1990s.[13] The insights of Douglas Meeks and Miroslav Volf will be especially important here.[14] Nevertheless, the topic has never broken through to the level of a common course offering in seminaries in the way, for instance, that the topic of science and religion has lately emerged in books and theological study.

In the meantime, a considerable vacuum still exits among those looking for a spiritual dimension in work. This vacuum is being supplied *outside theology* mostly by consultants in the area of business management, who have now become gurus of spirituality. They offer a mélange of spiritual remedies, Buddhist teachings, science, and new age inspirations. Publishers are producing their books like sausages.[15] Deepak Chopra and Stephen Covey's writings sell in the million-dollar range. As business understands it, "spirituality" means "access to a sacred force that impels life," promoting creativity, inner power, stability, drive, and openness to others. It can be possessed as an attribute without benefit of "organized religion," so that business people will say "I'm a very spiritual person, but I'm not religious."[16] It's a sense of spirituality making no strong claims on an ascetic commitment. It starts with an assurance that life is basically okay, and aims toward a personal success that will help one's company succeed, while glossing over any significant attention to the power of evil.

If a sound but effective theologically based spirituality of work could be bottled, it might seem that there would be a vast market for it. But only evangelical right-wing Christian expressions can be sanguine enough to believe that serving God in daily work brings with it a showy material prosperity and a completely contented soul. On the other hand, mainline church attitudes toward the world of business don't do any better by bending in another direction toward obscurantism. Many clergy tend to carry a deep suspicion that servants of business are servants of mammon. They are uneasy with the taint of "filthy lucre" even if there are business people in their pews whose activities lend solvency to their church's own financial position.[17] While the stresses of the workaday world can bring burnout, fear, moral ambiguity, depression, and a hunger for deeper meaning in life, these and other pressures operate within the structures of mammon, unfamiliar and suspiciously disdained by clergy, who tend to respond in a counseling mode that focuses on a happiness that is not coordinated with secular systemic causes.[18] A therapy of adjustment is used rather than trying to change the problem's origin.[19]

So if there is a rich theological vein to be mined implicit in the devotion that people give to their work, it is certainly neglected. The oddity of this negligence is only reinforced when other disciplinary alliances are considered. There is, for example, a sociology of work, a history of work, an ethics of work (business ethics), a psychology of work, an economics of work (labor economics), a management of work. Each of these amalgamations, and others like them, has its own experts, its own academic credentials, its own books and journals. But there are no journals, few (if any) specialists, few publications, and only rare academic course offerings in theology of work.

Theology of work, per se, also has difficulty getting launched because two different and worthy sidetracks immediately offer themselves when the subject of "work" is broached. One sidetrack is "spirituality of work," appealing in part because "spirituality" is a trendy concept made more pressing by the plethora of nonreligious spiritualities now being promoted. But a Christian spirituality of work also has a venerable tradition because it is possible to express and refresh a contemplative attitude in an active occupation. It takes a prayerful or meditative attitude toward work so that all is done with a subjective intention of glorifying God and serving others through work. This is part of the Benedictine rule of "pray and work," or Brother Lawrence with his pots and pans. Venerable as it may be, this spirituality doesn't provide a full expression that would be available if it were backed by a theology of work. A contemplative attitude might redirect the thoughts of a pipe fitter while at his job, but it doesn't address the basic issue of why pipe fitting, as such, is theologically significant.

The other sidetrack, equally appealing, goes off into the morality of work. Who can resist being drawn into moral questions of workplace fairness: the plight of the working poor or the unemployed? What about business ethics? What should a person do when she feels compromised or bored by her job? What about unjust economic systems? Such questions come naturally to mind, but they can easily lead one away from examining work as a theological concept. Conferences billed as "theology of work" often turn out to be nothing more than discussions of workplace ethics.

This book is meant for a readership already having some familiarity with theology and looking for a more thoroughgoing study of the topic of work on the model of Jeremiah's call: to "tear down and build up." It will tear down barriers that keep worldly work from being a holy calling and will build up a theological structure that can be found implicitly in the working world. However, since a theology of work cannot wholly succeed without questions of ethics and spirituality, the book will also investigate foundational questions regarding the spiritual and moral issues of work.

The concept "work" will be considered mostly as a remunerated activity, or one that would have to be paid if it couldn't be gotten for free. Homemaking falls into this latter category, as do a wide variety of volunteer services. But "work" is not a well-bounded concept. Even if not remunerated, but costly instead, student life is a form of work. There are also many hobbies and leisurely pursuits that require a strong work ethic. Even games and competitions can require work. Athletes, for instance, are praised if they have a "good work ethic." The concept is difficult to delineate, but does stay within a family resemblance most people can recognize.

Again let it be noted that the geography of standard theological doctrines will have difficulty accommodating the theology of work being posed here. Some serious tectonic shifts are required to make theological room for work. The first three chapters attempt to make these adjustments: first, as teachings about work adjust the doctrine of God; second, with regard to the genuine—but worldly—vocations as part of doing godly work; and third, as various doctrines need revision in order to reexamine the secular working world of Christian life.

These revisions set the stage for more positive suggestions about the meaning of work centered on the Trinity. Each person of the Trinity is the basis of a chapter using Miroslav Volf's distinction of the Son as *eschatological,* the Father/Mother as *protological,* and the Spirit as *pneumatological.*[20] A following chapter attempts to explain what "good" and "godly work" means and continues with more practical matters of ecclesiology,[21] liturgy, and the calling of the laity, whose work invests them with the primary identity of the church. This chapter serves some foundational issues theology can offer to a spirituality and an ethics of work. Then a concluding chapter offers a systematic summary of the book.

The book is meant to be provocative, written with appreciation of what has gone before, together with the hope that more will be studied, discussed, written, and refined in this yet not well explored nor mature area of theology.

1

Work and the Image of God

THIS CHAPTER HAS THREE PARTS. First, there are biblical teachings about work, its ambivalence and sustenance. The sustenance of God witnesses to the grace of God toward human work and, hence, to the image of God. Second, contributions from feminist theology have strong connections to women's growing participation in the workforce and the consequent ways that labor has been rethought and restructured. Feminist contributions to the doctrine of God can be shown to dovetail nicely with biblical teachings about the sustenance of God. Third, there are a variety of ways work has been devalued in Christian tradition. These devaluations display an implicit doctrine of God that is not accommodative toward work.

SOME BIBLICAL TEACHINGS ABOUT WORK

Work's Ambivalence

If word derivation reflects the accumulation of human wisdom over time, then many terms for work give the task a gloomy view: *labor* comes from the Latin *labor,* meaning "drudgery," "toil," "hardship," or "suffering." Similarly, there is a burdensome connotation for *travail,* as in the biblical "Come unto me all ye that travail and are heavy laden. . . ." The word seems to derive from the Latin *tripalium,* a three-pronged instrument of torture, possibly a prod. *Occupation* comes from *occupare,* "to seize hold and grapple." The middle high German *arbeit* meant "trouble" or "toil." The Slavic *rabota* (cousin to the English "robot") means "servitude." In Greek, *ponos,* the word for "work," also serves for "pain." Aristotle writes of a class of craftsmen and menial laborers, *banausoi,* whose work has a verbal counterpart, *banausotechneo,* or *banausourgeo,* and an adjective, *banausos,* meaning "base," or "vulgar."[1] Aristotle argued that such people are not worthy of citizenship, making it likely that they were mostly slaves.² And Plato, speaking through Callicles, states that "you would not wish to give your daughter in marriage" to the son of such a person.³

The dismal connotation of "toil," however, reflects only one side of the active life. Embedded in language-derived wisdom is a distinction found in many languages between *labor*, as toiling for subsistence, and *work*, which is valued for being worthwhile. In French, the distinction is carried by *travailler* and *ouvrier*; in German by *Arbeit* and *Werk*; in Latin by *laborare* and *facere*, in Greek by *ponos* and *ergon*. Among these pairs, the second terms, *work, Werk, ouvrier,* and *ergon,* lack the odious implication of drudgery.

A similar ambivalence occurs in Hebrew, where ʿ*ebed*, "servant" or "slave," has the same consonants as ʿ*abad*, "work." This dual character can be found in biblical foundation myths, notably in Genesis 2:4b–3:24. Working and serving God can both apply at the same time. Even before disobediently eating the fruit of the tree of knowledge, while still in an Edenic prelapsarian state, it is Adam's responsibility to "till and care for the land" (2:15). Here Adam obviously serves God, only partly working for himself, tending a garden he has not planted.

The ʿ*abad* of Adam also seems to imply some participation in creation, since Adam names the beasts and birds, reviewing them jointly with God as possible helpmates until a satisfactory mate is formed from Adam's rib. Cooperation is implied also at the opening of the story, where there are not even weeds on the earth, in part because God had not yet supplied rain, but also because there was not "any man to till the soil." In the story, there are three contrasted states of nature: one of weeds and wilderness, one of Eden, and one of cultivated land. Weeds and wilderness seem to appear as unwanted intruders into land that Adam attempts to cultivate. When Adam and Eve are expelled from Eden, the land is cursed such that Adam will suffer to get his food from it, yielding "brambles and thistles" (2:18). Expelled from Eden, where his work would have been much easier and free of weeds, Adam now works the ground from which he came: "by the sweat of your brow shall you eat your bread, until you return to the soil as you were taken from it" (2:19). So it is the condition and the environment, not the work itself, that is cursed.

Throughout the story, the word for "ground," "soil," or "land" is the same and a close cognate of "Adam," making it clear that Adam's role (he is taken from the ground to work the ground and return to the ground) is subservient to that of the Creator. Adam is constituted of little more than soil and must not overreach his status. Nevertheless, there is a workmanlike mutual respect implied by this story. Yahweh is dismayed at the disobedience, but provides Adam and Eve with clothing and declares that they "have become like one of us, with knowledge of good and evil" (2:22). But Adam still remains what he was before, the tiller of the soil, only now there is a slight Promethean twist, as the two have chosen for themselves what, where, and how they will plant, and how they will live. They have traded an Edenic life of easy work for knowledge and independence. But they remain co-workers with Yahweh, because Yahweh continues to provide the water. Nor does Adam create the plants he cultivates. Adam and Eve have some independence, but they still remain participants in the created order.

In his summary of the story, Göran Agrell finds the meaning of "work" to be ambivalent: it is partly toil, but it is partly service to God in creation. It has a double character. In Eden, Adam "tilled and cared for" the creation; the sustenance of Adam and Eve was provided. Now Adam must toil for his maintenance from a resisting earth, and Eve will have pain in childbirth, implying a toilsome role for her as well. They take over part of what had been God's work. Still, the Creator's work and humanity's disobedience exist together in the present. They are not artifacts of prehistory, but continue in tension. Humans may have sovereignty over creation (Gen. 1:28–31) and serve God by tilling, harvesting, and husbanding the gifts of God, but humans can, by overweening pride and ambition, perform work contrary to and ruinous of the created order, asserting themselves to "be like God."[4]

Sustenance

Work also provides a sustenance that is not merely bodily nutrition but also spiritual food. This comes in the awareness that the struggle for maintenance of life is not without godly assistance. Indeed, worthwhile work is never done alone. Psalm 127:1–2 illustrates this teaching:

> If Yahweh does not build the house,
>   in vain the masons toil;
> if Yahweh does not guard the city,
>   in vain the sentries watch.
>
> In vain you get up earlier,
>   and put off going to bed,
> sweating to make a living,
>   since he provides for his beloved as they sleep.

One may take the interpretative key to be given in the last line. It seems to say that those whom Yahweh loves are also given provision without need to work. But the meaning is that God labors even when his beloved ones sleep. The best biblical illustration of God's labor is agricultural: some things are done by people, but other things are done by God. God supplies the water, as noted earlier. But God is also at work during that time most critical, and most out of human control—gestation, when the seeds, having been planted, lie in the ground, and it is uncertain what sort of stand they will make. The gestation phase of agriculture is wholly in God's hands (Isa. 55:10). In the parable of the seed growing silently (Mark 4:26–29), the farmer plants the seed, and then little more can be done except to wait: "night and day, while he sleeps, and when he is awake," the seed is germinating. But it is not the farmer who makes it sprout. A similar teaching lies behind 1 Corinthians 3:7–9, where Paul uses plant gestation as an analogy for missionary work:

> I did the planting, Apollos did the watering, but God made things grow. Neither the planter nor the waterer matters; only God, who makes things grow. . . . We are fellow workers with God. . . .

Hence, the sustenance is found not entirely in the fruits of labor but also in a cooperative production of that labor. The beloved one can rest confident that the Creator continues with a helping, sustaining role. There is a grace present in the worker's effort, so that the mason of Psalm 127 cannot say it was *he alone* who built the house, nor can the sentries say that thanks *solely to them* the city was safely guarded.[5]

This cooperative nature of work, implied by both physical and spiritual sustenance, is the basis for a number of other teachings regarding work. If God and people work together, then the work must be ethical. According to Leviticus 26 and Deuteronomy 28, God blesses the work of those who follow his commandments and curses the work of those who don't. God produces rain at the right time so that the people can "thresh until vintage time and gather grapes until sowing time." They shall "eat their fill of bread and live secure in their land." There will be "fruit of body, soil, and livestock. Kneading trough and bread bin will be blessed," as will barns and all undertakings. And the converse will occur when people disobey God's laws: their efforts are cursed.

Sustenance and the Image of God

The sustaining work of God sounds a much deeper note of care, liberation, and equality in terms of the primal and ongoing created order. Dorothee Soelle (following Claus Westermann) interprets the opening story of creation in Genesis (1:1–2:4a) as purposely counterpoised against Babylonian creation myths. During the exile, the Israelites would have become well acquainted with Sumerian-Babylonian beliefs that in the beginning of the world there was inordinate chaos while many gods fought and vied for power. Eventually the strongest god subdued the others and became king. The vanquished gods were pressed into the king's service as his court and stripped of their independence. As time went by, these lesser deities became enervated by the increasing demands of this "sacred" king. They convened to resolve the problem and ultimately decided to create a servant for themselves. This servant was the first human being.[6]

In Babylonian beliefs, astral objects such as the sun, moon, and prominent stars were identified with various ranks of sky gods, who in fact populated not the sky but the king's court. Heavenly objects thereby gave an astral pedigree and hierarchy to the king and his retinue. In the Israelite version, by contrast, the stars, moon, and sun are simply objects of creation, set in the sky to provide light for day and night. And humans (as represented by Adam and Eve) are all of a single class and equally made in the image of God.

Meanwhile, God, unlike a resident king, is not to be identified with any specific aspect of creation. Instead of living in leisure while subjugating the underlings, the God of Israel assumes the role of a worker. This role has been felicitously expressed by Douglas Meeks as the one who creates and sustains "households." The operational term is the Greek *oikos* or the Hebrew *bayit*, and Meeks takes his lead from Paul's description of the *oikonomia tou theou*, the "management of the household of God" (Col. 1:25; cf. 1 Cor. 9:17; Eph. 3:2; 1 Tim. 1:4), and the notion of God's covenant with Israel as the constructor and guardian of the "house of Israel" (e.g., 2 Sam. 12:8; Pss. 98:3; 115:12; Isa. 63:7; Jer. 31:31; 33:14). The work of God as manager extends to the earth as an amalgam of households where God's wish is that people have reasonable access to life, where other creatures can also flourish, and where justice and peace can prevail. In this way, Meeks derives an ethical basis for work: God works in the various households of the creation, bidding humanity not only to cooperate but to do so within the context of fairness and justice, calling humans to a working environment that—as much as possible—affords meaningful work for everyone. The action of God is not automatic, nor impositional, but seeks to accomplish its purposes often through the action of love, which is sometimes perceived as weakness. The vocation of the ʿ*ebed Yahweh*, the "servant of God," in Isaiah 53 not only is an excellent example of the work of God but applies especially to Christ's own vocation.

The Greek word *oikonomia*, of course, is the progenitor of the modern word *economy* and, as with household relations and management, connotes a complexity most certainly present in the interdependent affairs of a modern economy. In any case, a God who works on behalf of creation is a strikingly different conception from the image of a God who achieves everything by fiat. Nothing about the image of God as "householder" is meant to connote the image of the *paterfamilias* as an idle and fearful potentate whose house (creation) is his castle, and whose sovereign will must be obeyed on pain of punishment. Feminist theology has greatly helped disabuse believers of the image of God as potentate.

THE IMPACT OF WOMEN ON WORK:
FEMINIST THEOLOGY AND THE IMAGE OF GOD

Probably the most important contributions to theology in the latter part of the twentieth century have come from feminist theologians, especially their influence on the image or doctrine of God. Much of the fruit of their efforts originates in the debates about sameness and difference regarding gender and sexual identity and the way labor management has evolved—or failed to evolve—at work both inside and outside the home.

Gender and sexual identity are slippery concepts and often get mixed together. It will be important here to acknowledge that they have different meanings. *Gender* will gather those attributes of men or women that are socially constructed, while *sex* will encompass those traits that are physically different, like physiognomy, pregnancy, birth, and lactation, plus possible neural characteristics.[7] Admittedly, sometimes the borderline between sex and gender is difficult to mark, as will become apparent a little further on.

Gender and the Sameness/Difference Debate

In the Victorian era, women were generally considered the "weaker vessel," not just physically but given to emotion rather than rational thought, easily susceptible to sexual temptation and therefore in need of masculine protection. In most of the twentieth century, a "Snow White" or "Sleeping Beauty" version of feminine development was promoted. For example, Sigmund Freud explains that at puberty, boys acquire a strong libido, while, in girls, libido is greeted by a "fresh wave of repression," compelling a girl to submit to "the fact of her castration," constituting a "wound to her narcissism" that develops "like a scar, a sense of inferiority." With Erik Erikson, boys, at puberty, go through a multistage process in order to overcome a crisis of self-esteem until they master some skill that they and others will acknowledge as suitable for a viable and independent adulthood. A girl, however, holds her identity in abeyance preparing to attract a man, whose name she will take for her identity and thereby fill her "lonely space" with a recognition that will rescue her from her loneliness. Similarly, Bruno Bettleheim takes puberty to be a time when male identity is won; he uses coming-of-age stories for boys that have to do with testing and hardship, while female identity must attach itself to masculinity and seek self-understanding through that relationship. He cites masculine stories of father–son conflict, where the son must become free of paternalism and struggle to find his own way of bringing value to the social order and individual esteem to himself. In contrast, at puberty, girls go into an involuted, repressed stage, waiting for a young man to find them and give them an identity, as in the stories of Snow White and Sleeping Beauty.[8]

The idea that women find their gender role only when they manage to submit themselves to a masculine schema, however, runs into disagreement. In 1964, in a conference at MIT sponsored by the Association of Women Students, keynote speaker Bruno Bettelheim stated that "we must start with the realization that, as much as women want to be good scientists or engineers, they want first and foremost to be womanly companions of men and to be mothers." The closing speaker, Erik Erikson warmly agreed, even though the intervening women speakers strongly disagreed, some arguing that, as a way of life, marriage was overrated.[9]

In the meantime, Betty Friedan's *Feminine Mystique* promoted liberation for housewives:

> "What do I do?" . . . Why nothing. I'm just a housewife. . . . I begin to feel I have no personality. I'm a server of food and a putter-on of pants and a bedmaker, somebody who can be called on when you want something. But who am I? . . . I just don't feel alive."[10]

Friedan contended that women could perform almost any occupation traditionally reserved for men and would lack full status and identity until such opportunities were available. Her view represents the *sameness* side of the sameness/difference debate, arguing that women in the workplace are just as capable as men. And there is no doubt that this thinking influenced a growing number of women to take jobs outside their homes.[11] The chance for women to find creditable positions in traditionally male-dominated fields is uneven but improving.[12]

On the other hand, Carol Gilligan argues that there is an inherent *difference* between men and women. Women are less inclined to approach problems aggressively, are more relational than confrontational, inclined to find ways to compromise and accommodate other points of view instead of vanquishing them, preferring cooperation over competition, seeking to nurture rather than demand. Even though these qualities may make them seem inferior when measured against a masculine schema, Gilligan insists that women are not inferior, only different.[13]

Ideal Worker and Domestic Partner

The sameness/difference gender debate is really a description of what Joan Williams calls two societal "force fields": that of the sole provider, bread-winner, or "ideal worker," on the one hand, and the domestic partner, on the other. Seemingly feminist attributes like sensitivity, tenderness, inclination toward relational problem solving, and self-sacrifice are part of a vortex in the force field of domestic caregiving. They serve as the opposite side of the gen-der coin, making it possible for the other partner to enter the marketplace of outside work unencumbered by domestic obligations. This partner is given more masculine attributes as breadwinner, set up by a social force field now a couple of centuries old. Joan Scott and Louise Tilly make a convincing case that these gender biases can be traced back to the industrial revolution. They claim that the work of men and women was originally oriented within a "fam-ily economy," where every member was required to work in order to con-tribute. Americans naturally think of subsistence farming as an example. But there were also landless proletarian families, in which all had to contribute by wage labor in whatever way they could: women and children engaged in "putting out" labor in their home, such as lace making or other piecework, while men worked in factories or in some other endeavor outside the home. Under these harsh conditions, the family unit took priority over any single member, especially children, who could be shipped off to work elsewhere.

Gradually the family economy became more dependent on a breadwinner, almost always the husband's role—who would go out into the world of com-merce and industry and wrest a living from it for the family. The amount of support the breadwinner could provide, of course, became a measure of mas-culinity. The family remained a family economy, but more in the sense of a consumer economy, and the concept of wage labor became detached from family. Wage labor took on an "ideal" sense: the ideal wage laborer was one who could accept the hours and responsibilities of a job without any familial encumbrance. This was made possible by a flow of domestic support at home.[14]

Thus, according to Nancy Cott, the work of women became "task oriented," while men were "time oriented," a distinction that may explain the saying "Man works from sun to sun, but a woman's work is never done." But Cott thinks that the woman's job was a sign of success because only one person was needed to support the family, and it became the wife's job to supply the comforts of home, hearth, and children, a sanctuary and a *cri de coeur* against the harsh demands of work and marketplace.[15]

The Effect of the Paradigm of the Ideal Worker on Working Women Today

The gender distinctions, or force fields, between ideal worker and domestic partner are not as entrenched now as they have been in recent years, but they are still strong. Strange and cavalier as it may be, assumptions about available work almost invariably include women in the same ideal worker envelope with men. Men and women are assessed on a par under the canon of the "ideal worker," and if a woman wishes to have a career, it is assumed that any family encumbrances are her problem and not the concern of the employer. Thus, she must be free to take assignments that could involve travel, overtime, extra training, or relocation. If a woman has children or family encumbrances, it will be very difficult for her to avoid the vortex of domesticity, and she may have to accede to that role, giving up her career.[16] This is falsely expressed in the rhetoric of "choice," regarded in somewhat the same way as Henry David Thoreau's having chosen to live at Walden Pond: a peculiar but voluntary submission. It follows—according to this strange way of thinking—that the disadvantaged position of women is something they themselves have chosen. For Thoreau, there were viable alternative paths open, while for women with children and an ideal-worker husband needing domestic backup, the choice to continue a career isn't as viable. Friedan and others who urge women to have careers and families with children have been too sanguine or superficial about the reality of a husband's insistence on continuing in his role as ideal worker. Moreover, support systems such as childcare centers and other services have not been adequate to allow wives to become ideal workers.[17]

Many wives, nevertheless, are forced to find outside work to bolster family income: about 70 percent among middle-class white families, and even more among minorities.[18] But women come home from outside work and take on what Arlie Hochschild calls a "second shift" of domestic duties.[19] Women still do 80 percent of the childcare in the United States, and two-thirds of the housework.[20] Hence, women find themselves leading dual lives, as domestic support caregivers and also ersatz ideal workers. The domestic gender image, however, also often follows them into their ideal worker aspirations, because most women are marginalized into lower-wage jobs and end up in the "pink collar ghetto." Even when they have jobs that require equal skill, studies of "comparable worth" reveal pay inequities.[21] Furthermore, women who are not the chief breadwinners receive short shrift when it comes to divorce.[22]

Thus, despite substantial gains among women in the workforce, the standard expectation of an ideal worker persists. Even when companies implement worker-friendly measures like time-sharing, flex-time, on-site day care, reduced hours, maternity leave, and the like, they are underutilized. People who choose to work within these family-friendly structures are often marginalized as lacking in dedication to the company and being indifferent to their career interests because they have "chosen" to devote a significant portion of their time to their families.[23] Hochschild cites the example of Eileen, a ceramics engineer, working as much as seventy hours some weeks. She asked to cut back her time to 60 percent after her first child was born, thinking that another engineer could take up the slack. But even though Eileen excelled at her job, her boss couldn't conceive of her as a part-timer. In the boss's view, part-time was like slicing something away from the whole, and therefore deficient for any person sincerely invested in a career.

> He said to me, "Eileen, I don't know how to do part time. My experience is that people who put in the hours are the ones who succeed." I said, "Measure my results." He replied, "No. It doesn't work that way. What matters is how much time you put into the job, the volume of work."[24]

The Larger Effect of the Ideal Worker Paradigm

Thus, the paradigm of the ideal worker hangs on. Indeed, in some ways it has gotten stronger. It reaches its zenith when loaded with special expectations. Certain sports figures, for example, like Ken Griffey, Jr., Shaquille O'Neal, or Kevin Garnett, are considered "franchise makers" because sports fans will flock in large numbers to see them play. Similar expectations are attached to college and professional football coaches, and also to top executives of companies. CEOs typically live in unreal worlds of luxury with salaries many times their employees' earnings; they are looked upon as kings, heroes, rescuers, and sustainers who, with their retainers, "go it alone" from the top as in a medieval fiefdom. They answer to a board usually made up of executives from other companies. Their only real fear is a stock market that requires them to show a rather steady and consistent profit, but even when profits aren't realized, they are usually still rewarded.[25] They claim that their huge salaries are justified by the competitive need to attract the best people, assuming that such people are exceedingly scarce and that being the "best" equates with being attracted by stupendous salaries. Harvard Business School's Kevin Murphy claims that "top executives are worth every nickel they get," and Leon Hirsch, who got $118 million in the early nineties from U.S. Surgical Corp., declared that he wasn't paid enough.[26] Something like this reasoning lies behind Warren

Buffett's claim that "You'll never pay a really top-notch executive . . . as much as they are worth. A million, $3 million, or $10 million, it's still peanuts."[27] By contrast, CEOs of Japanese corporations believe they will be out of touch with and lose the respect of their employees if their salaries become as bloated as those of their American counterparts. In 2000, Japanese executives received ten times as much as the average salary of their company employees, while the American ratio has grown steadily from a multiple of 40 in 1960, to over a hundred in 1990, to 180 times the average worker in the year 2000.[28]

If the "ideal worker" reaches its highest paradigmatic expression with industrial executives and professional athletes, it nevertheless has similar characteristics down the line in other areas of employment. There is a fixation on the notion that "one man can make the difference," whether it be a dean of an academic area at a university, a new partner in a law firm, a sought-after editor of a newspaper, or a hoped-for and well-suited new pastor of a church. And each ideal worker coming out of each family he/she supports is also looked upon as—in some measure—one who goes to work with a competence that "makes a difference."

Let it be noted here that the doctrine of God is necessarily based on analogies with human life that are extended and glorified. If God seems to be something like a "supreme being," upholding the fate of creation by an omnicompetence that is the best available, then God, depending on the century, is going to be the best possible oriental potentate, medieval monarch, or, in our own day, the ideal worker writ large in the form, say, of a CEO of a Fortune 500 company. An attack on this model is where feminist deconstructive techniques come in.

Management Systems Not Conforming to the Paradigm of the Ideal Worker

Before going to theology, a quick return to Joan Williams's critique of the force fields of domesticity and the ideal worker will be useful. The nurture and care of children, even if by day care, are still a family responsibility that cannot be avoided. Children cannot be given short shrift even if both parents work. This factor is what Williams calls an "unbending gender" trait, and it can attach to both equally, even if partially delegated to childcare facilities. Other obligations of domesticity can be equally shared, and, once these are shared, a good deal of importance is taken away from the ideal worker role. Instead of the role of "going it alone" outside the home, for many households there is no longer a single breadwinner, because both partners have outside jobs. Williams thinks that both force fields should be not only deconstructed but "deinstitutionalized," so that the domestic and vocational roles are shared in a horizontal expression of effort rather than a hierarchical structure of command.[29]

This caring and relational mode of working together has been attempted in America from time to time. In the Hawthorne Experiment of the 1920s, Western Electric in Chicago saw manufacturing productivity increase dramatically with a change not in the method of assembly but in relations between management and workers. Workers' opinions were solicited and carried through, giving a richer sense of participation. Again, Chris Argyris, in his *Personality and Organization*, argued that the human need for personal growth and fulfillment worked against the old Taylorist rational dissection of human action into machinelike motions. The need for "scientific" efficiency was making people apathetic, cynical, even ill. Job enrichment and participatory leadership are necessary if people are going to be employed to their full ability and satisfaction. Something like a *cri de coeur* was uttered against modern work relations in Douglas McGregor's "management by integration." Management, he noted, needs to be able to predict and therefore control its employees. "Theory X" management assumes (as in neoclassical economics) that humans dislike work and prefer leisure. Work, having no intrinsic value, is not supposed to be pleasurable: people do it for money, so they can have food and shelter. "Theory Y," by contrast, believes that work can have inherent value, that there is something to be said for work for its own sake as a means of self-fulfillment. Once people working under theory X have food and shelter, they are going to be churlish because, as human beings, they require higher forms of fulfillment. Management by coercion is no longer effective for these people; integration should be practiced instead. Workers should be able to share in the objectives of the company that employs them and participate in its decisions. Peter Drucker goes even further, suggesting that people in the work force need to be able to participate in the planning itself, not just in the execution.[30] Edwards Deming and the Quality Movement call for "driving out fear," "eliminating competition," and looking first at systems when things go wrong rather than isolating individuals and blaming them.[31] All these schemes bespeak a synergistic rather than a top-down power, and this kind of power is similar to the image of God promoted by feminist theologians.

Feminist Theologians' Image of God

Sallie McFague has criticized the monarchical model as one that separates creation from divinity. Just as a CEO slips quietly down from this top-most office suite and is driven off in a limousine, keeping at a distance from the *hoi polloi* whose fate he holds in his hands, so divine activity must bother itself to watch over a dependent and often rebellious humanity, "loved in spite of their unlovableness."[32] McFague notes Gordon Kaufman's observation that this model sets up an "asymmetrical dualism" that distances God from the world. God, having all power, evokes feelings of awe from his subjects, a close cousin of fear and condemnation, where God reigns out of a mixture of domination and undeserved benevolence. McFague observes:

> The relationship of a king to his subjects is necessarily a distant one: royalty is "untouchable." It is the distance, the difference, the otherness of God that is underscored with this imagery. God as king is in his kingdom—which is not of this earth—and we remain in another place, far from his dwelling.[33]

Following this line of thought, the work of Christ becomes a rescue operation, the action of "bailing out" an unworthy humanity. It is a substitutionary (forensic) atonement in which the love of God is mostly a matter of legalistic mercy, an act of undeserved and distant benevolence. The savior does it all; unmerited grace requires a complete rescue.

But the new way of understanding power makes the old monarchical model of God badly outmoded when one thinks about work. McFague suggests the model of the Creator as the "mother of creation," not according to old "stereotypes of maternal tenderness, softness, pity and sentimentality, but on gestation, birth, and lactation." This provides a model wherein God labors in order to give growth to her offspring, "an active defense of the young so that they may not only exist but be nourished and grow. Whatever thwarts such fulfillment is fought, often fiercely, as mother bears and tigers amply illustrate." There is, in other words, a "toughness in the model."[34] But it is in the interest of *having the creature thrive*. Power comes through "response and responsibility" rather than domination or fear. The love that comes from a maternal figure "operates by persuasion, care, attention, passion, and mutuality."[35]

Soelle suggests Carter Heyward's understanding of God as relational *in essence* rather than by accident: "reciprocal, dynamic, and of benefit to both parties." This is expressed in a cocreative partnership between humanity, the rest of nature, and God, where the power is proportionate to the quality of the relationship. It is not a raw, spontaneous, self-attributed, unlicensed power, not one that someone owns and might or might not share, but something that arises from mutuality. This relational contribution of Heyward serves well to enhance the cocreative role of human work.[36] The notion of a reciprocal dependency would go too far, however, if it failed to acknowledge the way God often initiates and prompts relationships.

Returning to an earlier theme, God as "householder," the Greek word *oikonomia*, as the progenitor of the modern word *economy,* connotes a complexity that is certainly present in the interdependent affairs of a modern economy, as in household relations and management. Modern economists are concerned with the efficient distribution of goods and services, and that seems to chime well with an image of God as an equitable householder. But the "efficiency" of economics springs from an agglomeration of sovereign individuals each pouring a pursuit of self-interest into a dynamism that somehow is supposed to bless all. But the deity who blesses this dynamism tends to be aloof, a deistic conception of a transcendent being who sets a competitive Darwinist law of nature in motion and approves of those who can compete successfully by their own wits.[37] This efficiency may increase wealth, but not equitably, because this god rewards freedom and fulfillment in proportion to accumulated property and wealth. This is no room here for a God of grace and justice who liberates the poor and the oppressed. Instead, it is a god who resembles the ideal worker writ large, wholly successful and entirely transcendent, leaving the game of life to be played like the game of monopoly. The rewards and blessings are there for those who can achieve them.

In contrast to this aloofness, feminist theologians suggest a panentheistic view of God's relation to the world. Rather than pantheism, which places God wholly within the creation, panentheism thinks of God as present and active in creation but also existing outside or beyond creation. More specifically, God is not completely and causally dependent on creation but, on the other hand, is not aloof from it either; rather, God permeates and affects creation both physically and spiritually.[38] In Elizabeth A. Johnson's words, "Here is a model of free, reciprocal relation: God in the world and the world in God while each remains radically distinct. The relation is mutual while differences remain and are respected."[39]

Panentheism allows creation to reflect in full measure the image of God from the vantage of the incarnation, and Jesus certainly reflects an image of God as co-worker and companion. Luke (ch. 10) tells of the disciples assisting his ministry. They looked after him and he them (John 4:31; 14:1). He hoped for their love (John 21) and wanted their companionship at Gethsemane (Mark 14). The Syrophoenician woman gave him instruction (Mark 7:28), and he considered his followers "partners" rather than "servants" in the work of the kingdom (John 15:15). These and many other interactions indicate a God who is free but thoroughly involved with creation and its human aspect. Such a demonstration of divine love is far from the potentate-monarchical image. A God who offers sustenance to creation can carry a more feminine image. Sally McFague suggests the images of "mother, lover, and friend," rather than fierce father, judge, and competitor. She writes of it in terms of other-regarding, agapic love, but the note of sustenance can be found here as well:

The agapic, just love that we have designated as parental, the love that gives without calculating the return, that wills the existence and fulfillment of other beings—this love is manifest in ways beyond counting. It is found in the teacher who gives extra time to the slow or gifted student, in the social worker whose clients are drug-addicted pregnant women, in the librarian who lovingly restores old books, in the specialist in world population control whose days are spent on planes and in board meetings, in the zoologist who patiently studies the behavior of the great apes in the wild, in the owner of the local supermarket who employs ex-juvenile delinquents, in the politician who supports more funds for public education, in the botanist who catalogues new strains of plants, in rock stars who give their talents to famine relief.[40]

Thus, part of the excitement of work comes in a sense of divine partnership.

TRADITIONAL CHRISTIAN BARRIERS AGAINST WORK

Today's Christians, especially among Protestants, are schooled to the idea that one cannot gain salvation by means of work, and over the centuries there have been a number of barriers put up against the value of work. These barriers help explain why even today Christians neglect the value of work. They also imply a persistent hesitancy to have God involved in the things of this earth. The medieval synthesis of Aristotle's philosophy with Christian theology yielded a cosmology with the earth at the center, surrounded by outer spheres of the sun, the moon, and the planets. The sphere farthest out was *primum mobile*, "prime mover," the dwelling place of God and the realm of paradise. A "great chain of being" devolved downward from God, through the angels, residing with the planets, down to earth and humanity. Humans lived amid an earth constituted of "base matter," the *excrementum mundi*. Focusing more closely within this earthly existence, there was a theological tripartite division of *oratores* (those in holy orders) at the highest level, then *bellatores* (soldiers), and finally *laborantes* (laborers), the latter assigned the least valuable calling. Most of these classifications belong to the dead hand of the past, except that Christian layfolk who are part of the working classes still tend to get a neglected second-class ranking from the church.

There is also the curse of the expulsion from Eden, often identified as the curse of having to work. The *Epistle of Barnabas,* for example, counsels "working with thy hands for the ransom of thy sins" (19.3), as if work were a matter of "doing time" for a criminal act. Or work is regarded as a way to deal with *ad corpus demandum*, a means to suppress undesirable bodily appetites.

Thomas Aquinas credits work with four purposes, none of them especially exalted: first, "to obtain food"; second, "to avoid idleness, from which many evils arise"; third, "to the restraining of concupiscence by mortifying the body"; and, fourth, for "almsgiving" (*Summa Theologiae* 2a–2ae, 187). He does, however, believe that work extends beyond the *opus manum*—to administering, teaching, writing, and so on—and that whether manual or otherwise, the objective purpose of one's work benefits a larger community, fitting into an ordered, architectonic society, like a grand pyramid, with everyone serving in his/her place and God at the top, encouraging all workers to serve within their respective stations. When people work unselfishly in this scheme, the result of their effort coincides with the will of God (ibid., *Suppl.* 41.2). Obviously, Thomas's teaching fit the static hierarchical society of his day. When he discusses the sort of perfection possible to attach to various stations of life, his answer is most unsatisfactory to the modern ear.[41] Ironically, the contemporary secular world often turns this classification on its head by dismissing religion as a confused and irrelevant tangle of wishful and outmoded thought. People who devote themselves to cloistered contemplation seem sidelined from the "real action."

The wisdom of *ora et labora*, the combination of activity and prayer/contemplation, runs deep in medieval life, especially through most of the history of monasticism. From the start, the common rules for monastic communities insisted on a regular regimen not only of prayer but also of labor for all monks, partly to provide the necessities of life but also for the sake of the charitable acts the monks might be able to exercise outside their gates. In addition, work was deemed a healthy counterweight to the regular round of reading and worship. The affliction of *acedia*, or sloth, the source of dryness of spirit, restlessness, fatigue, or boredom—a great enemy of the monks—was combated by the needed diversion of daily work.[42] Along with the renunciation of property, the requirement that all must work exerted a leveling, democratic effect on the community. The *Rule* of Benedict of Nursia prescribed manual labor for five hours a day and, by the formula *ora et labora*, enhanced labor with the dignity of something like an act of worship. Benedict also required that "the monastery ought, if possible, to be so constituted that all things necessary, such as water, a mill, a garden, and the various crafts, be contained within it."[43] The requirement of substantial daily amounts of reading, working, and prayer for *all* monks, finds frequent popular expression in many sermons on the story of Mary and Martha (Luke 10:38–42), where Mary is assumed to exemplify the contemplative life, and Martha the active. Sometimes it is baldly assumed that the monks have "chosen the better portion" with Mary; but more often, the one is understood as necessary to the other. Martha is understood as a necessary condition for Mary.

Just how successful this synthesis was is difficult to say. If one looks merely at the "official line" on work, then work seems to be the "poorer portion" of Martha, an obligation with disciplinary benefits to Mary's "better portion." The *opus Dei*, the "work of God" could never be "work of the hand" (*opus manum*); the "work of God" must reside in the worship of God. But if one looks at the flowering of technology, agriculture, and commerce, beginning especially in the tenth century, one can easily detect an enthusiasm for Martha's work as a good portion in its own way and for its own value. Unfortunately, the church could never bring itself officially to accept an inherent value to ordinary work, only an instrumental one; and gradually, as the medieval synthesis came unraveled, the dominion of work became a secular phenomenon with its own values.[44] The monks operated on an "edifying subsistence or gift economy." But coming to the fore was a profit economy. Lewis Mumford observes that long-accepted precepts were turned on their heads:

> Within a few centuries, the new capitalist spirit challenged the basic Christian ethic: the boundless ego of Sir Giles Overreach and his fellows in the marketplace had no room for charity or love in any of their ancient senses. The capitalist scheme of values in fact transformed five of the seven deadly sins of Christianity—pride, envy, greed, avarice, and lust—into positive social virtues, treating them as necessary incentives to all economic enterprise; while the cardinal virtues, beginning with love and humility, were rejected as "bad for business," except in the degree that they made the working class more docile and more amenable to cold-blooded exploitation.[45]

If Mumford exaggerates, he does so in a tone sympathetic to the suspicion churches still hold toward business.

But the main suspicion toward work, especially among Protestants, has to do with "works righteousness" and comes from Martin Luther's teachings on salvation by grace alone. Luther radically turns the tables on the value of vocations. Everyone, according to Luther, has a calling—whether milking cows, cutting hay, cooking meals, or administering a realm—to share Christ's *earthly* ministry, where the basic intent is to serve others out of love. It is not possible, according to Luther, to approach God by renouncing the fabric of ordinary life in favor of monastic piety or clerical institutionalism, because the religious and the clergy thereby structure their lives to avoid the role of serving humanity, to which Christ calls all his people.

Luther's primary interest, however, was with the gospel message of salvation, and in this regard works could amass no credit. Only faith, accepting the free gift of God's grace, is the means whereby one is saved. Faith is quite apart from any vocation, being something entirely free, unassociated with work. In order to describe the actions of faith and love, Luther gives each its proper realm or kingdom, one overlaid on the other in religious life: the kingdom of this world, and the kingdom of God. In the earthly kingdom, love belongs to the neighbor, where the believer is called to serve, thus participating in a creation that is also meant to serve the creature according to the downward-looking regard of God's love. In this kingdom, the righteousness of the law—both religious and civil—prevails. Here also people have free will and serve their neighbor well or poorly. In serving well, they become familiar with the burden, suffering, and frustration Christ himself knew in his ministry.

In any case, however, neither a love well spent nor a vocation well exercised counts for anything more than so much sinfulness in the kingdom of heaven, where God alone is sovereign and good, and where only forgiveness and the gracious gift of Christ's righteousness, taken from the cross and given to us—even in our undeservingness—count for anything. The only response required in heaven is faith. Love, as part of the other kingdom, goes to the neighbor. In this way, Luther provides that every sort of work, however humble, serves God if it serves humanity. Such work is also cocreative, acts out of love, and has the added feature of being valued on earth even if morally ambiguous, ephemeral, and certainly not an end in itself. But ultimately, in the kingdom of heaven, work has no value, and in this regard Luther returns it to ashes and dust, like our mortal bodies.[46]

Luther's way of putting up a firewall to keep the value of work out of the kingdom of heaven is reminiscent of the way Augustine set up the firewall doctrine of unearned divine election in his debate with Pelagius over the worth and responsibility of human activity.[47] No one doubts that Luther's insistence on the efficacy of divine grace was an important corrective to ecclesiastical abuses of the time, and there is still sympathy for Augustine's side of his debate with Pelagius, but both positions do a disservice to the value of human work and promote an image of an aloof, distant, and sovereign God, the sort of image feminist theologians have convincingly worked against.

The liberation theologian José Míguez Bonino offers a useful solution to the problem of works righteousness. Latin theology engages the powerful Marxist conceptual tool of alienation, since so much of peasant work is exploitative and has little chance of reaching the godly calling any human ought to have. For liberation theology, good work is understood as something inhering in the worker, or something *internally related*, such that to affect the work is to affect the worker, or—put another way—the worker is affected by the work she produces. Put yet another way, the Marxists would say that the worker defines herself through her work. It follows that treating work as something for sale on the market is a misuse of the nature of both work and worker, because it presumes that work is only *externally related*, an impersonal commodity on the same level as a tool. This is the sort of "work" Paul (and Luther) found objectionable: detachable work, whereby one might buy justification. Detachable work fits into a cycle of work–commodity–salary–consumption. When the work is performed, there is marketable value to the vendor, consumption value to the buyer, and, eventually, only throwaway value to all parties involved because nothing personal has occurred. These relations are external, whereas in a godly calling, one performs an open-hearted service with the opportunity of self and family maintenance and community betterment. Such work always involves soul making as a significant part of its value. In this case, the relation can be integral because the worker is of value to herself and others by virtue of her work, and this work also carries an inherent value in itself.[48] The scriptural warrant "By your fruits you shall know them" describes a way of discerning true from false prophets (Matt. 7:15–20). A similar situation holds for work: a person who does good work will find that her efforts contribute to the definition of who she is. She is like the "good and faithful servant" whom the landlord knows, from experience, he can trust (Matt. 25:21). These character traits cannot be bought like a commodity; they have to be proven through the quality of work. In the same way, a person who has good working character traits cannot sell them to someone else.

There is, therefore, an important way that work fits into the kingdom of heaven. God is not aloof, merely bestowing saving grace on some and denying it to others according to some inscrutable sovereign plan of election. Instead, a panentheistic theology offers the possibility of a God who delights in working and encouraging the efforts of people in gracious partnership, hoping and leading them toward good work.

The import of this present chapter has been to demonstrate from three different points of view that God is gracious and cooperative toward good work. The next chapter will describe the contributive power that working with God has toward spiritual formation under the argument that *what there is to be* is the foundation issue of *what there is to do*.

2

Getting a Focus on Vocation

IN CONVERSATIONS WITH YOUNG PEOPLE about vocation, an appropriate but rarely asked question is, What do you want to be? Invariably, the response comes as if one asked, What do you want to do? where the answer is "I want to be an engineer," "I want to be an elementary school teacher," "I want to be a football coach, a nurse, join the merchant marine, or fly an airplane." But within vocations, *there is something to be* and not just *something to do*. And *what there is to be* stands behind *what there is to do*. A person can be a lazy or inattentive airplane pilot, a neglectful nurse, or an abusive football coach. On the other hand, there are skilled, highly reliable pilots, caring, devoted nurses, and football coaches who do a memorable job of molding young people to meet the challenges ahead.

The question of *what there is to be* should be addressed before asking *what there is to do*, especially when considering the concept of "vocation." The Latin root for *vocation* means "to be called," suggesting that God calls people to their livelihoods. But there is a prior call that urges a person to be not just a truck driver but a reliable truck driver; not just a homemaker but a caring, nurturing homemaker; not just a grade school teacher but a creative and inspiring teacher. Even though they find their expression in the doing of a job, such traits as reliability, caring, inspiration, nurture, and creativity are prior, or more basic, features of being. Hence, rather than simply fitting oneself into a given occupation, the calling of *what there is to be* operates at a deeper level, and this more basic aspect ought to be included in what it means to have a vocation. Even though secular parlance no longer carries this implication of a divine call,[1] Christians should honor the old meaning because there is a certain kind of spiritual power to be found in persons who believe they are responsible to a divine call in their lives, a divine purpose that they serve.[2] The first part of this chapter will attempt to investigate the spiritual dynamics of that special kind of call and what is distinctive about it. The second part of the chapter will challenge some traditional theological assumptions about perfection and spirituality that stand in the way of *what there is to be* as a vocation. While the theme is "vocation," the chapter may also be taken as a foundational study for the spirituality of work.

WHAT THERE IS TO BE: VOCATIONAL CREATIVITY

The philosopher Dorothy Emmet distinguishes "person" from "role" by the creativity exercised in a role. Personal creativity within a role, she believes, is best captured by the Christian notion of "vocation."

> "Vocation" is a term which indicates that an individual can make his own first-hand and creative contribution in working within some context in which he has a loyalty. The language in which people try to talk of vocation is thus likely to be not the organic functional language nor the political purpose language, but religious language. It may indeed turn out that the discovery and development of vocation is one of the main things that religious language is about.[3]

Emmet observes that "vocation" in Christian thought tended to champion a seemingly higher calling modeled on monasticism, as if Christians should be lured by an "Honors Degree" rather than a "Pass" into salvation.[4] This implied denigration of a "pass" as compared with "honors" is part of the scheme that unfortunately fails to appreciate the active working life to which the majority of Christians must be called if the fabric of society is to be maintained. To some ears, "having a vocation" means having a call to holy orders or to an avowed religious life, but the term ought to apply to all sorts of honorable work because that is part of *what there is to be*.

What there is to be can stand out as a moral question about the virtues one might like to have, but people don't usually think that way. Instead they tend to aspire to be like some person they hold in esteem. Wanting to become like one or more admired personalities means that there is a spiritual level that carries the moral level. People are respected and imitated for the manner, history, and practice their convictions bring to bear on the changes and chances of their life's work. Paradigmatic people leave a footprint, a mark that reflects the center of their effort and intention. It can be called "personality," but because, more than seeming touched and animated by mere survival or "getting by" it seems to be responding to a prompting beyond itself, we designate it with added respect and call it "spirit." We tend to admire and imitate people who not only exemplify virtuous behavior but are steadfast and creative in their work.

A paradigmatic character of *what there is to be* can be exemplified by story-telling. There is nothing as powerful as narrative for showing virtues as they are put into practice and thereby exemplify a spiritual footprint. In Harper Lee's *To Kill a Mockingbird*, Tom Robinson, a black man falsely accused of rape, trusts his life to Atticus Finch, a lawyer appointed without fee to take on the unpopular task of Robinson's defense. For Atticus, *what there is to be* is a southern Christian gentleman, and he exemplifies this to his son, Jem, who eventually says, "Atticus is a gentleman and so am I." Atticus's challenge is to make his best professional effort for a black man named Robinson, despite strong social pressures to find Robinson guilty. Robinson has been accused of the rape and murder of a white girl. A weak, perfunctory defense would suit the townspeople. But Atticus cannot permit himself to do less than his best. He expresses his southern code eloquently when he says, "I can't live one way in town and another way at home." His integrity requires that his life be of one piece.

The character development of Mary Follet, homemaker, in James Agee's *Death in the Family* is another example of *what there is to be.* The Follet family, strongly centered in father and husband Jay Follet finds itself suddenly and tragically bereft when Jay is killed in a car accident, leaving Mary alone with two small children. With parents of little help, an atheist brother, an alcoholic and immature brother-in-law, and a cold-hearted priest, there is little source of comfort or strength, except for an aunt, Hannah, and the resources for wholeness the immediate family can recover for itself. After the first shock of death has passed, Hannah and Mary kneel together to say a faltering *Our Father,* Hannah to an uncertain darkness, but Mary to a less patriarchal God, her God, one who can receive and speak to the experience of being a woman. Hannah senses Mary's progress toward meeting the challenge of *what she ought to be* and later prays in her own way of Mary: "Here she is and she is adequate to the worst and she has done it for herself, not through my help or even particularly through Yours. See to it that you appreciate her."[5]

A remarkable person named Dolores Dante emerges from the pages of Studs Terkel's *Working.* She began her job as a waitress when her husband left her with debts and three small children and has worked the 5:00 P.M. to 2:00 A.M. shift six days a week in the same restaurant for twenty-three years. In terms of *what there is to be,* Dolores has what Terkel calls "ebullience," a way of conducting her work with dignity and art as a "professional."

> "When somebody says to me, 'You're great, how come you're just a waitress?' I say, 'Why, don't you think you deserve to be served by me?' It's implying that he's not worthy, not that I'm not worthy. It makes me irate. I don't feel lowly at all. I myself feel sure. I don't want to change the job. I love it." . . .
>
> "To be a waitress, it's an art. I feel like a ballerina, too. I have to go between those tables, between those chairs. . . Maybe that's the reason I always stayed

slim. It is a certain way I can go through a chair no one else can do. I do it with an air. If I drop a fork, there's a certain way I pick it up. I know they can see how delicately I do it. I'm on stage.

"I tell everyone I'm a waitress and I'm proud. If a nurse gives service, I say, 'You're a professional.' Whatever you do, be a professional. I always compliment people."[6]

Another paradigm is Vernon Johns, virtually unknown to white people, but a legend among blacks. He served as pastor of the Dexter Avenue Baptist Church in Montgomery, Alabama, and was the one who primed that congregation for its next pastor, Martin Luther King, Jr., and what was to follow with the civil rights movement. Johns was a man of prodigious mental powers, proficient in several languages and widely read. When driving on lecture and preaching circuits, he measured distances by how much poetry could be recited between towns. He also maintained ties with his humble beginnings on an Alabama farm and frequently returned there for a few days to help with the work. What *there was for him to be* was embodied in the belief that "the dignity and security of a people derived from its masses, and that without the stability and character in the masses an elite could live above them only in fantasy."[7]

The Dexter congregation considered itself among the "elite," imitators of white status, and shunned the symbols of their own roots. So, after services, Johns would shed his Sunday robes, put on overalls, and sell produce or fish from the back of his truck to the Methodists and whoever else would buy as they came out of church. On one occasion, after selling fish, he was summoned before the deacons to account for his unseemly lower-class behavior. He defended himself by saying:

"Gentlemen, I have a duty to provide you with the Gospel, and I have a right to provide you with food. As far as I'm concerned, I will sell anything except whiskey and contraceptives. Besides, I get forty calls about fish for every one I get about religion."

Taylor Branch says of Johns that he

was both the highest and the lowest, the most learned and the most common, the most glorious reflection of their intellectual tastes and most obnoxious challenge to their dignity. He enjoyed reminding them that the same Moses who talked to God on Mount Sinai also rejected his status as the adopted grandson of Pharaoh to lead the Hebrew slaves out of Egypt.

Even though Johns's time was in the 1950s, when severe punishment of blacks was a normal happening, he could also stand up to white authority. When officers stopped a black man for speeding and used a tire iron to beat him nearly to death, Johns posted the topic of his sermon on his outdoor sign. It read: "It's Safe to Murder Negroes in Montgomery." Before Sunday arrived, he was brought before the judge to explain his presumptuous sermon title and was asked to remove it.

> Johns replied with a brief lecture on the meaning of signs in history—how civil authorities had pressured men to take down their signs in ancient Greece and Egypt, in Rome, and in Europe during the Reformation. Then the judge asked why anyone would want to preach on so inflammatory a subject as murder between the races. "Because everywhere I go in the South, the Negro is forced to choose between his hide and his soul," Johns replied. "Mostly he chooses his hide. I'm going to tell him that his hide is not worth it."

These and similar confrontations, some with whites, some with blacks, eventually led Johns to submit his fifth resignation. Previously his people had begged him to stay, but in the fifth instance, his resignation was accepted. By then, however, Johns, and others like him, had cleared away the safe isolation mentality of an upper-class pietism and prepared the way among black churches for the necessary leadership and prophetic engagement with the civil rights struggle.

What is it that makes people stand out as exemplary role models? What sort of equipment does a person have who is admired in his or her vocation as an admirable *way to be* a lawyer, a homemaker, a waitress, a preacher? What drives people to strive for "honors" rather than just a "pass" in their life's work? Part of the answer has to do with native talent and disposition, while other aspects are developed with discipline and practice. But lying beneath these aspects as a foundational necessity is a person's spirituality, or what will here be called a person's ROS, or Religious Operating System.

THE ROS

Spirituality has to do with spiritual issues. But what is a spiritual issue? It is different from physical issues such as breaking an arm, the ability to jump vertically, or sweating in hot weather. It is also different from psychological issues, such as compulsive hand washing, nervous ticks, or kleptomania. But the spiritual can influence the physical and the psychological because of its foundational nature. Regrettably, however, therapists often don't recognize spiritual issues or tend to reduce them to psychological issues. Nevertheless, once isolated and defined, spiritual issues can be shown to have a direct bearing on *what there is to be* in terms of vocation.

Spiritual issues can be brought into focus by adapting Paul Tillich's existential polarities as presented in *The Courage to Be.* He uses "being" and "nothingness" as genus terms to cover more specific lived conditions that are set in a relation of polar tension. The following array is a slight adaptation of his oppositions:[8]

Being		Nothingness
Meaningful	*in tension with*	Meaningless
Fruitful	*in tension with*	Fruitless
Approval	*in tension with*	Condemnation

These tensions pervade life and crop up in specific forms. The profession of journalism, for example, finds itself—under the pressure of ratings and market share—tempted to compromise responsible news gathering substituting sensationalism. As a young producer a generation ago, Don Hewitt, who is responsible for CBS's *60 Minutes*, says that the ethic has now changed from "Make us proud" to "Make us money."[9] This reflects a tension between *meaningful* work and *meaningless* work. Or again, in medicine, physicians complain that the danger of liability suits can pressure them toward excessive diagnostic tests, while at the same time managed care offers them incentives and penalties to limit such tests. *Meaningful* medical practice can have difficulty coping with these kinds of tensions. Another example can be taken from the growing field of genetics. When Jonas Salk created a vaccine for polio in the 1950s, he disdained any possibility of a patent, thinking that it would be like taking a patent out on the sun. But while in France it is illegal to patent genes, that is not the case in the United States, where a great many patent applications have been submitted. The difficulty here is not just with ownership but with the way in which meaningful scientific information will not be shared—a basic violation of the free exchange of information science usually enjoys.[10] One well-known geneticist remarked (anonymously):

> It's created chaos in the interface between the public [and] the private spheres. It's created chaos because of patenting and cross-patenting and reach-through patenting and ambiguity of legal regulation and ambiguity of discrimination legislation. . . . Who owns what, what right do individuals have, how do we balance the need to do research in order to continue to make progress with people's fears?[11]

With respect to the tension between *fruitfulness* and *fruitlessness*, consider the age-old problem of farming. Weather, soil, disease, and pests can cause crop damage sometimes beyond repair. And even if a crop is fruitful, the price of the commodity may not allow sufficient profit. Market forces also affect many other people with respect to fruitful versus fruitless pressures, as when inflation overtakes the purchasing power of pension allowances, or when recessions throw people out of work. Another example of the fruitful/fruitless tension comes from the fact that mass media tend to concentrate recognition of talent in the hands of a very few. There are many more musicians, painters, poets, actors, athletes, and speakers than those who achieve great recognition or even make a living at their craft.

A recent news clip, for example, reported that more than 60 percent of NCAA Division I college basketball starters believe they will eventually start for a National Basketball Association (NBA) team, whereas the actual proportion is less than 5 percent.[12]

Claudia Schiffer . . . and a handful of other supermodels dominate the fashion magazine covers, earning between two and three million dollars each year in modeling fees alone. Their earnings from workout tapes, MTV series, and endorsements add considerably to these totals. . . . however, an average model does not come close to earning $150,000 a year. In fact, the annual income of most models, now as in the 1940s, is zero—even negative, if allowance is made for money spent on portfolios and modeling schools by the many thousands of aspiring models who never land a professional booking.[13]

Moral questions are involved when it comes to the tension between *approval* and *condemnation*. Gene therapy, for example, holds out great promise for treating diseases heretofore beyond the scope of the healing arts, but is it moral to experiment with human stem cells? Fertilized human eggs, embryos created *ex utero* and frozen for use with couples otherwise unable to conceive, possess a small number of stem cells that could be useful for replacing diseased cells. Moral *approval* is available for implanting an embryo *in utero*, even though more than enough embryos for a couple usually remain unneeded in cold storage. To many, it seems ironic that these extra frozen embryos languish when their stem cells could be harvested. Yet that would meet with *condemnation* by others, since these embryos possess the information and potential to become human beings.

Again, risk takers like Atticus Finch or Vernon Johns walk a fine line between *approval* and *condemnation*. They had an inner and transcendental sense of what is right, which they heeded for self-approval even though a significant part of society strongly condemned what they did and said. Such people are striking because they manage to live within a tension that is difficult to maintain.

The way these various tensions have been illustrated thus far falls into the category of structural or systemic conundrums, where people are set down within difficulties they cannot entirely control. It is beyond the control of a single farmer to tame market forces, or a single doctor to entirely change the economy of medicine, or for Atticus Finch to transform entrenched prejudice.

But there are also a great many ways that these polarities of *being* and *non-being* can show up within the purely personal sphere. It is not uncommon, for example, for married couples to face the feeling that a once *meaningful* relationship now seems *meaningless*. A person in her twenties can enter a profession that seems *fruitful* but by midlife seems utterly *fruitless*. Many—perhaps most—people hide a personal moral foible, hidden failing, or repository of guilt that meets their own disapproval and would likely meet the disapproval of others if it were known. Certainly the way people seek *approval* is an indicator of a tension between *approval* and *condemnation*.

These tensions between the various forms of being and non-being create anxiety, according to Tillich, an anxiety that is a normal and abiding state of life. In itself, this anxiety is not necessarily bad, because it can promote creative and healthy ways of coping; but—if one is not careful—it can also lead to despair and destruction. Coping with the tensions between being and non-being is what constitutes *the spiritual issue*, and it always manifests itself religiously; that is to say, this sort of coping is always basically spiritual and *must necessarily* require a religious answer.

The following illustration uses the analogy of a computer operating system to suggest a Religious Operating System, or ROS, on the analogy of Microsoft's DOS, or Disk Operating System. First, a DOS is necessary as a platform to support all other programs; second, it has default modes: while an operator can choose how the DOS is set up, she doesn't necessarily have to because the system can take on modes by default. A ROS has the same features: it is the necessary framework for how life is lived, and one can choose its settings or let them come into existence by default. (Note, however, that a ROS has one serious element that is not analogous to a DOS that will be mentioned later.)

The definition of religion for purposes of a ROS needs to be broad. Robert Bellah's will serve well: "a set of symbolic forms and acts which relate humanity to ultimate conditions of human existence."[14] This definition does not require one to have a formal belief in God, nor does it entail belief or membership in an organized religion. It does, however, require commitment to a meaning that is "ultimate" in the sense of being self-transcendent, that is, a projection—either real or imagined—that seeks a meaning for living that goes beyond one's own self and circumstances at any given moment in order to provide a rationale and support for existence. It follows that since everyone is confronted with spiritual issues in many forms and is obliged to cope one way or another, everyone *must* be religious (as defined above) either on purpose or by default.

There may be other ways to represent a ROS, but the schema of a priority pyramid is useful and clear.

Priority Pyramid

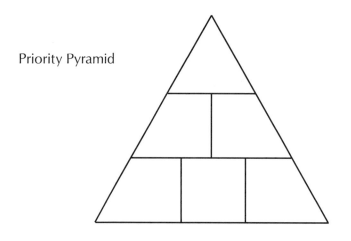

Priority Pyramid
for a
College Professor

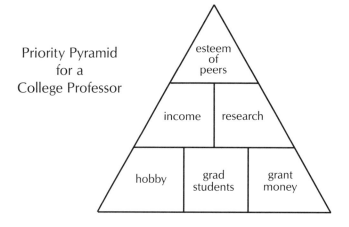

Priority Pyramid
for a
Used-car Salesman

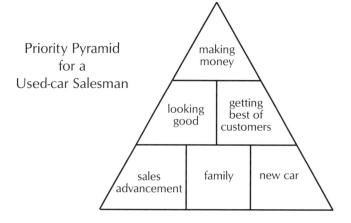

The pyramid on the preceding page has six compartments arranged according to priority of concern, whatever one cares about the most, so that the highest priority is at the top, those ranking next below the top, and so on down to the lower levels.

To illustrate more fully, imagine what a priority pyramid for a college professor might look like. It would not be unusual for such a person to have as his top priority *the esteem of his peers;* next down would be his *research* and his *income,* since both are significant indicators of the esteem he seeks. On the third tier would be other supportive issues like *grant money* and *graduate students* he can command, and then, possibly, his *family* or a *hobby.*

What about a used car salesman? Such a person might have as a top priority *making money.* Next down might be *getting the best of customers,* and *looking good.* Next would be the *new car* he wants, then *advancement in sales,* and somewhere down the line, his family.

These pyramids are simplistic and perhaps cynical. The same person could have several pyramid configurations depending on variables such as the time of day, location, or present company, so that a person might be one way as a shop foreman, but have a different ROS at home, and yet another at a bar or an Elk's convention. It is also possible to have more than one top-priority concern, a kind of polytheistic position—service to more than one god.

In any case, the important thing to note is that when a person loses a top-priority concern, the spiritual nature of that concern is exposed because that person is thrown into a spiritual crisis. Thus, for example, if the college professor or the used car salesman should be fired, it would be like having the rug pulled out from under her/him. Such crises can sometimes be so severe that people will take their own lives. Obviously, then, top-priority concerns have a transcendent aspect because they provide people with a meaning for their lives, a reason for being, an answer that keeps them creative, helps them find an interest in life, and keeps them from slipping into despair. So even if a top-priority concern does not have any of the marks of a standard notion of what would ordinarily be called "religion," it is, nevertheless, serving a religious function.

Notice also that these top-priority concerns dictate a person's moral system. The used car salesman, for example, is interested in getting the best of his customers, a concern that ranks above his desire to be honest. That means his ROS will recommend that he choose to be a liar, if necessary, in circumstances where he can "put one over" on a customer. That top-priority concerns dictate moral behavior is another characteristic of religion.

An important question to ask about a ROS is how adequately it corresponds to reality. A person whose main preoccupation in life is where to get his next drug fix is seriously out of harmony with reality. Similarly, a college student whose whole life is devoted to a dubious love affair can find himself out of touch with the way things really are. It is therefore of the utmost importance to find concerns that are adequate to reality. For this reason theology occupies itself with doctrines of creation (how reality is made up and what its purpose might be), together with doctrines of humanity (what it is to be a creature, and what purpose creaturely life is supposed to have). Organized religions encourage people to organize their ROSes into schemes that work in harmony with creation and with whatever meaning they believe creation to have.

But it is here that the ROS analogy and the pyramid schema become disanalogous to the way a DOS works. To be fair to the used car salesman or the professor, it may very well occur to them from time to time that they are spiritually vulnerable by worshiping idols of clay feet, and that they ought to have the true God at the top of their pyramids the way one might purposely rearrange a DOS. But the possibility of putting God at the top of a ROS is rarely available, except perhaps with mystics. With most people, such attempts are on the order of ambitious efforts at self-improvement, where God is employed, however sincerely, to serve some higher personal need. A DOS can be reconfigured, but setting out to put God at the top of one's ROS is a vain hope. That's because God is rarely summoned; instead, God encounters people often by surprise. Sometimes suddenly, sometimes very gradually, but these encounters usually occur when some kind of spiritual crisis loosens up an otherwise rather tight set of priorities, making room for unaccustomed spiritual resources. And unexpected resources do occur: an especially helpful friend intervenes, an undeserved act of reconciliation happens, an unanticipated source of courage asserts itself, an unwarranted strength finds a place to help, an unimagined development comes to the fore. One who is already attuned to such events knows that divine encounters work in this way, knows them for what they are—unmerited gifts that serve as a foundation for life.

But even for people who have a sensitivity toward the divine, God is not "at the top" of their priority pyramids. Instead, people begin gradually and progressively to care about the things God cares about; they are "made over," as it were, to participate, however modestly, in God's concerns, sharing in the spiritual strength this offers. This strength, however, never occurs to enhance one's standing in a vocation, but only to enhance the servanthood of a vocation to a larger purpose as one begins to care about the things God cares about.

The top concern becomes sharing the concern of God as it applies to a given vocation. With Atticus Finch, serving God was invested in being a southern gentleman of a rather high order. For Mary Follet, the call was toward the courage needed to restore her family to wholeness. Dolores Dante seems to have been fulfilled by serving her clientele with unusual grace, while Vernon Johns invested his life in preserving and uplifting the roots of black dignity.[15] None of these people necessarily concentrated their thoughts on God the way a mystic might. For the most part, working people are not contemplative in the classical Christian sense. Nevertheless, they can be authentically called out by God in a genuinely spirited way.

But when the contemplative life is held up as the best paradigm of spirituality, other authentic callings are denigrated or obscured. A similar danger occurs with the misleading way various forms of Christian perfection are promoted. For far too long, theology, biblical translations, and liturgical language have misled people to believing they are called to perfection.

WHAT ONE CANNOT BE: PERFECT

Perfection tends to obstruct a spirituality of work at several levels, because the term implies a root meaning from which a variety of others are taken. At this root is the common spiritual yearning for paradise, expressed mythically in primordial time. The Garden of Eden is the most familiar instance of a paradise lost but nostalgically remembered, and Plato's myth in the *Phaedrus* is another example. But there are many others, with common themes, found around the world. In a variety of ways they describe a paradise of immortal existence where men and women enjoy friendship and conversation with the gods and animals, having dominion over the rest of creation, easy access to heaven, and no earthly mishap, sorrow, or toil. But through some error or fall, all this is lost, and humankind is corrupted. The ladder, mountain, vine, tree, or other means of access to heaven, is removed (or in the case of Eden, an angel with a flaming sword denies reentry), leaving human existence no longer immortal but flawed and estranged from what it had known. As an event in mythic time, it does not occur in history; instead, it is a primordial condition and a very real yearning for something that never existed, expressed as an event that never actually happened.[16]

In many primitive cultures, shamans claim, by ecstatic trance or other means, to temporarily reenter paradise, thus communicating more directly with the gods, reestablishing harmony with other living things, and even temporarily reconnecting heaven with earth. The desire to return, or to be restored, is part of this spiritual yearning.

In Christian literature, the incarnation and the atonement are often taken to be restorative. John of Damascus (sixth century), for example, echoing the earlier Cappadocian fathers (fourth century), takes humanity to be the connecting link between the visible world and the invisible world; the former was created perfect but was subsequently tainted and estranged by the fall. Christ's incarnation as the second Adam reunites the Godhead to human nature, heaven to earth; and Christ's atonement, by his perfect humanity, opens the way for humans back to communion by a paradisical illumination and communion with God.[17] This communion, however, is, like the paradise for which it yearns, outside time, ahistorical, an abolition of history.[18]

Following Aristotle, Thomas Aquinas expands the notion of perfection. For Aristotle, the explanation of things, both living and nonliving, includes their purpose. Each occupies a niche in an overall scheme: a rock has the built-in proclivity of being a rock; similarly, a bird has a place where it belongs, but is higher on the scale of existence because it has a rudimentary kind of soul, being capable of nutrition and self-directed motion. Aristotle's scheme amounts to a graduated kingdom of ends, with humanity just below the top of the scale, since humans—if given leisure for contemplation—can engage in abstract thought. At the top of the pinnacle, Aristotle posits a philosophical god with the property of aseity: self-sufficient, self-contemplative, unmoved but moving everything else to be the best each can be within its niche. Thus, everything has a purpose to fulfill, a *telos* or perfectibility, while Aristotle's god has a perfection that is *sui generis*, a category to itself. Humanity is best fulfilled when engaged in thinking thoughts akin to the thoughts of this god.[19]

With Aquinas, Aristotle's isolated but magnetic deity becomes creative, active, and loving, while retaining the quality of drawing what perfection there may be out of each creature according to its purpose in the order of things. In the Garden of Eden, Adam and Eve possessed a divinely infused knowledge of God's goodness and love, from which they became estranged. Perfection requires a restoration of that Edenic harmony, toward which humanity may aspire through the redeeming work of Christ. Just as Aristotle finds the highest human fulfillment in contemplating the thoughts of the deity, so with Aquinas, contemplative inner communion with God is preferable to the active life. Anyone truly wise will follow the counsels of perfection and take the extra vows of the religious. Perfection is an inward state or experience of both seeing God in a mystical sense and participating in God's love. Absolute perfection belongs to God alone, but in the next life, completeness of the believer's spiritual yearning is gained by enjoying the direct, unmediated vision of God. In this way Aquinas weaves three senses of perfection together: the nostalgia for a mystical lost Eden, the Greek sense of *telos*, and, third, the perfection of aseity which resides with God alone.[20]

In Protestant tradition, there has been a stream of perfectionism surrounding Christ's powers of atonement. There was, for example, the Anabaptist belief that, once born again, the believer entered a sinless or perfect state, not by virtue of any ability within the believer, but by the perfecting power of Christ's atoning sacrifice. If such a convert did sin again, then there was no further hope except to purge the congregation of the backslider so as not to soil the body of Christ among the people with whom the sinner had worshiped. Luther and Calvin both reacted against these teachings. Luther taught that the believer was in a state of *simul justus et peccator,* that is, justified by Christ, but unable to reach a state entirely purged of sin. For Calvin, the best character traits were those of humility and watchfulness.[21]

Closely related to the idea of perfection by Christ's sacrificial atonement is an *experiential* perfection, used to answer the deep need among evangelical Protestants for what they call "assurance," some emotional sign indicating that their own salvation is in good working order. A thread of this tendency is found in John Wesley's essay "Christian Perfection," a sanguine, yet humble belief in the possibility of moral and spiritual progress after conversion. According to the Holiness movement, this was hardened into a strong notion of believer perfection through an "added grace," received after baptism. Something similar occurs with Pentecostals, who claim an overwhelming assurance by receiving the "gift of the Holy Spirit" through the laying on of hands after baptism and authenticated when the believer speaks in tongues. This blends with another perfectionist tendency that seeks to restore the church to the pristine primitive state known to the first apostles, by replicating their experience at Pentecost. Finally, many evangelicals have become fixated on the end times, when they believe Christ will take his own into heaven so they might avoid the tribulation to come. This more extreme Protestantism seems to have one foot in the primordium and the other in the millennium, dismissing as virtually irrelevant whatever occurs between.[22]

At bottom, all of these notions of perfection, both Catholic and Protestant, tend to contain the universal yearning explicated by the Greeks as the desire to reach a flawless ideal and denigrate or escape the earthly everyday existence so realistically found in the spiritual tension between various forms of being and not-being. Are these concepts of perfection also biblical? The most common root with this meaning in Hebrew, *tm,* sometimes translated "perfect," has the sense of being complete, whole, finished, having integrity, in the sense of an accomplished maturity. It is applied to God's knowledge, justice, or fidelity (Job 37:16; Ps. 18:30; etc.), or to moral uprightness among humans (Gen. 6:9; Prov. 2:21; etc.), but also to the ripeness of fruit (Ezek. 47:12) or even to the utter destruction of a people (Num. 14:33). Rather than the Greek notion of conforming to an ideal, *tm* refers to the quality or character of a relational activity or disposition among persons. In Deuteronomy 32:4, for instance, *tm* is attributed not to Yahweh but to his work, because "his ways are just"; he is "a God of faithfulness." Similarly, Noah is called *tm* because "he walked with God" (Gen. 6:9). If there is a standard for *tm*, it is invested in the historical quality of a relationship, as when Abraham is bidden by God to "walk before me and be blameless" (Gen. 17:1) or in the sense of Deuteronomy 18:17: "You shall be wholehearted [*tm*] before Yahweh your God."

Although it doesn't use the word *tm*, perhaps the most important ascription of something like perfection occurs in Leviticus 19:2, with the demand "You shall be holy, for I the Lord your God am holy." It seems to be echoed in a very demanding way by Jesus in Matthew 5:48: "Be perfect even as your Father in heaven is perfect." The holiness which God rouses his people to imitate in Leviticus requires separation from what is ordinary or profane, partly for cultic reasons, but more for the ethical principles of faithfulness and justice. The call hearkens to a rich and time-tested historical relationship in which Yahweh has proved his constancy and bids a reciprocal response from his people. Jesus' demand uses the Greek *teleios* (often used to translate *tm* in the Septuagint), which conforms to his Jewish heritage if it reflects the quality of a relationship built up over time: "be true" or "wholehearted," rather than the Greek sense of flawless conformity to an ideal.[23]

Other uses of "perfect" (*teleios*) in the New Testament are similar to *tm* inasmuch as they connote a completeness in the sense of "maturity" rather than flawlessness. Thus, Christ becomes mature through his sufferings (Heb. 2:10; 5:9; 7:28). For his part, Paul says that he has not yet reached maturity (Phil. 3:12) but projects his hopes for completeness in the life to come (Phil. 3:8–21). Of course, in keeping with the New Testament, there is more emphasis on maturity as a relationship initiated and brought to fruition in the believer by the action of Christ (Heb. 10:14). But there is no compelling evidence that this maturity indicates a restoration to the lost purity of paradise or a conformity to a faultless ideal. Instead, "perfection" reflects the quality of an open-hearted or true relationship with God and other people that finds its completeness through ordinary worldly events rather than apart from them.

But in that case, why use the word "perfection" at all? "Mature," "complete," or "open-hearted" would be more accurate without evoking nonbiblical notions of a flawless ideal or the universal yearning to be returned to an Edenic existence. Nevertheless, "perfection" has widespread use in contemporary Christian literature regarding liturgy, spiritual formation, and theology of work. What a travesty that this is so! Why should a word that is so misleading continue to be invoked so uncritically?[24]

This same kind of yearning toward a flawless ideal can appear also in the context of work. It may seem that a perfectionist would be the best kind of worker, but in fact perfection is the enemy of excellence. An excellent worker can utilize criticism, is not defeated by failure, can be venturesome at risk taking, but open and understanding toward others, whereas a perfectionist is never satisfied, is fragile when criticized, crushed by failure, not likely to try risky projects, and lacks tolerance toward other people's mistakes.[25] Thus, both at work and at devotions, a perfectionist spirit can be a very different thing from the biblical concepts of faithful relationships, open-heartedness, or maturity.

But just as misleading ideals of perfection do not belong to *what there is to be* in a Christian vocation, so also are the traditional categories of spirituality misplaced. In discussing the formation of a realistic Religious Operating System, it was noted that one's top-priority concern ought to be caring about the things God cares about, given what there is to be and do within a particular occupation. In the workaday life, assuming their work is moral, people ought to care greatly about the object of their work. But does God care about such things? Does God care about honey bees, or Otis elevators, or Gortex, or arc welding, or ladies ready-to-wear, or two-cycle engines? The answer has to be *yes*, but there isn't a category in the area of spirituality to accommodate that yes—at least not yet.

A WORKER'S OBJECT OF CONTEMPLATION

How would an ordinary Christian working person develop a spirituality? A conventional answer might require sufficient church activity to be in good standing. Beyond that, she might become a tertiary member of a religious order, set aside time for a life of prayer and meditation, be guided by a spiritual director, attend quiet retreats, and otherwise follow a life of extra discipline, as a kind of avocation. Or, from a more Protestant point of view, someone seeking spiritual enrichment could be encouraged to attend regular Bible studies, possibly seek the gift of tongues, travel to renewal conferences, find a soul friend, and teach Sunday school. Such part-time commitments would seem necessary because one's spirituality seems to grow or diminish with the amount of time it can be given *outside an active working life.* But suppose this person finds her calling and enthusiasm in politics, in the laboratory, in merchandising, or child rearing? It is entirely possible that the standard requirements for spiritual development would then be a distraction and a hindrance. Looking over the prospects of spiritual formation, a working person could well say that she has little or no spirituality, or has no time for it. What might serve a monk eminently well serves the average working man or woman poorly.

On the other hand, it seems unfair to dismiss spirituality as irrelevant for working people. The path toward spiritual formation is an authentic tradition, a time-tested fund of observations and disciplines for developing a spiritual life, and many laypeople have participated. Nevertheless, three factors are especially unsuited for working people: the emphasis on contemplation, the way in which things of this earth are valued, and (as already argued) the urge toward perfection.

All three factors come out of the Greek crucible of thought. The Greeks denigrated work as necessary for most people but brutish, leaving little time for the higher pursuits of contemplation. Spiritual yearnings were best satisfied by those with the necessary leisure to live in the realm of ideas. The world of appearances in which the rank and file toiled, reflected only imperfect copies of what could be grasped through thought in more perfect form and order.

Contemplation requires leisure, or at least some freedom from constant work. As early as Ambrose, a division was recommended whereby all Christians were expected to live by basic moral precepts, while only a few could follow an upward path given in the "counsels of perfection," the extended disciplines of poverty, chastity, and obedience.[26] In the eleventh century, this distinction was further solidified under Pope Gregory VII, so that the chief concern of the laity was tied to morality, shifting from "spiritual growth to avoidance of sin."[27]

The fifth-century monastic rule of St. Benedict of Nursia is praised for having placed the *opus manum* (work of the hands) in a position interdependent with *opus Dei* (liturgy, prayer, and contemplation), where each is essential to the monk for maintenance of community and spirit. *Ora et labora,* "work and pray" was the watchword of this teaching. But by the eleventh century, in abbeys that could afford it, a division had arisen where "lay brothers" performed most of the physical labor and were excused from most of the liturgy, allowing "choir monks" to devote themselves more exclusively to the *opus Dei.* Benedict's synthesis came apart because the demands of ordinary labor were perceived to stand in the way of those whose goal was the contemplation and vision of God.[28] In the thirteenth century, Aquinas carried on a debate as to whether the religious life or the priesthood constituted a state of perfection.[29] Neither side of the debate considered the spirituality of all the baptized.[30] The idea that spirituality requires contemplation, which, in turn, requires time off from ordinary work, persists to this day, as can be seen in Parker Palmer's eloquent expression:

Contemporary images of what it means to be spiritual tend to value the inward search over the outward act, silence over sound, solitude over interaction, centeredness, quietude and balance over engagement and animation and struggle. If one is called to monastic life, those images can be empowering. But if one is called to the world of action, the same images can disenfranchise the soul, for they tend to devalue the energies of active life rather than encourage us to move with those energies toward wholeness.[31]

Instead of requiring a work-free context for contemplation, consider the possibility of *active contemplation*, as when someone becomes "lost in her work" or where, like an athlete, one enters into a "zone" with an activity. The possibility of active contemplation will become clearer with an adjustment in traditional meditative paths.[32]

Patrick Carroll and Katherine Dyckman define spirituality as "the style of a person's response to Christ before the challenge of everyday life, in a given historical and cultural environment."[33] As it stands, this definition is acceptable and workmanlike, but in classical spirituality, the "response to Christ" occurs by devaluing the things of this life, either by *kataphatic* or *apophatic* means. The *kataphatic* theme claims that the visible finds its value by pointing to the invisible: one must look through external appearances to the divine reality standing beyond the appearance. Yves Congar calls this tendency "divinism," and Alfons Auer claims that it is a manifestation of the monophysite heresy, because in devaluing earthly things it devalues the incarnation.[34] But according to the kataphatic approach, meditative progress requires going from the material to the spiritual. Brother Lawrence's pots and pans, for example, or other implements of work, have no intrinsic worth except to serve others and express the love of God. Or again, the order and beauty of creation stir the heart of the believer to reflect on the design and intent of the Creator, standing behind her handiwork, and thus one comes close to God.

It follows that the paradigm of ultimate spiritual experience will be simple contemplation of God, bypassing things of this world and going directly to apprehension of the divine. This ultimate spiritual experience comes by means of the *apophatic* path. It is known as the *via negativa*, stressing that God, by not being this and not being that or any other thing, is wholly other and ineffable. This-worldly affections are expunged from the mind, and, by recollecting the soul's true home, attention is focused toward communion with the Deity.

There is certainly wisdom in these paths: the need to avoid excessive attachment to material goods, the caution to look behind the surface significance of things, the call away from mindless busy-ness toward quietude. Yet they neglect another kind of spiritual experience especially important to laypeople.

This is the experience of satisfaction over something for *what it is in itself,* for its intrinsic worth. There is a sense in which a marriage ought to reflect (*kataphatically*) the union between Christ and his church, but when husband and wife take one another, they choose each other not primarily for their suitability to this mystical union but because each loves the other *as is.* Again, one does not become a scientist or an artist because it provides a point from which to bear witness to the gospel, but because there is some aspect of art or science that in itself seems worthy of pursuit. This opens up quite a different category in spiritual experience: players in a string quartet become as one in their rapture over a particular passage of music, and at one with the audience. It is a spiritual experience, but concentrated *in* the music rather than *beyond* it to something else. *But it can nevertheless be a moment at one with God insofar as God too is enraptured by the music.* Why not? Similar observations can be made with regard to a finely wrought object of art, a well-turned phrase in literature, a carefully honed movement of thought, an especially useful tool, a good architectural design, or an elegantly conducted and successful experiment.

When the psalmist says, "The heavens declare the glory of God and the firmament shows his handiwork," he is speaking kataphatically. And when the psalmist says of the Lord, "He is not impressed by the might of a horse; he has no pleasure in the strength of a man," the expression is *apophatic.* But these two categories omit a third way, as when Jesus speaks of the Father's care for the lilies of the field, the birds of the air, or the hairs on one's head. Here earthly things are not pointing beyond themselves or being denied altogether, but they are valued intrinsically for what they are. A different category of spirituality needs to be added.[35]

Spiritual experiences are essential to life because people cannot live by bread alone. They thirst for incentives, excitements, and motivations that will call out their abilities toward fruitful undertakings. But the spiritual excitement that bears up the laypeople in their everyday activity tends to be of a different category from that so extensively developed and cultivated by the church. Indeed, Auer thinks a different theology is needed, one that he calls a "theology of earthly realities." He writes of a theology that "is not confined to a study of God; indeed it is concerned primarily with his relationship to mankind in the world."[36] It will be sufficient here, however, to mark off this different category of spiritual experience by coining a contrasting term. Instead of *kataphatic,* in which objects or events point beyond themselves toward God, let the term *metemphatic* designate those experiences where an event or thing is felt to be valuable in itself. The root word *phatikos* means "appearing" and has a customary English usage in the word *emphatic,* "to appear strongly." *Metemphatic* has the sense of "emphatic," but the prefix, deriving from *meta*, "among," indicates a shared value between one or more people *as well as God*, regarding some event or thing.[37] Thus, for example, when God declares the various phases of the creation to be "good," one's own sense of the goodness of creation is available to share with its Maker, and that would be a *metemphatic* experience or value. In the psalm, "The heavens declare the glory of God and the firmament shows his handiwork," the experience is clearly *kataphatic*, but when Jesus speaks of the value of the fallen sparrow, the lily of the field, or the hairs on one's head, the sense of value being elicited is *metemphatic*.

One of the ways God encounters people and begins to reorder their ROSes is by having them lose themselves in something worthwhile about their work and in this way begin to share a common concern with God. Mihaly Csikszentmihalyi,[38] investigator of "flow" experiences (where one becomes totally lost but involved in a performance of some kind),[39] thinks that such events occur more at work than anywhere else. Among his examples is Serafina, an old woman of the Italian Alps who gets up at five in the morning, milks cows, cooks breakfast, and takes a herd of cows to high mountain meadows, several miles from the barn. On the way back, she "could reach the barn in half the time if she took a direct route; but she prefers following invisible winding trails to save the slopes from erosion. . . . Serafina knows every tree, every boulder, every feature of the mountains as if they were old friends." Another is Joe Kramer, "a welder in a South Chicago plant where railroad cars are assembled." It is a dark, noisy, uncomfortable place to work, and he has worked there for more than thirty years, and eschews ever becoming a foreman. "Although he stood at the lowest rung of the hierarchy in the plant, everyone knew Joe, and everyone agreed that he was the most important person in the entire factory. The manager stated that if he had five more people like Joe, his plant would be the most efficient in the business." It is Joe's gift to be a natural tinkerer with a high mechanical aptitude, able to lose himself in how things get fixed or put together. A third example concerns a surgical team who find "flow" experiences in performing surgery. One speaks of the "gratification of taking an extremely difficult problem and making it go." While with another:

> It's very satisfying and if it is somewhat difficult it is also exciting. It's very nice to make things work again, to put things in their right place so that it looks like it should, and fits neatly. This is very pleasant, particularly when the group works together in a smooth and efficient manner: then the aesthetics of the whole situation can be appreciated.[40]

Cases of flow experience at work are instances of transcendental concentration and admirable as examples of *what there is to be*. But it should be recalled that the biblical doctrine of work treats work as ambiguous—as sometimes a joyful activity but at other times a dreary toil. The duality of common parlance in many languages also reflects that experience.[41] It is not necessarily bad that this duality exists, because it is the duality and the tension it generates that urge workers to be creative. The examples that opened the chapter portrayed people who gained in spiritual stature under conflicting pressures or, in the case of Dolores Dante, found a professional kind of creativity in what most people would call a humdrum job. But what of people who feel constricted by circumstances they can't control?

Howard Gardner, Mihaly Csikszentmihalyi, and William Damon's *Good Work* attempts to describe instances of job creativity under this sort of stress. "Creating new institutions" is one possibility. The Council of Responsible Genetics is one example. Or making sure that the values of existing institutions are upheld, as in the case of Bill Kovach of the *Times*, who is responsible for spotting and nurturing young talent with an "intellectual dress code," wherein he fostered a supported community of professional interdependence and integrity: "I care about each and every sentence in this paper and I care how we get them, and I have very clear views of how they are to be gotten. . . . Make the calls, and I'll back you."

One can also take a personal stand, as Daniel Ellsberg did by making the Pentagon Papers available, or as Nobel Prize–winning Linus Pauling did when he thought the cold war infringed on doing good science and took up the cause of peaceful protest even though he was harassed by the FBI and Congress and had his passport withdrawn. Or again, John Gardner, who left plum positions in government to found Common Cause and other grass-roots organizations. In other cases, it might be necessary to step outside normal environs in order to exercise a profession more meaningfully, as would be the case in Doctors Without Borders, or Partners in Medicine, organizations that work with victims of tuberculosis and AIDS in Haiti.[42] Other solutions are also worth noting. Assembly line workers, for example, find their work more rewarding if they can trade jobs with one another as they do making New Balance shoes or Volvo automobiles. In many cases they are also a vital part of the feedback loop; Nucor Steel, for example, considers its workers a vital part of its system of knowledge sharing. And, of course, there is strength in numbers, which is often effective in labor unions.

This chapter began by asking what it is about vocation that leads some people to strive for "honors" rather than just a "pass" in their jobs. This question focuses on *what there is to be*, a vocational issue that is anterior to the concern over *what there is to do*. This prior question of vocation is brought into focus by asking what constitutes a spiritual issue, described as every person's anxiety when stretched between tensions of fruitful and fruitless efforts or mean-ingful and meaningless outcomes, or embroiled in moral questions that can bring approval or condemnation. Since these are deep and universal anxieties resonating at the spiritual level, they require religious solutions, obliging everyone to seek—either purposefully or by default—an ordering of their life concerns so as to come up with a purpose that takes on transcendental power—real or made up but in any case needed—to cope with the abiding polar tensions no one can escape. While it is entirely possible to invoke pow-ers that are idolatrous and destructive, it is not possible simply to put God at the top, as people are often wont to do out of shallow motives of self-improve-ment. Instead, one must wait for God to come and reorder a person's priori-ties or hark back to instances where God has already been invasive and cultivate those experiences in order to make one's highest concern match the things that God cares about.

But this raises a difficult question for people whose livelihood engages them in the things of this world. Does God really care about such things? The answer is yes, so long as the work in question is moral and honorable. This argues against an urge toward perfection, because it is deceitful to believe that human work should strive for perfection. Instead an openness toward the Creator is encouraged, to whom one must continually return to order one's life realistically. Finally, a new category of spirituality is coined in order to account for how God would care about the things of ordinary working life, that of the *metemphatic.* This strong avoidance of perfection and recourse to the metemphatic will be further explicated in chapter 4, where the incarnation is assessed in terms of its great value for a theology of work.

3

Making Space for a Theology of Work

MORE CATEGORY CHANGES are needed to accommodate a theology of work than just those touching on individual persons. Hardly any gainful employment serves only the worker and no one else. Instead, all such work entails a public domain made up of people and structures far beyond an employee's personal acquaintance. It follows that theology cannot be purely private and still be relevant to one's occupation.

This chapter begins by arguing that privacy in religion does not make sense. We turn attention next to corporate or superpersonal structures as an important context of a workaday world. In view of these structures, a substitutionary view of the crucifixion is rejected as not just repugnant but inadequate, in favor of the idea of Christus Victor. The theme of salvation is further discussed in terms of a more expansive notion of the kingdom of God; and the kingdom is seen not just in human structures but in nature as well, where humanity has become increasingly aware of its own peculiar interdependence with the natural world. The place of humanity within nature leads to a rejection of "redemption" or "reconciliation" as the umbrella term for the calling of God and humanity in favor of "creativity" and "cocreativity," respectively. This rearrangement of categories implies also that Christian laity should be the focus of primary identity for the church since they, rather than the ordained, are the ones who serve the creation. Finally, humanity and human work cannot be put into the context of nature without extensive reliance on natural theology, a field out of favor until recently. So a revival of natural theology will be defended together with the metemphatic as an intuitive spiritual path of knowing in the relation of God and nature.

AVOID THE BELIEF THAT ONE'S FAITH
IS A PRIVATE MATTER

William James takes religion to be "the feelings, acts, and experiences of individual men in their solitude . . . in relation to whatever they may consider divine."[1] His definition reflects a popular mind-set. It has a close analogue in the way people think of freedom of speech. Freedom of speech not only means freedom of expression but also seems to imply that each person is entitled to a personal opinion about almost anything; and being entitled seems to carry over, *ipso facto*, into *having* an opinion whether qualified or not. Fortunately, opinions are usually molded and tested in the marketplace of ideas, such that outlandish notions are not, for the most part, put into practice. Here, however, is where the analogy breaks down. Religion, being more a variety of interior solitudes—at least according to James's definition—is not necessarily subject to public scrutiny.

Another popular notion contributing to the idea of religion as something done in solitude, comes from the assumption of "private access." Private access assumes that no one can be privy to the innermost thoughts and feelings of another. T. S. Eliot, for example, writes of the typical married couple as

> Two people who do not understand each other
> Breeding children whom they do not understand
> And who will never understand them.[2]

Yet another instance of this view comes from B. F. Skinner, who observes that when someone reports about a private mental event by saying, for example, "my tooth aches," there are difficulties because "each speaker possesses a small but important private world of stimuli," which others can only "infer."[3] To further complicate matters, the *cogito ergo sum* argument of Descartes asserts that, if not the content, then at least the occurrence of mental activity is the most impossible to dispute of all phenomena.

Religion, proposed to stem from private religious experience, therefore, can seem, on the one hand, publicly inaccessible and, on the other hand, veridical, or self-authenticating, just for being there. No wonder people say that one's religion is a very personal matter, or that one man's religious convictions are as good as another's, so long as he keeps them to himself. Of course, both the assumption of privacy and that of authenticity in religious experience fit very well with pietism. A strong ecclesiology and theology of work, however, must have more than a notion of people who are alone, even if somehow "alone together" in their religious convictions and communion with God and labor. If St. Paul's analogy of the church as the body of Christ is correct, there is an interdependence among individual Christians in which mutual cooperation and understanding are essential.

As it happens, the opinion that religious belief must be private, together with the notion that all mental events are necessarily private, are both humbug. Feelings, thoughts, and emotions, insofar as they are coherently understood, are within the public domain.[4] Suppose, for example, that Jones has perfect pitch. His sensation of a musical tone is an interior mental event, but it is informed by the public criteria of the mean-tempered scale and an A that beats at 440 cycles per second. Or again, suppose Jones is having the sharp sensation of a shooting pain down his back and into his leg. The sensation belongs to Jones, but he must see his doctor to understand what sort of coherent description can be made of the pain—whether a muscle strain, a slipped disk, or a crushed vertebra.

What truly belongs to oneself personally is what is sometimes called one's "point of view," or, after Martin Heidegger, could also be called *dasein*, "being-there," that is, occupying a specific time and situation from which a personal narrative can be built like a personal fingerprint in history. This fingerprint is unique, but it is not inaccessible to others, because they too have fingerprints. If they did not, one could not understand one's own.

It follows that there is nothing sacrosanct, hidden, or of primary truth regarding personal religious experience or convictions except as they are woven into some sort of coherent story within the public domain. St. Paul, for example, may have had an intense personal conversion experience, but the *sense* of it came from his discussions with the disciple to whom he was sent in Damascus. The church is a much stronger entity than simply an agglomeration of people who are "alone together." Its teaching constitutes a coherent story capable of making sense of individual experience.

ACKNOWLEDGE CORPORATE, SUPERPERSONAL STRUCTURES AND THE CHRISTUS VICTOR ATONEMENT

There is such a thing as *alterity*, the state of being alone, even when surrounded by others. Strangers standing in line for a bus, for example, are each an atomic unit, isolated and alone. This sense of lonely anonymity-alongside-others can be felt also in the context of work. Literature about work very frequently uses Kafkaesque portrayals of people indifferently caught in structures they cannot control.[5] However isolated or powerless people may feel, they are nevertheless enmeshed within corporate contexts. The trivial act of cashing a check, for example, requires more than just Jones and the teller. The act entails banking as an institution, the economic multiplier effect of checking accounts, the use of currency, and other large-scale practices that are inexplicable if one is restricted just to the actions of two isolated individuals engaged in cashing a check.[6] Adam Smith ascribed the virtue of market economies to what he called the "invisible hand," that seemingly beneficent force, which, from the synergism of competing self-interests, brings about the prosperity of all participants.

It is ironic but true: people can feel very isolated and alone despite this inevitable milieu of involvement. The mood of the 1950s brought out Sloan Wilson's *Man in the Gray Flannel Suit*, or David Riesman's *Lonely Crowd*, describing a worker's stark alterity under the irony of isolation within a corporate structure. The man in the gray flannel suit seems to be part of a community only to the limited extent of conformity to a middle-management dress code. The woman in the lonely crowd confirms the possibility of people gathered without any mutual solidarity. The "blue-collar blues" is a repeated theme in the corpus about work.[7] Meaningless jobs in authoritarian settings with only extrinsic rewards are the lot of many.

Equipping oneself for *what there is to be* requires a larger theological dimension than the interior privacy of pietism. One must be able to work realistically within structures and systems to have, as St. Paul put it, "the whole armor of God": loins girded with truth, the "breastplate of righteousness," "the shield of faith," "the helmet of salvation," "the sword of the Spirit" (Eph. 6:14–17). Pietism tends to be blind to the biblical vision of moral agency in the context of corporate structures. Such structures are capable of enormous good and enormous harm. Note the Pauline injunction:

> We are not contending against flesh and blood, but against the principalities, against the powers, against the world rulers of this present darkness, against the spiritual hosts of wickedness in the heavenly places. (Eph. 6:12)

Paul makes a clear distinction between two levels of existence: that of the individual personal life, on the one hand, and corporate life on the other. Pietism generally tries to ignore the clear indication that a "contending" takes place on the level of corporate life; or if it does try to contend with the corporate level, it does so by mistakenly addressing it as the personal level of "flesh and blood."

Therefore working people should appreciate that there is a superpersonal category of existence, powerful and able to act for good or for harm. However murky, it participates in reality because of its ability to do good or to do evil. Its category of existence can be difficult to individuate, since, at bottom, it is constituted by a solidity of human relations, some formally constituted, some enduring through custom and language, some very fleeting, as in the action of a mob. However short- or long-lived, these corporate structures exist in multilayered complexity, interwoven through human existence. Although without human participation these entities cease to exist, with participation, ironically, they seem to gain an overarching life of their own that can be unpredictable, intentional, stubbornly static, and morally ambiguous.[8]

This systemic dimension becomes especially obvious when one tries to explain the causal agents involved in large-scale events. What happens in history can rarely be accounted for through the actions of individual persons. Instead, historians resort to "traditions," "economic" or "political forces," and other kinds of superpersonal agencies. The Great Depression, for instance, occurred not as a result of the action of any single individual but because of people engaged in a vast tangle of market policy, economic incentive, equity capital, borrowing, and the like.

But the kind of existence these superpersonal agencies have is murky and difficult to define. They are "agencies" capable of acting for good or ill, and since they have a moral impact, they also have an intentionality of some sort, which, in turn, gives them a spiritual aspect. Adopting biblical terminology, Walter Wink calls them "powers" and suggests that they have a spiritual and a visible pole:

> . . . as the inner aspect, they are the spirituality of institutions, the "within" of corporate structures and systems, the inner essence of outer organizations of power. As the outer aspect, they are political systems, appointed officials, the "chair" of an organization, laws—in short, all the tangible manifestations which power takes. Every Power tends to have a visible pole, an inner spirit or driving force that animates, legitimizes, and regulates its physical manifestation in the world. Neither pole is the cause of the other. Both come into existence together and cease to exist together.[9]

In any account of work, superpersonal agencies need to be recognized because people work within a web of many of these agencies. Fortunately, there is also a strong biblical recognition of this superpersonal environment, especially in the New Testament. There the death and resurrection of Christ and the kingdom of God range against the "powers" that threaten creation.

The scenario for the crucifixion of Jesus involves the machinery of forces beyond any single human's control. When Pontius Pilate washes his hands, it is not entirely an act of cowardice; he is also expressing a feeling of helplessness. In the Gospel of Luke, for example, at the end of the trial in the wilderness, after Satan has failed to succeed with his temptations, the Gospel explains that the "devil . . . departed . . . until an opportune time" (4:13). Satan does not appear again until he "entered into Judas" (22:3) to motivate Judas's betrayal. What drives the plot on a mythical level combines with the superpersonal agencies toward an inevitability. It is as if the two best systems of that day, the Jewish religion and the *pax Romana*, find the crucifixion a necessity. This does not mean that humans aren't thoroughly involved and responsible; but there is also an overarching dimension of larger-than-life agencies playing a strong hand in the action. Human beings can make a difference in contending with such overarching structures, but they should have knowledge of how this is done and should take strength from Jesus' own way of overcoming these powers. The plot of crucifixion has a Kafkaesque reality that should be incorporated into the triumph of the cross.

A harmful belief is one that takes Satan as a strictly personal tempter, thus fitting the devil into a pietistic scheme. That scheme continues with a substitutionary doctrine of atonement, teaching that God's wrath for humanity's sinfulness under Satan *must be satisfied* by an offering more morally perfect than any single human can manage. Therefore God offers his son *to himself* as a substitute, and thus Jesus propitiates God's anger. The struggle and resolution take place within the Godhead on the legal (forensic) model of a civil suit requiring satisfaction and a criminal suit requiring punishment. Salvation is freely offered through the substitutionary sacrifice of Christ. Principalities and powers are ignored, and the character of God—as someone sacrificing his son to satisfy his outrage—is most strange.

A better explanation for the "helmet of salvation" comes in the more ancient Christus Victor version of the atonement. Here the death of Christ is accomplished by human beings constituted into powerful civil and religious relationships. These principalities and powers—probably the best of their time—tragically accomplish the crucifixion. But Jesus is raised from the dead, alive again to his promise for the world and beyond the effective reach of the worst that malevolent powers can accomplish. He thereby stands not as a *substitute* but as a *representative* whose liberating path humanity can follow. The triumph of God in the cross and resurrection certainly conforms better with Paul's "armor of God" than does the language of a propitiatory sacrifice. It assures the final outcome of Christian contending as prefigured by the resurrection.[10]

A doctrine of Christus Victor does not focus exclusively on systemic powers; it can include personal matters within its scope. But present-day contentions with principalities and powers must often be clothed and carried on at the superpersonal level or through what are often called "mediating structures." Rather than work alone, for example, on environmental problems, one should become part of, say, Greenpeace or some other organized effort. Or again, when churches urged their members to boycott Nestle for promoting infant formula over breast-feeding to the detriment of infant nutrition in the third world, the churches were engaging a power at the proper level. The necessary theological space for this dimension requires a Christus Victor doctrine of atonement and a broader notion of the kingdom of God.

CLARIFY THE PLACE AND VITALITY
OF THE KINGDOM OF GOD

When Christianity is prophetic, making moral judgments about the course of history, it invokes explanations at this more corporate level, even if at times it runs the risk of later finding itself mistaken. The reason for this vantage point lies in its belief in the "kingdom" or "reign" of God. The kingdom of God should be one of the most important doctrines for working people because it is the shared venue for the work of God and the work of the people. It signifies the locus of God's reign and activity. It has its roots in the historical Hebrew experience of Yahweh as the one who chooses and makes a covenant with them, leads them out of Egypt to their own country, and imparts his will and teaching through the prophets. The prophets attribute to Yahweh a high notion of righteousness with respect to fairness and fidelity. This righteousness is required of the people and is to be accomplished with favorable divine aid but within the dimensions of ordinary human instrumentality. Unlike the Greek gods, jealous, fickle, and behaving amorally, Yahweh is esteemed not just for power, or for being the only God, but for high ethical principles and faithful care of the people. God's nature and purpose of working to bring the people and creation to their fruitful destiny will not be thwarted. But the people must be persuaded to freely conform to that will as it is accomplished through love and justice, culminating in a final "day of the Lord" at the end of history, when judgment will take place and all will be set in order.

The day of the Lord, as an act of God, is outside the divine action that might be found within human hands, plain history, real politics, or human instrumentality, and represents the first shift from prophetic to apocalyptic teaching. The apocalyptic vision takes in a larger historical theater, where powers come into conflict that overarch individual human capacities beyond any person's control. The apocalyptic theater sets Satan and his demonic hosts against God and the angelic minions of heaven. Also among the belligerents are armies, political powers, and other human institutions opposed to God's reign, including some human systems that are perhaps well meaning but misguided, or else malevolent but disguised to appear well meaning. Apocalyptic writing, as a combat among superpowers, reflects the helplessness of a small Jewish state, repeatedly a doormat for much larger Middle Eastern nations. The fate of God's people seemed to be out of their hands; to whom else would they look for help except God? God with the heavenly hosts alone could successfully oppose the enemies of the people and would surely do this in God's good time.

While the kingdom, as the reign and activity of God in history, begins as a concept with the prophets, it is, by the time of Jesus, mixed and laden with a thorough tradition of apocalyptic freight. And since apocalypse implies a final consummation in which the purposes and sovereignty of God are triumphant, it culminates in the old prophetic day of the Lord. In the Synoptic Gospels, Jesus subordinates himself and his message to the context of a kingdom of God that is "now at hand." His miracles and sending out his followers are meant to be signs of how the kingdom is impinging on human affairs. The parables impart the urgency with which people must seize the opportunity Jesus offers so as to conform to the new order and not miss out. In addition, his teachings break free of legalistic constraint, applying the principle of other-regarding love and the attentive care of a creator, who, rather than a stern judge, is better compared to a familial father.

Edward Schillebeeckx describes the inbreaking kingdom as "a new world in which suffering is done away with, a world of completely whole or healed people in a society no longer dominated by master–servant relationships.[11] Others find different hallmarks to emphasize. Augustine, in equating the final kingdom with the heavenly city, looked to a "new creation where the old has passed away" (*City of God* 20.16–17).[12] Albrecht Ritschl, following Immanuel Kant's idea of a "kingdom of ends," envisions a fellowship of moral behavior based on the paradigms of Jesus' own acts and teachings. Wolfhart Pannenberg thinks that the kingdom works toward a unity, reconciling opposition by love, bringing coherence to what is shattered and discontinuous in history. Jürgen Moltmann emphasizes the glory of God shown forth in a new creation suffused with righteousness.[13]

These expectations are all eschatological, looking to a consummation in some future end-time. But the kingdom of God is not necessarily something to expect just at the end of time. Jesus speaks of it as "at hand," and "among you," in his time, continuing to manifest itself, and eventually a finished work. Unfortunately his references seem sufficiently ambiguous to have allowed a variety of interpretations. A kingdom that is paradoxically already-but-not-yet is said by C. H. Dodd to be "realized" in view of the power with which the early Christians spread the gospel and established the faith. Reginald Fuller takes it to be "inaugurated," since Jesus' ministry begins it, but the full consequences of his crucifixion and resurrection are yet to be realized.[14] These writers tacitly imply what others make explicit:[15] namely, that there is a current of history working its way through the larger ocean of historical events—much as the Gulf Stream passes through the Atlantic—called "salvation history," traceable back to biblical events and expanding outward with the church. Pannenberg, however, takes the kingdom and the whole of history as coextensive, so that whatever happens in history generally, with the Christ-event—his appearance, ministry, crucifixion, and resurrection—stands as a determining foretaste, a *prolepsis*, for the sure end result of the kingdom.[16]

Another problem of interpretation surrounds the credibility of the kingdom to a modern mind. Perhaps it should be dismissed the way one might dismiss a literal belief in the existence of Satan. Johannes Weiss, the late-nineteenth-century scholar whose New Testament investigations convinced others that the kingdom of God was indeed an apocalyptic message, nevertheless did not himself believe that it was a credible concept and reduced the value of its meaning for his day to Ritschl's collective but interior moral pilgrimage. Rudolf Bultmann thought the apocalyptic element unacceptable because it was "prescientific," and he demythologized it into an existential scheme of decision and authenticity.[17]

On the other hand, it has already been argued that the theme of God and the people of God contending with superhuman agencies of good and evil has been accepted by others as a viable notion—even if couched in mythical expression—of what is meant by contending with such things as social, military, political, or economic systems. Norman Perrin suggests that the "freedom riders" of the 1960s conceived of their activities in a context fully accepting of an apocalyptic dimension, as expressed in their slogan, "Go out into the world and find out what in the world God is doing in the world." Perrin also cites Walter Rauschenbusch as a similar example.[18] The latter openly used the kingdom as the theological underpinning for his social gospel:

> The Kingdom of God is still a collective conception, involving the whole social life of man. It is not a matter of saving human atoms, but of saving the social organism. It is not a matter of getting individuals to heaven, but of transforming the life on earth into a harmony of heaven.[19]

Even if one does accept the kingdom as a viable concept, there is still disagreement about where it is. One theory says that the kingdom of God is *within* the believer.[20] Nineteenth-century theologians, wishing to avoid any connection Jesus might have had with apocalyptic ideas, spiritualized the kingdom as an *interior* phenomenon. Adolf Harnack, for example, wrote:

> The Kingdom of God comes by coming to the individual, by entering into his soul and laying hold of it. True, the Kingdom of God is the rule of God; but it is the rule of the Holy God in the hearts of individuals; *it is God himself in his power*. From this point of view everything that is dramatic in the external and historical sense has vanished; and gone, too, are all the external hopes for the future. Take whatever parable you will, the parable of the sower, of the pearl of great price, of the treasure buried in the field—the word of God, God himself, is the Kingdom. It is not a question of angels and devils, thrones and principalities, but of God and the soul, the soul and its God.[21]

Second, there is the *enclave* theory, which holds that the kingdom of God and the church are one and the same. An enclave kingdom is especially popular when that part of the world outside the church seems apathetic or hostile. Augustine, for example, wrote the *City of God* when Rome was being overrun by the Visigoths. It seemed to him axiomatic that God's reign extended only over the redeemed, certainly not the godless, and since there were "tares among the wheat" in the church, the kingdom was only perfectly realized at the eschaton as the heavenly city.

> For the city of the saints is up above, although it produces citizens here below, and in their persons the City is on pilgrimage until the time its kingdom comes. At that time it will assemble all those citizens as they rise again in their bodies; and then they will be given the promised kingdom, where with their Prince, they will reign, world without end. (*City of God* 15.1)

The enclave theory became bedrock belief for centuries in the Catholic tradition, and led to such distinctions as the "church militant" versus the "church triumphant," corresponding to the inaugurated and finalized kingdom stretched out over time and confined to the church. It is a natural assumption to make: the church as the body of Christ, ought, after all, to be the place where God reigns, since those obedient to God are there. The analogy is to a civil ruler: if a king is going to reign, it must be over loyal subjects: the king of England, for example, doesn't rule over Germany. The distinction also led to the doctrine of the "two swords," separating realms of civil and ecclesiastical rule, and to the difference between "sacred" and "secular."

A third theory is that of *indefinite postponement,* where the signs of the kingdom had best not be a worldly hope of earnest Christian people because humanity is still engulfed in sin. This view is a corrective to Rauschenbusch's liberal overconfidence in the possible perfecting of worldly social systems. There is simply too much suffering and misconduct in all areas of history to imagine that the kingdom is on its way, let alone present. The Niebuhrs especially typify this view. Richard Niebuhr, in *The Kingdom of God in America,* believed that the history of American religion can be strung on the thematic thread of the hope to establish the kingdom of God, but he parenthetically remarks:

> Though Pilgrims, Puritans, Quakers, and sectarians may have believed that in America they might construct a society of secure institutions in which to dwell until the end of time, their obedience to the sovereign God led them to produce something better—a life directed toward the infinite goal.[22]

He seems to be implying that one may aim at the kingdom, but it cannot be captured and made concrete in the context of ordinary history. His brother, Reinhold Niebuhr, says this explicitly:

Apocalypticism in terms of a specific interpretation of history may thus be regarded as the consequence and not the cause of Jesus' religion and ethic. The apocalypse is a mythical expression of the impossible possibility under which all human life stands. The Kingdom of God is always at hand in the sense that impossibilities are really possible, and lead to new actualities in given moments of history. Nevertheless every actuality of history reveals itself, after the event, as only an approximation of the ideal; and the Kingdom of God is therefore not here. It is in fact always coming but never here.[23]

Finally, there is the *coextensive* theory, which holds that the kingdom of God is coextensive with the whole of history. This view is taken in the spirit of Amos 9:7, which indicates that while Yahweh may have reason to expect loyalty from the Hebrews, it does not follow that divine action is confined exclusively to them: "'Are you not like the Ethiopians to me, O people of Israel?' says the Lord. 'Did I not bring up Israel from the land of Egypt, and the Philistines from Caphtor and the Syrians from Kir?'"

The paradigm that seems to dominate the enclave theory is that of a king who, in order to rule at all, must have consenting subjects, auguring a kingdom that equals the church. But a coextensive theory insists on a pervasive activity of the Creator working in nature and history, going beyond any territorial franchise the church might claim. A God of continuing creativity puts a different light on the analogy of kingship, but is necessary nonetheless, if such activity is not to be restricted. The same may be said of the renewing and enabling activity of God. This coextensive position is one held by a number of modern theologians, notably Pannenberg, Moltmann, and Schillebeeckx. It has also been important for those wishing to provide adequate theological room for a theology of the laity, such as Alfons Auer, Yves Congar, Hendrik Kraemer, and Karl Rahner. It is a view that is indispensable for a theology of work, since the other theories remove the kingdom from the everyday working world.

As one might expect, a variety of linkages can occur between these different interpretations of the kingdom.[24] A spiritualized *interior* kingdom works well for pietists, who acknowledge no superhuman moral agency. They may acknowledge an end-time, possibly a "rapture," but it is only for vindication of the faithful as individuals with no concern for whatever human or natural structures might exist.

The enclave theory has a better grasp of reality inasmuch as it can acknowledge the existence of "principalities" and "powers," but such things are outside the church. Only with difficulty does it allow that the church might, at times, be a "spiritual host of wickedness in a heavenly place," since the church is the kingdom of God, and therefore cannot seriously err. However, the most serious deficiency of the enclave theory comes in its severe limitation on the activity of God. It requires the logic that God is only active in the church. In the case of pietism, of course, this restriction is even worse, because there God's activity is solely within each isolated human heart. But in either case, the world outside the church is not only godless, but it is, in principle, bereft of God. The saying of St. Teresa of Avila, eloquent as it may be, is based on the enclave assumption:

> Christ has no body now on earth but yours; no hands but yours, no feet but yours. Yours are the eyes through which Christ's compassion is to look out to the world. Yours are the feet with which he is to go about doing good. Yours are the hands with which he is to bless now.

St. Teresa's plea reflects a long-standing disposition of church people. Concerned about the church and its obligation to serve the world, they forget the lesson of the Gospels, where the disciples discover a perfect stranger who is nevertheless working effectively and well in Jesus' name. They ask that it be stopped because this activity, however laudable, is not within their circle, nor under their control. Jesus, however, observes that whoever is not against him must be for him (Mark 9:38–41). Moreover, the prologue of John's Gospel and the Nicene Creed both speak of a preexistent Logos/Son who participates in a creation vaster than just the church. But, alas, people who do not hold the enclave view in theory often cling to it in fact.

For Christians and others who work in the world, neither the interior kingdom nor the enclave version is acceptable as exclusive parameters, because neither allows the activity of God to occur in the world generally. Weekday working people must be able to say, with the freedom riders, "Go into the world and see what in the world God is doing in the world." The *postponed* kingdom is another matter, having to do with problems surrounding the concept and progress of "perfection." The kingdom is postponed because too much is expected of it except as a way of finishing history. It has been argued earlier that while perfection is a universal human longing, when it is defined in the Greek way, as "conforming to an ideal paradigm," it is not biblical, even though many Christians believe that this Greek notion is what "perfection" means. It will be argued later that the Greek concept of perfection can be unmasked like the Wizard of Oz, found to be inconceivable in any strict way, and replaced by something both more reasonable and plausible as the true object of spiritual hunger.

But this raises a larger question of the signs or criteria by which the kingdom is recognized. If the kingdom is available for workers, then the evidence of its presence must be both discernible and worthwhile. If not the universal hunger to be restored to a Greek perfection, then the positive worth of the kingdom and the mission of God's people should answer some other deep longing in terms of what there is to be and to do. A mission of cocreativity is the best way to enfold this longing and put it to active use.

REJECT RECONCILIATION OR REDEMPTION AS THE BROADEST CATEGORIES OF MINISTRY: USE "COCREATOR" INSTEAD TO DESIGNATE WHAT THERE IS TO BE

The term used most frequently to describe the task of the people of God is "reconciliation." It is biblical and seems to characterize God's purpose: God is reconciling or redeeming a rebellious humanity and humanity's systems. Reconciliation tends to be a broad description of what the church does, winning people to Christ, healing troubled souls, turning the spirit Godward, carrying forward a servant ministry, and the like. All of these activities—laudable as they may be—are people-oriented and point toward an enclave notion of the church. But what is the ministry of a pipe fitter, an auto mechanic, a supermarket checker, or a forest ranger? None of these occupations is primarily aimed at serving people in terms of redemption or reconciliation. Someone with a clerical prejudice might answer by suggesting opportunities for ministry to other people in the context of the job, but people don't choose their jobs primarily so they can have a platform for witnessing. When people value their jobs, they value them out of an excitement for the creativity a job offers, with a view to the job's intrinsic rewards, and because a job offers a platform of usefulness and self-worth. The concepts of redemption and reconciliation don't cover this excitement in any straightforward way. Once more they betray an implicit enclave view of the kingdom and an institutional church with a clericalized emphasis on membership. Redemption and reconciliation have their place, as do the church and its membership, but they belong under the umbrella of a broader, more inclusive term for human vocations. That term should be cocreativity, and its fuller description awaits the chapters on how human work is complemented by the work of the Trinity.

Using *reconciliation* as the master term for what constitutes ministry also reflects a turning away from a cocreative role in the history of the church. Thomas Berry argues that, prior to the fourteenth century, the church's "story" was integrated with a stewardship of nature. But the black death's devastation shocked the church out of confidence in nature, reinforcing a focus on redemption, the need to be sure one left this uncertain world as a saved soul.

> Such excessive emphasis on redemption, to the neglect of the revelatory import of the natural world, had from the beginning been one of the possibilities in Christian development. The creed itself is overbalanced in favor of redemption. Thus the integrity of the Christian story is affected. Creation becomes increasingly less important. This response, with its emphasis on redemptive spirituality, continued through the religious upheavals of the sixteenth century and on through the Puritanism and Jansenism of the seventeenth century. This attitude was further strengthened by the shock of the Enlightenment and Revolution periods of the eighteenth and nineteenth centuries.
>
> The American version of the ancient Christian story has functioned well in its institutional efficiency and its moral efficacy, but it is no longer the story of the earth. Nor is it the integral story of the human community. It is a sectarian story. At its center there is an intensive preoccupation with the personality of the Savior, with the interior spiritual life of the faithful, and with the salvific community. The difficulty is that we came to accept this situation as the normal, even desirable, thing.[25]

If these very strong statements are followed to a logical conclusion, a different doctrine of the laity will be required because it is principally the laity who work with the creation. They are not just a clutch of people whom the clergy try to get into heaven but a people at the core of life as it is to be lived now. Part of the reason theologies of work get so little attention is that the gatekeepers of theology are mostly clericalized professionals, few of whom have spent their lives—or else forgotten—working in factories, raising crops, or in other ways affording themselves a laboring layperson's point of view. Indeed, the conventional wisdom of church professionals perfunctorily screens out or only nods at the seemingly secular world and its occupations. The pull of attention toward the institutional church and its Sunday observance is too strong to make room for the other days and other institutions that make up the majority of people's time. Nevertheless, the laity constitute that part of the church that serves the world, and that role demands recognition.

GIVE THE LAITY THE PLACE
OF PRIMARY IDENTITY

When eloquence is needed to express the gulf between the faith of the church and the work of its members, no one has more power of expression than the laity. Dorothy Sayers, for example, writing fifty years ago, protested:

In nothing has the Church so lost her hold on reality as in her failure to understand and respect the secular vocation. She has allowed work and religion to become separate departments, and is astonished to find that, as a result, the secular work of the world is turned to purely selfish and destructive ends, and that the greater part of the world's intelligent workers have become irreligious, or at least, uninterested in religion. But is it astonishing? How can any one remain interested in a religion which seems to have no concern with ninetenths of his life? The Church's approach to an intelligent carpenter is usually confined to exhorting him not to be drunk and disorderly in his leisure hours, and to come to church on Sundays. What the Church should be telling him is this: that the very first demand that his religion makes upon him is that he should make good tables. Church by all means, and decent forms of amusement, certainly—but what use is all that if in the very center of his life and occupation he is insulting God with bad carpentry?[26]

Another Anglican layperson, Mark Gibbs, recites the old saying that church membership consists of "turn up, sit up, pay up, and shut up."[27] Lutheran layman William Diehl, former sales manager for a major steel company, writes that his church asks him to be a "little Christ" with those he meets at work, but does "very little" to help him implement this request. It never calls him to account for his on-the-job ministry, never asks him if he needs any support, never inquires into the kinds of ethical decisions he makes. "In short, I must conclude that my church really doesn't have the least interest in whether or how I minister in my daily work.[28]

One of the most eloquent statements of the gap between the church and the working world comes from the 1977 "Chicago Declaration of Christian Concern," composed and signed by forty-seven Roman Catholics from all walks of life. It protests the church's tendency to channel lay energy into avenues of institutional work and outreach that the clergy and religious can no longer perform because of the scarcity of "vocations." It also chafes at the irony of being bypassed, as laity, on issues of social, political, or economic concern over which elitist church groups claim sudden ownership and authority, even when these issues are often at the heart of lay expertise in everyday occupations. The signers reaffirm what ought to be obvious: that the best place for the laity to exercise their Christianity is in their occupations, and they urge the church to rethink its relationship with its laity, the vastest part of its body.[29]

While other churches are making modest strides in this direction,[30] it is instructive to follow developments in the Roman Catholic Church, where the position of the laity moves from what can be called a *client* status, to an *instrumental* status, to a *primary identity* status.[31] In earlier times, the church acted toward the laity by dispensing the sacraments and maintaining an acceptable level of morality, so that the ordained hierarchy could usher the laity heavenward. The laity were a clientele dependent on the hierarchy. But since the time of the social encyclicals of this century, the earlier transcendental vision has had to make room for healing the great secular and worldly problems of humanity. Its members are called more toward responsible and transforming this-world citizenship than toward world renunciation. The laity are now seen as instruments meant to act as bridges between hierarchy and world so that the hierarchy can accomplish, through the laity, measures of justice, freedom, and peace in the secular world. But this leaves, say, a Catholic plumber to assume, alas, that his working life is purely secular.

Yves Congar is one of the first to advance and undergird a *primary identity* thesis for the laity by assigning them a distinct calling. He sets out the "position of the laity through the fullness of Christ's messianic powers as King, priest, and prophet." The kingly function includes a salvific power exerted in the world apart from the church, a sphere especially occupied by the laity. The priestly function denotes sacrifice, where the laity—by virtue of their baptisms—participate in the royal priesthood noted in the First Letter of Peter. All Christians are called to sacrifice by works of mercy and other-regarding love. With respect to the prophetic, Congar argues that the spiritual gift of knowledge is not necessarily confined to the clergy. Indeed, in certain areas, for example, scientific knowledge, the laity have as much insight as the clergy, or perhaps more. Finally, every Christian, whether religious, clergy, or lay, is called to be an apostle, and each pursues this call with respective differences. The religious apostolate is exercised by keeping in solitude and apart from the world, emphasizing a direct, "vertical" path to God. The priest is "in the world, but not of it," having the vocation to "make his way to God, guiding others with him by use of spiritual means." But the vocation proper for the laity "requires making their way to God while doing this world's work." Thus, activity in temporal affairs of the world and its history, is the realm where laypeople are called, a realm that is not the natural ground, vocation, or acquaintance of the religious or the clergy.[32]

Congar's theology is more appreciated today because it ties into anointing at baptism. He cites numerous early church fathers, all of whom understand the anointing by oil to be the generic and foundational status of priesthood that all Christians share.[33] These days, however, baptism has become something like a high school diploma, widely held but not greatly valued. Of highest value is a Ph.D., the so-called "terminal degree," because no greater accreditation is granted than to hold a doctorate. Similarly, a person ambitious to climb the ecclesiastical rungs, would seek to be a priest or an ordained minister. A growing consensus would now argue, however, that baptism is the "terminal degree" for a Christian, since Christ beckons all—regardless of station—to serve his interests, which are constituted in servanthood, making each Christian a *servi servorum Dei*. Aidan Kavanagh, a recent apologist of this view, argues:

> Christians thus do not ordain to priesthood, they baptize to it. While the episcopacy and the presbyterate do come upon one for the first time at ordination, priesthood *per se* does not; it comes upon one in baptism, and thus *laos* is a priestly term for a priestly person.[34]

Finally, there is the influence of Pope John Paul II's *Laborem exercens*, in which the thesis is that all good work is cocreative with the work of God. A believer who is a shipbuilder should be concerned about humane and fair treatment among workers, that part of the vocation Congar called the "priestly" vocation. But the "kingly" and "prophetic," involving mastery and knowledge, are cocreative. The shipbuilder is mostly concerned about the building of ships, and *that* must be God's work too.

A resolution to this discussion is found in Vatican II's Dogmatic Constitution on the Church (*Lumen Gentium*), where the laity, not the hierarchy, are given primary identity with respect to the church:

> What specifically characterizes the laity is their secular nature. . . . the laity, by their special vocation, seek the Kingdom of God by engaging in temporal affairs and by ordering them according to the plan of God. They live in the world, that is, in each and in all of secular professions and occupations. . . . Today they are called by God, that by exercising their proper function, and led by the spirit of the Gospel, they may work for the sanctification of the world from within as a leaven. (§31)[35]

For Protestants, some of this reasoning sounds like Luther *redivivus*. The priesthood of all believers was, in part, an effort to break the church hierarchy's exclusive franchise on the means of grace, but, in his discussion of ordinary work, Luther turned old hierarchical priorities on their heads. He argued that any sort of work serving humanity ought to be called a "vocation" or "calling." His key text in this regard is 1 Corinthians 7:20, where Paul counsels new Christians to "remain in the same vocation (*klēsis*) in which [they were] called." Luther takes this to be equivalent to a *Beruf*, a "calling," peculiar to Christians, which obliges them, in all their daily activities, to share Christ's earthly ministry, whose basic intent was to serve others out of love. It is not possible, according to Luther, to approach God by renouncing the fabric of ordinary life in favor of monastic piety or clerical institutionalism, because the religious and the clergy thereby structure their lives to avoid the role of serving humanity, to which Christ calls all his people. Thus, Luther radically turns the tables on the traditional notion of "vocation," making it of no special importance to those in Holy Orders or special vows and finding it instead with the laity, whose work had been earlier thought to be either profane or simply secular.

The priesthood of all believers easily follows from this conclusion, thereby putting all Christians on level ground: "All Christians truly belong to the priestly class, and there is no difference among them": every believer is *vocatus, conversus,* and *religiosus* by virtue of the call of God.[36] Thus, Luther issues a clarion call to the primacy of the laity, expressed in many ways in Protestant tradition. Unfortunately, however, this call is meant more to break the exclusivity of clergy as indispensable professionals holding franchise to the means of grace, than it is to affirm the laity by virtue of the work they perform in the day-to-day world.[37] The firewall Luther puts up against any salvation by work remains intact.

Yves Congar sparked a Protestant counterpart in Hendrik Kraemer. In his influential *Theology of the Laity,* Kraemer uses and praises Congar's conceptual basis (Christ as priest, prophet, and king) and argues that the *diakonia,* the servant role exemplified by Christ, must be the underlying rationale for all these themes.[38] The church should see itself primarily in a servant role toward the world, and all baptized people are equally part of that community. Laity uniquely constitute those who serve in the world, and therefore their position is vital and integral to the church. It is a mistake to value laity only insofar as they are clericalized.[39]

In actuality, a church with clear vision regarding institutional maintenance but myopia when it comes to the daily work of its laity, may be compared to a Sunday gas station. Consider the following parody:

> Imagine a gas station whose stated reason for existence is to maintain and fuel its customer's cars, and equip them to go out on the road. In practice, however, this never happens. Instead, the cars never go out. Indeed, they aren't even serviced for this purpose. They are just polished, maintained, and driven home again. They are exclusively Sunday cars, driven by people, who, for one reason or another, are aficionados of the Sunday station. When it comes to getting out on the road for week-day work, these people, like everyone else, drive a different car, maintained and fueled at a different station. Sometimes the Sunday-only station will provide a bus to take its members out for social service work, but that's the only outward venture it makes.[40]

If the laity are acknowledged to have a unique position as those who are called to occupations in the world, then as a theology of laity is expanded, it will logically lead toward a theology of work. But the expansion will also lead logically to two other developments and a shift in the church's educational efforts: one would be away from producing a professionally elite and credentialed clerical caste and toward more appropriate ways of equipping the laity; the other development would be a genuine theology produced by the laity themselves, for their use and from their point of view.[41]

In the early 1980s, James Hopewell published a paper entitled "The Congregational Paradigm for Theological Education."[42] It was an attempt to get "beyond clericalism" by redirecting theological education away from a professional elite and instead primarily toward the local congregation. He suggests comparing a congregation to a ship, where maritime education would not focus exclusively on training the officers how to get themselves to port but on teaching the entire crew how to reach its destination—namely, its self-understanding and moral development.

Hopewell's suggestion stirred a good deal of discussion, including an article by John Cobb, who argues that a better paradigm shift would be a change in what constitutes a professional. These days a professional is thought to be someone having "access to esoteric lore that enables one to solve the problems of those who do not share the knowledge." Clergy have the double enhancement of a divine calling and a seminary education, plus—for some at least—certain sacerdotal powers. They can fit quite well into this exclusive-provider paradigm. Unfortunately, this paradigm is linked to laity and congregation primarily on the basis of dependence.

Instead, Cobb proposes the professional paradigm of the "reflective practitioner." He uses the analogy of an emerging kind of medical practitioner who moves away from treating a narrow range of symptoms of disease and instead sees her role as a proactive one, encouraging, guiding, and inspiring people to seek and adopt healthful lifestyles for themselves. A clerical profession following this paradigm would exist for purposes of inspiring and empowering, which naturally leads away from dependency. Cobb further argues that the congregation cannot itself be the educational goal. If the congregation has the world as its horizon of self-understanding and mission, then the educational program that serves best is one that equips the laity to serve its Lord in the world.

> My counterproposal is not that we should ignore congregations, but that we should focus more on the world than on the church. Norms for congregations and for ministry in congregations should come out of judgments about God's mission in the world.[43]

Cobb takes the matter no further, however, even though the logical force of it begs to go on. An important share of God's mission in the world surely must connect with the workaday lives of the laity. Unfortunately, once this is realized, an enormous barrier comes up, because the seminaries and clergy they produce are rarely qualified to speak with any measure of sophistication about the manifold details and intricacies involved in weekday lay occupations. Obviously only the laity can do that. The force of this logic necessarily reaches the point where it demands not only a theology of the laity but also a corpus of lay theology. One naturally leads to the other.[44] The church should do more to nurture and use such efforts.

Finally, the place of the laity is especially important at the Eucharist. Tradition finds the real presence of Christ in three ways: in the presider as the *alter Christus,* the one who acts in Christ's place as host; in the bread and wine as the body and blood of Christ; and in the people as the assembled body of Christ.[45] These people, receiving the sacrament and seeking its strength, are mostly laity, who will be dismissed after praying words like "And now, Father, send us out to do the work you have given us to do." The rich variety of worldly work they bring to the table should not be short-changed by failing to give it the attention it deserves.

BRING BACK NATURAL THEOLOGY AND ACKNOWLEDGE THE CONFIDENCE OF METEMPHATIC SPIRITUALITY

A full-bodied theology of work requires some grounding in a theology of nature, but the general trend has moved away from any sort of accommodation to nature or culture. Friedrich Schleiermacher's retreat into a religion of subjectivity was influential, but the most perspicuous example is Karl Barth's stark opposition to "German Christianity" and its developing creed of blood and soil. To be a Christian, according to Barth, is to follow a revealed religion, not known through ordinary life experience, with a radical gospel that calls its people out into obedience to a God who is "over against" culture and stands in judgment of it. It was echoed in the Barmen Declaration of the Confessing Church in Germany and in the "religionless Christianity" of Dietrich Bonhoeffer, where faith is set apart as distinctly different from culture.[46] A similar theme comes from Reinhold Niebuhr's criticism of the social gospel movement in America and his strong reminders of how culture is shot through with human fallibility.[47] There is also the resistance fundamentalist Christians have put up against evolution and a cosmos of considerable age, while science, for its part, has—to the popular mind—abjured any association with religion.

Yet another tributary of the trend toward an involuted religion came in the convenient way science and religion were carved at the joint between questions of how and why. Each was given its own domain: science asks how, and religion asks why, and each legitimately runs entirely on its own track. The work of Ian Barbour and others, however, has overcome this simplistic separation by detailing the numerous places where science and religion interface in dialogue over issues of common interest. As a result, there is now a considerable flowering in natural theology, the effort to discern the mind and hand of God according to current understanding of nature without benefit of divine revelation.[48] Natural theology can be seen to reconcile knowledge of nature with theological commitments. Indeed, one dovetails the other because science must look elsewhere for the ethics and ultimate explanations theology can provide. On the other hand, the results of science—for example, in evolution and cosmology—have brought considerable change to theological views. Furthermore, both theology and science may be said to have a common methodology insofar as their truth claims depend on the adequacy of what they explain.[49]

A generous part of the science–religion dialogue has focused on evolution and an acceptance by mainstream Christians of the Darwinian theory of a slow evolutionary process achieved by means of the natural selection of genetic variations and differential reproductive success. Even though the process is given great developmental freedom, the context for divine action in this scheme comes in setting boundary conditions, the overall context, form, and direction taken by evolution.[50] *Homo sapiens* expresses a nodal point in evolution, because life functions for humans are much less "hard-wired" than for other life forms. Instead, a consciousness has emerged, giving a keen sense of self-identity and community, a facility for thought transcending the here and now, a vast language capability, and an imagination that can explore and stretch ideas. This human nodal point can also be called the *homo artifex,* because humans are creative beings, capable of enormous global constructive and destructive impact. Humans are *ad adsum*, meaning more than "being here"; but "I am here" and "I am toward" all that is here: "I am given to it," a *homo viator.* In Emmanuel Mounier's words, "I am not present to myself if I do not give myself to the world."[51] A sense of responsibility toward the creation follows: not to exploit, pillage, ruin, or exhaust but to use the environment in a protective, enhancing way. The challenge is to be creative yet conserving, and it places the *homo faber* in a position and vocation of co-creativity—a "created co-creator."[52]

A metemphatic way of knowing occurs because human beings are as much children of nature as children of God and one bespeaks the other. A good worker is someone who can fit into the harmony of nature, taking, shaping, yet respecting what is there with a resourceful kind of familiarity. George Sturt, for example, in his classic book on wheelwrights, explains that a skilled wheelwright is found not so much in making wheels and wagons as in "jobbing," that is, going out in the field with limited tools and resources, and yet confident to make whatever on-site repair might be required:

> From repairs, in fact, came the teaching which kept the wheelwrights' art strongly alive. A lad might learn from older workmen all about the tradition— all that antiquity had to teach—but at repairs he found out what was needful for the current day; what this road required, and that hill; what would satisfy Farmer So-and-So's temper, or suit his pocket; what the farmer's carter favoured or his team wanted. While new work was largely controlled by proven theories and well-tried fashions, on the other hand repairs called for ingenuity, adaptiveness, readiness to make shift. It wasn't quite enough to know about why, and to be ready to think of alternative dodges for improvising a temporary effect.... What was wanted was an experienced man, sure of himself and well versed in the use of odd apparatus and handy tackle for emergencies.[53]

Thus it is with anyone's work: it is not slavishly routine but requires innovation and resourcefulness. An intuitive sense of sustaining cooperation and confidence can occur between Creator and cocreator that allows nature to become more open to the possibilities that work affords. Hence, what one feels in cooperating with nature, including human nature, comes in a metemphatic way, and for the worker who has an eye of faith, such things are a gift of the Creator as divine companion. Consider these lines by Wendell Berry:

> Who makes a clearing makes a work of art,
> The true world's Sabbath trees in festival
> Around it. And the stepping stream, a part
> Of Sabbath also, flows past, by its fall
> Made musical, making the hillslope by
> Its fall, and still at rest in falling, song
> Rising. The field is made by hand and eye,
> By daily work, by hope outreaching wrong,
> And yet the Sabbath, parted, still must stay
> In the dark mazings of the soil no hand
> May light, the great Life, broken, made its way
> Along the stemmy footholds of the ant
> Bewildered in our timely dwelling place,
> Where we arrive by work, we stay by grace.[54]

This chapter has been concerned with breaking loose from pietistic categories that attempt to confine religion to a private personal sphere: first to appreciate the reality of superpersonal structures in which people work and live; second, to become attuned to a doctrine of the atonement toward a saving dimension which encompasses this reality; third, to appreciate the possibility of a kingdom of God that includes not just the church's stream of history but also all other historical streams; fourth, to make "cocreativity" the master concept for describing Christian vocation so that cocreativity ranges above but includes the activities of redemption or reconciliation rather than vice-versa; fifth, to put the laity in a position that conforms to cocreativity; and, sixth and seventh, to a return to natural theology for a theology of work, since so much of work and the metemphatic intuition that comes from work is embedded in nature.

4

The Eschatological Christ
and Homo Artifex

THE SCHEME OF THIS and the next two chapters considers how God enables human work based on a trinitarian economy with designations suggested by Miroslav Volf: the Father may be thought of as *protological,* the Son as *eschatological,* and the Holy Spirit as *pneumatological.*[1] The role of God the Son as the eschatological exemplar and promise of new things is the main concern of this chapter, but we begin with a doctrine of humanity as an evolved creator based on Philip Hefner's anthropology of the "created co-creator." Since the creation, through Christ, offers the possibility of a cocreative humanity participating in new things, and since this creativity is given in a context of freedom, bad things can also result. The chapter concludes with a discussion of bad things.

THE CREATED COCREATOR

Hefner has suggested that humanity be called "created co-creator." The force of this term can be better appreciated if other similar terms are imagined, like organized-organizer, built-builder, modeled-modeler, purchased-purchaser, enabled-enabler, powered-empowerer, or elected-elector. These all imply a person equipped for a purposely composed role. And that role occurs within a context; that is, someone intentionally equipped to be an organizer functions within the task of organizing, or someone elected to be an elector performs within that role, and so on. There is the further implication that a created cocreator depends on the initial enabling of creation by an antecedent power, but thereafter takes on a measure of free creativity alongside and responsible to the initiating creator.

For Philip Hefner, a theologian, the role and destiny of humanity are found in God the Creator's intentional equipping of humans as cocreators.[2] But since they are not self-created but contingent, like the rest of creation, their creative power is not *ex nihilo* but contextual, within God's broader creation, and not *de novo;* it gradually builds on whatever knowledge and materials have already accumulated. The transistor, for example, wasn't created before the vacuum tube, and the microchip followed only after both tube and transistor had been invented. Hefner uses the word *culture* as a label for that fund of human accomplishments from the past. Like the system of a library, human work must maintain what has been accomplished in order to move forward because whatever is new carries with it some transformation of the old. The cocreator's job can be divided into two aspects: *maintenance* of the cultural stock that has gone before, and *creativity* acting on the cutting edge of that stock. These aspects harmonize with the *protological* and *eschatological* aspects of the Trinity. The third aspect, the *pneumatological,* is concerned with how the created cocreator is equipped for the role he or she plays in creation. This chapter is concerned with the *eschatological* part of work, the next chapter with the *protological,* and the following chapter with the *pneumatological.*

Natural theology plays a key role in defining created cocreativity, because the creation must be understood within the context of evolution, and humans find their origin and activity there as well. They share a homologous bone structure, for example, with other vertebrates and, going deeper, are encoded by the nucleotide sequences within DNA, the same scheme that describes all forms of life, making it hard to deny Darwin's thesis of common origin with variation arising through natural selection. Yet among the many genotypes, *homo sapiens* shows a uniqueness that Theodosius Dobzhansky calls "a genetically controlled adaptive plasticity of phenotype."[3] Dobzhansky is pointing to the fact that there are examples of *homo sapiens* living successfully in a wide variety of environments, not only capable of adapting to a given surrounding—whether the arctic, the tropics, or even the moon—but also able to adapt the environment itself by, say, heating in the arctic, cooling in the tropics, or using the moon's gravity as a device to sling them around that orb and back earthward. The reason for this plasticity comes in the emergence of a central nervous system capable of conscious assessment among alternatives, carrying a memory not just of a single life experience but of knowledge and equipment passed through many generations, a culture of information that grows much faster than the random accretions of genetic learning. Genetic learning works like an editor, carefully refining a specie within a specific ecological niche, where it operates well so long as the environment supporting that niche doesn't change. But should environmental change come about, genetic change lacks the "phenotypic plasticity" humans possess through a fund of knowledge about nature. No other animal keeps charts of the ocean tides; maintains seed archives; or knows the genome sequence of flatworms, how to generate and harness electrical power, or what measures to take during an epidemic.

In addition to this vast fund of human how-to knowledge, there are narratives, traditions, and explanations for the courses of action humans have taken. Implicit in this accumulated culture is a freedom implying choice in paths taken and not taken, and with that freedom a sense of responsibility over success or failure, achievement or debacle, acts of goodness, and acts of evil. Tied to the aspect of freedom and responsibility in accumulated human culture are also myths, rituals, and discursive thought regarding ultimate meanings of things and events—the whys and wherefores of having been created into a role of cocreativity. In the present technological civilization in which humans find themselves, physical systems and biosystems are so thoroughly impacted on "this fragile earth, our island home," that a keener sense of cocreative responsibility calls out, for example, not to deplete aquatic ocean life, or risk further global warming, or burst population beyond sustaining capacity. Such considerations have led to a nonexploitative, stewardship interpretation of the meaning of Genesis 1:28: "Be fruitful and multiply and fill the earth and subdue it; and have dominion."

But what does the notion of humans as created cocreators have to say for the *homo artifex* and the theology of work? Not everything a created cocreator does is going to be under the category of work, but work, as such, fits nicely within the created cocreator category. There are also the ancillary concepts of human work embedded in the context of creation, set there intentionally by a Creator for whom cocreators can sense an ultimate calling, not just to the Creator but also to the integrity (Hefner uses the term "wholesomeness")[4] of creation. There is a freedom to do well or ill and a vast cultural assemblage of knowledge, both practical and theoretical, that extends over into the dedication and wisdom that religion imparts, together with a bedrock of moral precepts collected in written law and backed by the moral language that guides everyday conduct. As to self-fulfillment, it was remarked earlier that a crucial part of enrichment in life comes from being able to serve beyond oneself for the sake of others often too remote to ever be known. Daily work offers a connection with Christ's teaching that humans must lose themselves for the sake of others if they are to gain themselves. The mailman, for example, delivers the mail mostly to people he doesn't know, and while it is true that he is paid for his work, the job satisfaction he derives is not exhausted simply by that remuneration. When people are "let go" or "laid off," they often feel unhooked from any valuable contribution to humanity because they have lost their primary opportunity for this element of altruistic expression.

CHRIST'S ESCHATOLOGICAL PROMISE:
THE DOING OF NEW THINGS

Hefner thinks the creation has a built-in propensity to "stretch":

> God is able to provide new possibilities and new futures without destroying the
> life-giving continuities with our origins . . . the tendency to create continually
> new conditions in which the [human] genotype must survive and flourish.[5]

And this serves to introduce the eschatological promise of Christ, beckoning toward the doing of new things.[6] It is this aspect of work that is deemed especially exciting and worthwhile even to the point of life-dedication toward its realization. People who participate in devising a new teaching technique, a reliable insulin pump, a prestressed concrete beam, a fuel-efficient hybrid car, a self-help housing program, or a drip irrigation system feel that they've been part of a creative accomplishment, something worthwhile, and they will say that they've "made a contribution." Such a contribution often constitutes the highest point in the working lives of those who are fortunate enough to have a hand in this sort of creativity.

Alas, theology has difficulty honoring this dedication. Anything salvific, says theology, must be by grace, not by effort. In the tradition of Luther and Augustine, the old firewalls go up to keep "work" out of the domain of "grace." God might love a self-help housing program, but that God would love an insulin pump, a prestressed beam, or a hybrid car seems to go too far. No Tower of Babel is going to make it into heaven. Furthermore, human strivings pass away, are superseded, and are forgotten. In the measure of time against eternity they are as nothing.

Nevertheless—and even more ironic—within the context of work, an eschatological Christ is a *temporal* phenomenon, not restricted to eternity, coming into the context of human history, leading with the exemplification and promise of new things and new creation, things and creations open for humans to accomplish in their work. Jesus did not postpone this fulfillment until the end of time but demonstrated it every day during his life, in his transformative teachings, in his new and startling insights, in his action toward civil authority, in his reconciling acts among people he touched, and in his healings. These demonstrations form the basis of the proleptic promise of the Christ-event. They are nothing more than exhibitions of how breakthroughs, large and small, are possible in an evolving creation that can be "stretched" for doing new things. What constitutes a "new thing" or "new creation," however, needs to be spelled out rather carefully.

Defining New Things

Some theologies tend to founder at the point of defining what a new thing might be. Miroslav Volf, for example, seems to think that a "new creation" may involve a return to Eden and beyond. On the other hand, he sees (rightly) that it cannot involve an *annihilatio mundi* because that would put new creativity beyond the reach of workers. But so would Eden. History gives no evidence of anyone working in Eden. Indeed, the angel with the flaming sword prevents return; the expulsion is permanent.

Other writers make reference to perfection, since no conceptualized honorific seems too good when speaking of the fulfillment toward which eschatology beckons. John Haughey, for instance, writes: "Whatever is beautiful, true and good in human cultures will be cleansed, perfected, and transfigured, and become part of the new creation." And quoting the Pastoral Constitution on the Church in the Modern World (*Gaudium et Spes*), he adds,

> If by our labors, we have nurtured on earth the values of human dignity, brotherhood, and freedom, and indeed all the good fruits of our nature and enterprise, we will find them again, but freed of stain, burnished and transfigured. This will be so when Christ hands over to the Father a kingdom eternal and universal.

Yet despite these quotations indicating that there is no new creation until the end, Haughey also quotes Johannes Metz with approval, even though the latter indicates that present-day work does indeed contribute to the new creation:

> We are workers building this future and not just interpreters of this future. The power of God's promises for the future moves us to form this world into the eschatological city of God.[7]

Honorific notions of the fulfilled end-time, especially when hardened into concepts of perfection, are like "language on holiday," unhooked from ordinary conceptual connections, so that one hardly knows what to make of them. When the book of Revelation looks toward "new heavens and a new earth," for example, that language is poetic and ruminative, not discursive and connotative, much less denotative of anything specific. Still, it is all too possible to think of the end-time as one of fulfillment-cum-perfection and to allow the old Greek idea of paradigmatic perfection to slip back in with the stultifying effect it has on human attempts to do good and godly work.

Further, as already argued in a previous chapter, wherever Christian fulfillment is invested in an eschatological perfection, apophatic and kataphatic spiritualities make war on metemphatic spirituality. Yet the emphasis that Jürgen Moltmann, Miroslav Volf, and others place on eschatology as the means by which the Christian faith interprets life seems correct. But they tread a fine line in doing so.

Consider Moltmann for a moment. His influence comes from Ernst Bloch, whose understanding of humanity as *homo viator* ("man on the way") always led toward some utopian hope. Bloch uses Marx's "kingdom of freedom" as a goal of perfectibility toward which humans might work.[8] Moltmann, while agreeing that the pull of future expectation can draw humanity along, does not believe that a specific goal, even a perfect state, or utopia ought to be spelled out when it comes to Christian expectation.[9] Christian hope dominates Christian belief, but the faithfulness of God and the newness of what God does always "overflow" and surprise human expectation at any given stage or advance on life's way.[10] Thus, rather than the promise of a specified state of being (e.g., real streets of gold or pearly gates), Christian hope is invested in the promise of God's righteousness and faithfulness as attested through biblical history and beyond. But it is centrally exemplified in the cross and resurrection of Christ. The cross embraces the depth of what is tragic and suffering about history, and, on the other hand, Christ is raised from the consequent death history had brought him. The resurrection thereby represents an already profound reversal or contradiction to what one might more cynically expect of history, but it is set in the not yet of Christ's reign at the end of time. That much can be said, but anything more would lead toward a "transcendental eschatology" that would, by its majesty, devalue any historical stage along the way.[11] *As it is, Christians have warrant for hope that the same God who raised Jesus will also make room for new creations in history as it proceeds toward the end-time.*[12]

Moltmann's own thought then proceeds toward mission and political theology, but something like the same careful path he treads opens a way to value new things: the way Christ especially exemplifies, and is exemplified, in the working world.

A Method for Defining New Things

Consider the following two columns:

column 1:	column 2:
innocence	knowing good and evil
heavenly	mixture of heaven and hell
peaceful	unsettled
reasonable	absurd
perfect	imperfect
utopian	reality
understandable	confused
good	compromised
Garden of Eden	in this world

These terms are set in a kind of opposition to suggest two different worlds: one is ideal, the other real. If a working group or an individual worker were asked which column accurately reflects working life (or, for that matter, any other aspect of life), the answer would have to be column 2.

What, then, is the function of the first? One might think that column 1 serves as that toward which one ought to strive. On second thought, however, striving toward column 1, with the hope of reaching it, is a chimera. Toyota, compared to other manufacturers, for example, has the most defect-free cars coming off their assembly line, but there has never been such a thing as a *totally* defect-free car. A seemingly perfectly machined bolt, when examined under a microscope, is pitted with flaws. The efforts of humans never reach an ideal perfection. Part of the process of maturity is to realize that the concepts in column 1 are always out of reach. Indeed, when taken too seriously, the terms in column 1 have a way of denigrating those in column 2 as things of little worth. But this conclusion (that column 2 is of little worth) runs counter to the gospel, which affirms human beings in love, "accepts the unacceptable," as Paul Tillich put it.[13] Indeed, it is a mark of maturity with most human beings that, while they know they fall short of what they *ideally* (and impossibly) could be, they are not ashamed of who they are. In other words, there is a difference between being sorry and being a "sorry person." No one likes to see the latter. A certain dignity is required even in humility. Job stubbornly sits on a dung heap, covered with sores but resolute in his sense of dignity. And when Yahweh comes to confront Job, he says, "Gird up your loins and I will confess to you that you are a man" (Job 40:7), acknowledging that same dignity.

There is another reason for abandoning column 1—it doesn't exist: none of these attributes or states exists in any perfect way. "Utopia" literally means "no place." Yet column 1 is often, and in many ways, something toward which humanity seems to strive. But the notions in column 1 are always vague, not well formed, and chimerical. They function in somewhat the same way as certain kinds of honorific universals. In Plato's *Theatetus*, for example, Socrates asks what "knowledge" is, and he is given replies following specific uses: knowledge is wisdom, knowledge is knowing a body of theories such as geometry, or it is a craft like carpentry. But Socrates disparages these answers by giving a paradigm of what he wants:

> If anyone should ask us about some common everyday thing, for instance, what clay is, and we should reply that it is the potter's clay and the oven-maker's clay, and the brick-maker's clay, should we not be ridiculous? . . . in the question about clay, the everyday simple thing would be to say "clay is earth mixed with moisture," without regard to whose clay it is.[14]

Socrates wants to know what all the versions of "knowledge" have in common: he wants the real or essential definition of "knowledge," as if there were one, since there seems to be one of "clay." But there isn't one for "knowledge." Instead, there are just instances, some having common features with others, but without every instance having all of the same common features, and some instances being entirely discontinuous with others yet still recognizable as an instance of "knowledge." Ludwig Wittgenstein calls this a "family resemblance," where a word is meant to cover a number of somewhat similar cases. One can recognize a certain sameness, as with family members, because one has the same chin as another, while a different member has a similar nose, but not the chin, another a similar forehead, but neither the same nose or chin, and so on as in a composite resemblance.[15]

Similarly, column 1 consists of nothing but vague honorific composites coming from many sources. The perfect CEO, the perfect boss, the perfect manager is a similar kind of composite: a visionary who facilitates the ideas of the people, commanding but conciliatory, empathetic but uncompromising, young and energetic but also of mature wisdom, loyal to the company yet always ready to support the employee.

Among the most obvious composites of column 1 are those offered through advertising. The superwoman as glimpsed in television commercials is young, attractive, vivacious, a caregiver to her children yet also professionally successful. There is no indication that a career takes time away from attention to children or detracts from a quality marital relationship, that she may grow old, lose her job, or expect anything less than perfection. Similarly, the successful man drives an expensive car, is a top performer in his work, has a reputation for excellence on the golf course, is young and attractive, married well, lives in the suburbs with bright promising children, and so on.[16]

Psychologist Steven Hendlin gives an example of a fifty-seven-year-old man earning $300,000 per year, with season tickets on the fifty yard line at (what were then) Rams games and corporate seats to watch the Lakers, membership in a private country club, trips to Europe every year with his wife, and an expensive customized car. Yet he did not feel he was enjoying life the way he was supposed to.

> I never really seemed to be focused on where I was in my race to the top. I was always looking forward to the next big deal or next promotion. As soon as I reached one plateau, I couldn't stop and enjoy it; I had to go like hell to outdo myself and everyone else around me. That became the game—to outdo myself no matter what it took. When I look back on it, I can see how afraid I was of not making it; I can see how anxious and driven I was and how much I was willing to give up just to get the glory of making it to the top. I was always afraid of not

having enough money, of struggling like my father did just to take care of the bills. And I was afraid that my life wouldn't amount to much if I didn't strive to be the best. Excellence for me was taken for granted—I wanted everything to be perfect.[17]

It follows that pursuit of column 1 ought to be abandoned because it denigrates a column 2 existence, and because it (column 1) doesn't exist. Try as one might, no one lives there. Column 2, for all its faults, must be affirmed. But when column 1 is abandoned, an existential vacuum occurs. Affirming column 2 and giving up column 1 seems to give up on hope as well. Quoting again from Hendlin's patient:

> I get anxious when I think of giving up the goal of perfection. Even though I don't think I'm feeling the joy in life that I ought to, it scares me to think of not having that end goal to shoot for—the goal of being perfect. I know that I can't achieve complete perfection but I still use it as the target. I have used it pretty well, I believe. Without seeking perfection what would I use as the goal to keep me productive, to keep achieving more? So don't ask me to stop striving for perfection unless you've got something better to replace it with.[18]

The difficulty with column 1 goals is that they remain vague, remote, and unachievable, like an ever-receding horizon. Indeed, if there is to be any hope at all, it must be without renouncing column 2; that is, it must somehow embrace column 2.

But the resolution to give up pursuing column 1 and to accept and live within column 2 can create an existential vacuum or crisis. The crisis is similar to what alcoholics call "unhappy sobriety," a state in which a disciplined life lived honestly within one's limitations offers no satisfaction because the oxygen of any hopeful goal has been sucked away. According to the argument being made here, a Christian should find her hope in the beckoning of an eschatological Christ, that is, a goal offered by Christ. This goal, however, cannot be a first-column goal. Instead, Christ, as the built-in rationale, the *logos* of creation, exemplifies and provides for a creation that (in Hefner's words) "stretches," or—in terms of the argument presented here—adds the possibility of doing more within second-column existence, without disparaging that existence. And it is here that the eschatological hope lies.

An Example

Consider the following, somewhat lengthy example from the world of work. The difference between wishing for a column 1 fulfillment and a realistic hope within column 2 can be appreciated in the contrast between science fiction, on the one hand, and scientific discovery and invention on the other. It is sometimes said that, for all the fanciful adventures of Jules Verne's novels, he nevertheless foresaw a great many later inventions. Yet he is not credited with actually having invented anything. A real invention requires not just vision, but a good deal of background information, technical know-how, and practical application—all attributes within column 2. Otherwise the early Incas, for example, might have said (in the fashion of column 1), "Why don't we invent the wheel?" and it would have happened. But such things don't occur out of fancy, or *de novo*; there must be something already in reality that leads up to them—some prior knowledge upon which to build. It is like Jesus' little saying that "every scribe who has been trained for the kingdom of heaven is like a householder who brings out of his treasure what is new and what is old" (Matt. 13:52). The new is always some transformation of the old. Therein lie hope and the possibility of doing a new thing. This is where the incarnation "gives evidence."

The specific example concerns Ernest Rutherford's work on radiation. It has to do with the artificial transmutation of the elements and finds its column 1 fanciful representation in alchemy. It seemed to many ancient students of nature that substances could be changed from one to another: food into flesh, ice to water, and ore to metal were examples where this change appeared to take place. Alchemists supposed that tin could be transformed into gold; and because metals were associated with astrological signs, they were supposed to have special powers. Gold, thought to be the perfect metal, could not only make one rich; when transformed from some other metal, it could open the possibility of creating other perfect substances, such as the *panacea*, the perfect medicine. Thus alchemy was an ill-defined composite concept aimed at a perfection conjured out of a number of different notions. But it eventually had to be given up. By the end of the nineteenth century, the possibility of this sort of transubstantiation was widely rejected.

Rutherford's contribution came not by cherishing the alchemist's dream but by investigating radioactivity, a task within the confines of column 2. Pierre and Marie Curie had noticed fluorescence in minerals, but only Rutherford proposed that these rays might be the result of disintegrating atoms. Among heavy metals there is a natural change that occurs when radium, for example, decays to lead. Assuming that radium might be giving off particles in this process, Rutherford set up a device in which these particles ("alpha particles") would be emitted into a gas chamber with a screen detector on one end. He noticed "long-range scintillations" when he injected very dry air, and these scintillations increased when he added more nitrogen, even though the resultant gas had more hydrogen. He hypothesized that the alpha particles were colliding with nitrogen and creating hydrogen atoms that registered as the long-range scintillations. But a hypothesis wasn't enough: he had to show that it was a "natural extension of theories already well established," and this he did even as a "householder might bring out of his treasure what is old and what is new." He may not have been a "scribe . . . trained for the kingdom of heaven," but he nevertheless found the "stretching" factor in nature and human knowledge that gave him hope without the fanciful column 1 wishes of alchemy. One could say that he "stretched" column 2 and did "more" with it.

Rutherford also exhibited the "stretching" of nature by suggesting a fruitful experimental program that has since been followed extensively in physics. He speculated that "if alpha particles—or similar projectiles—of still greater energy were available for experiment, we might expect to break down the nuclear structure of many of the lighter atoms." And this has led to the extensive experiments and results with particle accelerators, age dating by atomic decay, and the like.[19]

The faith that science has in advancing and stretching the knowledge of nature is an example of faith in the possibility of a new thing showing up in a seemingly secular context. But the same faith can be expressed theologically. The restriction that one's hopes must remain within column 2 raises a very important question: it asks whether, while without denying the confines of column 2, one might do more. This question is important because it is the question of the incarnation: Would it be possible to live within column 2 and yet do more with it? Could someone do this? Has someone done this? The "more" in this special case of "doing more" amounts to doing a "new thing," participating in a "new creation." The idea of participation is important because, following biblical teaching, there is always an element of sustenance, grace (others say "luck"), a Godward side to the action of such creativity, even as the concept of a "created cocreator" implies.

But "new things" are not necessarily religious. The invention of the wheel is a new thing; likewise Rutherford's work with particle physics. In general, any new development out of something already in column 2 existence that can contribute to the goodness of creation is a new thing. A new thing is a hoped-for achievement carried out within column 2 that can work to the good of creation. Some new things, like Rutherford's discovery, are momentous; others, like having a new baby, are both routine and momentous; still others, like achieving reconciliation after personal estrangement, can be small but gratifying. But the biggest emphasis here should be on those new things gained in the working world, like cleaning up a polluted river, devising a new algorithm, finding the cause for ulcers, rearranging an assembly line for improved safety, solving an engineering problem in bridge construction, settling a better labor contract, and so on. Thus, Christ gives concrete evidence of the eschatological promise in the working world. His exemplification of new things is picked up and carried on by the created cocreator. Again, column 2 is stretched thereby to encompass a new aspect of reality.

Christ's Exemplification of New Things

Much of what Christ does in his own early life epitomizes the doing of new things. The temptation in the wilderness represents his rejection of a column 1 mission to the world. His favoring of the servant role of Second Isaiah indicates a thorough embrace of a column 2 existence, identifying with the situation in which all humanity finds itself. His teaching is not *de novo*, but, as he says, "brings out . . . what is new and what is old."

The resurrection might seem to be a column 1 event, but not so in view of the thoroughgoing passion that precedes it and the fact that Jesus endures death at the hands of all-too-human corporate structures. There were plenty of column 1 alternatives, especially that of a triumphal or militaristic messiah. Following the logic of column 2, the resurrection must issue from the dead and must be a historical event. As a triumph, it is not a column 1 assertion of a living deity, but a column 2 surety where grounds for hope can realistically be expected to drive through history on both a personal and a corporate level. The resurrection is the *ne plus ultra* of new things, but it is not *sui generis*. It could be called the climax of Jesus' demonstration of how *more* can happen within a column 2 existence and a promise extended for the created cocreator to use as well. This is why a Christus Victor theory of atonement is to be preferred over the substitutionary theory. As Christus Victor, Christ is a representative, showing the way, not a substitute for humans. The created cocreator does not need to stand aside for a substitute; instead the cocreator's creative role is underlined, beckoned, and encouraged by the demonstrative representation that Christ has made.

If the demonstration of new things is a central feature of Jesus' ministry, then a notion of the cosmic Christ is also important. The wheel was a new thing—likely invented several times over in different civilizations. Similarly, the discovery of herbal medicines for healing or the arch as a building technique. As a participant in creation, Christ represents the aspect of creation that has the possibility of new things built into it. And such possibilities are not the exclusive franchise of the church but may be done by anyone. Furthermore, the possibility of new things reflects a kind of innate hunger within humans. The church tends to emphasize the category of new things having to do with human relations, but the doing of new things obviously extends to other areas, like machinery or architecture, horticulture or immunology, conservation or medicine, to which many people devote their working lives and find justifiable gratification in their achievements.

Equivocating over New Things

The struggle to overcome the attraction to column 1 occurs again and again. The church, for example, seems forever caught in the equivocation of what constitutes Christian fulfillment when it uses a word like *reconciliation* to mean "restoration" to an Edenic column 1 existence. The tendency is very much like the popular tendency to believe technology is a magically promised approach to a column 1 utopia. But the promises of God go through column 2. St. Paul's struggle to overcome his lifelong commitment to the Law is an example of a perfectionist whom Christ turned in another direction (Rom. 7). Whatever affliction he had was not taken away; instead the Lord told him, "My grace is all you need; power comes to its full strength in weakness" (2 Cor. 12:9).

In summary, Christ is the exemplar of new things. Almost every aspect of his life is constituted by this activity, including his death and resurrection. The resurrection puts a surety on God's promise, making the Christ-event a prolepsis that draws history toward him. He is also the exemplar of the kingdom of God because the activity of this kingdom has its cutting edge in the doing of new things. It is as if the Father sends his Son and cocreator to end the distraction of perfectionism and to demonstrate instead how the creation works with respect to new things. But doing new things can come in many guises and walks of life, not just those that the church especially seems to like but also the kind that give satisfaction to people at their work. Christ thereby represents the yeast of creation, that energy which opens human work to new possibilities through the course of history. As civil rights workers said in the 1960s, "Go into the world and see what in the world God is doing in the world." The invitation of Jesus himself also gives reinforcement to this image of activity in the world, or what Pierre Teilhard de Chardin called "God forward":

> . . . the one who believes in me will also do the works that I do and, in fact, will do greater works than these, because I am going to the Father. I will do whatever you ask in my name, so that the Father may be glorified in the Son. If in my name you ask me for anything, I will do it. (John 14:12–13)

BAD THINGS

Sadly, a creation that leaves open the possibility of good new things also leaves open possible bad developments as well. The terrorist attack on the World

Trade Center in New York City is just one of many examples, where sophisti-cated technology and planning were required to work devastating harm. The development of weapons of mass destruction, both nuclear and chemical, are large-scale instances of bad things that have come into reality. But there are also smaller ones, as when the mail systems make fraud possible, guns are used for shooting sprees, or advanced harvesting techniques in the seas and forests seriously deplete natural resources. The danger of havoc wreaked on creation comes in part because people cannot foresee the consequences of technologi-cal development. People build atomic power stations, for instance, without knowing how to dispose adequately of nuclear waste. Sophisticated medicine becomes so expensive that access is limited, leaving many in need but unable to be helped. And as population increases, world trade and communication weave a web of delicate interdependence, where old social practices must be given up. Adam Smith's seemingly benevolent "invisible hand," thought to guarantee fairness in a free-market economy, wasn't sufficient to prevent the oligarchic monopolies of the gilded age; antitrust measures had to be enacted.

The created cocreator, *homo artifex,* is an evolved being who has managed to weave complex social systems into a high degree of interdependence. If var-ious human social traits are thought to be "selected" in an evolutionary process, then a spirit of compromise and cooperation must surely have come to the fore for the modern social system to continue. It may be that hedonic "winner takes all" behavior was, at one time, a key to survival, followed by a fierce tribal loyalty or ethnocentrism, and, in turn, a nationalism. But this social development runs counter to genetic evolution. Quoting Donald T. Campbell,

> The survival value of complex social coordination, with full division of labor, professional soldiers, and apartment house living, has been achieved in man as a socially-evolutionary product which has had to inculcate behavioral disposi-tions directly counter to the selfish tendencies being produced by genetic selec-tion.[20]

The genetic selection Campbell has in mind was brought to the fore problem-atically by E. O. Wilson. On the first page of his *Sociobiology, a New Synthesis,* he writes: "This brings us to the central theoretical problem of sociobiology: how can altruism, which by definition reduces personal fitness, possibly evolve by natural selection?"[21] Various auxiliary hypotheses have been suggested in order to circumvent this difficulty: kin selection, reciprocal altruism, or inclu-sive fitness,[22] but none of these explains the trans-kin altruism a complex soci-ety requires, where people—especially in the context of work—serve others they will never see or know. Campbell believes scientists must look to sin and temptation in the folk morality that our religious traditions provide. The commandments, the proverbs, the religious "law" represent social-evolutionary products directed at inculcating tendencies that are in direct opposition to the "temptations" which for the most part represent dispositional tendencies produced by biological evolution. For every commandment we may reasonably hypothesize a biological tendency running counter to some social-systematic optimum.[23]

The eye of the believer will find the altruistic impulse originating not in the cocreator, but coming from the Creator, as an emergent phenomenon in the cocreator, not explainable entirely by whatever historical factors preceded it.

Christians will see the love command of Jesus, an other-regarding renunciation of self for the sake of others without hope of being reciprocated, as a specific endorsement of altruistic behavior. Such is the situation especially in religious communities, where not only inward- but outward-regarding expressions of self-sacrifice are expected and common. Following Campbell, it is the key that redirects the impulse to find and do bad things.

Looking back on this chapter and the themes listed at its beginning, the main task has been to show how the work of Christ "gives evidence" in the work of humanity. Humans can be described as *animalia laborantia,* not just because of a need to subsist, but because they are an integral part of creation, in that "they are like the beasts that perish" (Ps. 49:11b). Therefore natural theology is useful because it grounds humanity in the context of evolution. But humankind can also be described as *homo artifex* and *homo faber,* capable of making intelligent artifacts, while they themselves are "made . . . but little lower than the angels" (Ps. 8:6a), having a commissioned status as created cocreators, uniquely equipped with a "phenotypic plasticity." Humans are also *homines viatores,* going somewhere as spiritual beings who are obliged to have a transcendental purpose that can go destructively off course, but comports best when grounded in God-given reality. Christ, as the eschatological dimension of work, pulls human effort toward himself as the *anakephalaiōsis,* as the "head" or consummation of creation.[24] Despite however much Christian language might imply that Christ thus beckons *homines viatores* toward perfection, this is not the case. Instead, the call is toward ever stretching or doing more with an imperfect reality, here called the doing of "new things." And this is probably the most exciting part of human work.

The next chapter, while reinforcing this call toward innovation, will shift the emphasis of work to that aspect requiring by far the most of labor's time with the *homo conservans.*

5

The Protological Creator
and Homo Conservans

THE PREVIOUS CHAPTER'S TOPIC, how Christ exemplifies the doing of new
things, presents an incomplete picture, because the actions are seen from
a human point of view, focusing on the created cocreator's call to the possibility of the new in everyday work. But work, day-in and day-out, is hardly constituted entirely of doing new things. Instead, most human work is *not* new
but routine, with a familiar round of sameness: ledger entries must be made,
clerks must answer the same inquiries repeatedly, bills must be paid, employees must punch in at the time clock, agendas must be drawn up for monthly
meetings. None of these activities is new. And what is new doesn't spring up
out of a vacuum, but, like the increase of knowledge, always rests on the
accomplishments of what has gone before. Innovation must come out of a
reservoir of preserved possibilities.

New creation's requirement to emerge from what was already there presupposes two preexisting theological conditions: an original creation *ex nihilo*,
requiring nothing preceding it except the Uncreated Creator, and, once that is
done, a continuing maintenance of a creation that is in flux. It requires also
some discarding of what becomes obsolete, undesirable, or harmful. This
function depends on God as the original Creator and continuing Maintainer,
the acts of *creatio ex nihilo* and the *creatio continua* respectively, whose functions are foundational and protological but intertwined with doing new
things, that facet which is especially represented by Christ as the preexisting
Word whose rationale of new from old is built into creation. This intertwin-
ing of the Uncreated Creator and the preexistent Word bespeaks part of the
way the self-revelation of the Trinity takes place. Thus, as the perichoretic doctrine of the Trinity implies, these two persons of the Trinity, Father and Son,
are distinct but rely on and witness to each other. A similar case—from the
point of view of human work—will be made for the Holy Spirit's distinct but

interdependent role in the Trinity. The purpose of this chapter, however, is to ponder the continuing work of God the Creator as a guide to the role of maintenance in human endeavor, the role of *homo conservans*.

Since the central theme for this theology of work views humanity in the context of humans as created cocreators, natural theology once again becomes necessary as a way to describe current views about the creation and the implications these views have for how faith understands the work of its Creator. Contemporary results in science can plausibly be said to evince a creation that is tailor-made for human inquiry and work.

THE WORK OF GOD AS CREATOR AND MAINTAINER

An Apology for Natural Theology

All talk of divine-human endeavor may well appear doubtful in the context of a worldview given by science. Science seems to have virtually shut God out of the picture, leaving *homo laborans* to toil on alone. A Christian might say "so much the worse for science," but scientific endeavors are part of the world of work for many Christians and should be honored even if it obliges a believer to scramble and search for plausible windows and clues to the work of God and the complementary place for the work of people. The method of science is bounded in order to clear itself from the ultimate questions posed in theology. But theories and speculations within science often interface with questions of interest to theology in such a way that, within the mind of a believer, the limits of science can be taken over meaningfully into the realm of theology. Fortunately, these days scientific worldviews open up some new possibilities for a natural theology.

The point of special interest here involves current thinking about creation in order to detect those places where cocreative settings for work seem especially evident. Even though old answers about the order and design of creation are no longer plausible, new approaches and discoveries reveal new possibilities for how human and divine work can be seen to join forces. First, humans are in a remarkably good position to survey the creation. The rational abilities of *homo sapiens* seem to have a special congruence with the structure of the universe. Second, the universe—in order to come into being the way it is—has been exceedingly fine-tuned, plausibly indicating an intended goodness and a home for living things. Third, while from ancient times the creative act has been one of somehow subduing chaos, there is now a much clearer understanding of how energy is utilized in the midst of chaos. As it turns out, "chaos" is not subdued—at least as this term has come to define aperiodic events with a deterministic feedback loop. In this case, creation requires a chaos that is both encouraged and controlled, especially among living beings, but with a different sort of order. Call it a "creative chaos." Fourth, as this creative chaos develops, it follows certain "lures," "attractors," or "trajectories," some leading nowhere but others leading to a fecundity fulfilling virtually every viable niche, but especially leading to *emergent* levels, levels of novel difference not anticipated by what went before. Most interesting from the human point of view is the emergence of consciousness, the intentional construction of culture, history, and a treasury of knowledge to assist human effort, which we discussed in the previous chapter. The foregoing points will be considered on a more cosmological scale, using the now-discarded Paley's "watchmaker" as a stalking horse. Finally, a fifth consideration will switch from the macro to the micro and the strange consequences that seem to come from the world of quantum theory.

Virtually every educated Englishman of the time knew William Paley's *Natural Theology* (1802) and his argument that God must exist because the natural order compared favorably to a finely made watch, which in turn implied an intelligent Designer. Furthermore, as a mechanical contrivance, the universe was so well put together that it could run on its own with little interference or adjustment, just as Isaac Newton's laws of motion had said a hundred years earlier. Newton had also provided a "sensorium" for God, a universe with space and time everywhere absolutely fixed, a kind of divine window so that God could survey all.

But this vision of God in his heaven and everything right with the world suffered a serious blow when Charles Darwin adapted Adam Smith's theory of marketplace competition to living things along with Thomas Malthus's theory of population pressure, coming up with a theory of common origin through survival and speciation based on the pressures of natural selection and differential reproduction. If humans and apes descended from a common ancestor, then they could hardly claim to be specially created or, for that matter, exempt from eventual extinction. Furthermore, the ingenious design one might claim to find in living organisms is not something intentionally wrought by a clever and benevolent Designer, but simply the accumulation of gradual evolutionary change over millions of years: a *blind* watchmaker at best. As to Newton's sensorium of God, Albert Einstein's general theory of relativity blends space and time into a geometric scheme where the universe has no single *now* through which all of space can be seen. Nor can the universe be controlled from a single point: both cause and time are relative to place. The old picture of God on a throne, seeing and directing all, now seems impossible, leaving the whole idea dispensable. And humanity, having sprung up accidentally in an inconsequential corner, also merits no special treatment.

The Placement of Human Intelligence

More recent developments, however, have revived interest in a designing God and a centered place for humanity. Even if the earth is not in the middle of things, there is a coincidence of scale that puts the size of a planet at a geometric mean between the size of the universe and the size of an atom; and, similarly, the mass of a man is at a geometric mean between that of a star, like the sun, and a proton, implying that humans stand at an advantageously knowing place between the smallest and the largest aspects of the universe.[1] Aside from the size and position, there is also mental power. Three pounds of brain yield a complexity and neural connective capability that beggars any other known constellation of matter in the universe.[2] And human comprehension is mysteriously in harmony with the universe. Information found in nature is decipherable to the human mind. This strange congruence between mind and matter is especially conspicuous in mathematics. Work done in pure computation seems to be nothing more than drawing out the consequences of abstract mathematical concepts: logically elegant, perhaps, but of no more connection to the world than doodles on paper. Yet such results are often subsequently adapted by scientists because they capture orderings and regularities in nature that had not been understood before. Without Georg Riemann's speculations in non-Euclidean geometry, for instance, Einstein couldn't have worked out his theory of general relativity.[3]

The Anthropic Principle

The centering of humanity and the possibility of a deliberately designed universe are also of renewed interest because of what is called the "anthropic principle." If one asks, Why this universe and not some other? Or many others? an awesome mystery arises. The universe is here because of a few basic physical constants expressing the relation between basic forces governing such things as gravitation and nuclear reaction.[4] For example, if certain constants had different values, chemical elements heavier than helium would not have formed because stars would either never have evolved or would not have lasted long enough to cook up, eventually explode, and spew out the heavier elements upon which life depends. But the life of stars alone doesn't guarantee these elements; more coincidences are required. Pressure on two helium nuclei forms an unstable beryllium, which would quickly decay except that the resonance of nuclear matter within a star is in a fruitful harmony that allows the combination of another helium nucleus to change beryllium to carbon, so crucial to organic life. But the happy coincidence does not end there. Carbon might then easily decay to form oxygen. But the resonance needed to form oxygen lies just below the star's thermal energy, preventing carbon from being entirely dissipated. Fred Hoyle, who noticed this delicately tuned interaction, remarked:

> A common sense interpretation of the facts suggests that a super intellect has monkeyed with physics, as well as chemistry and biology, and that there are no blind forces worth speaking of in nature.[5]

Again, the force of gravity is relatively weak when matter is sufficiently spread out, but gets stronger by the square of diminishing distance between objects. If, at the big bang, the expulsive force had been too great, there would have been too much dispersion to allow astral constellations like the solar system and galaxies to form. On the other hand, if the big bang had been less powerful, an implosion would have followed, causing a stillborn universe. As it is, the universe is dispersed well enough to keep the initial expansion going, but clumpy enough to allow suns and planets to form. If the universe were not homogenous, some portions would have been dense enough to suffer gravitational collapse, pulling other portions after them. So the acceleration of a universe moving outward from an initial big bang and the relative evenness of its distribution seem also to be in delicate adjustment.[6]

Such painstaking balance among fundamental forces of the universe is not only improbable to an ultra degree, but even more improbable because it represents an ensemble of such individual balances, each improbable in its own right. In this respect, it augers for something reminiscent of the watch Paley had in mind two centuries ago—except now the watch is not only finely made but finely tuned as well. The "anthropic principle," which attempts to comprehend this fine tuning, is often expressed in two basic versions—one weak, one strong. The weak version merely says that, among the myriad of possible universes one could imagine, this universe exists because it contains, among other things, the recognition of intelligent carbonaceous life. Claiming that a particular kind of universe is here because humanity is here only asserts the obvious. This weak version is trivially true. The strong version says that this universe *must* be such as to admit the creation of intelligent life. The strength of this expression lies in its claim that this universe did not arrive by accident but somehow *had to be*. Physicist Paul Davies remarks:

> the strong anthropic principle is founded on a quite different philosophical basis from the weak principle. Indeed, it represents a radical departure from the conventional concept of scientific explanation. In essence, it claims that the uni-

verse is tailor-made for habitation, and that both the laws of physics and the initial conditions obligingly arrange themselves in such a way that living organisms are subsequently assured of existence. In this respect the strong anthropic principle is akin to the traditional religious explanation of the world: that God made the world for mankind to inhabit.[7]

A "radical departure" indeed. Science usually constrains itself to explanations involving only efficient causes rather than final causes. Consider the following illustration. Suppose a hiker in Alaska enters a region so remote that no one has been there before. She looks up and sees some rocks on a grassy slope so configured as to spell out the words "Made by God." Restricting itself to explanations involving efficient cause, science would have to say that there is no intention behind those words: they are there by accident. After all, rocks roll down many grassy slopes in this world, and it is not unthinkable that among many such events, an accident could occur where the rocks would line up to spell out "Made by God." On the other hand, if the reasoning is from final rather than efficient cause, one looks for purpose and intention rather than accident, and it would be reasonable to conclude that the rocks were placed there by intelligent life.

Of course, there is no overt message occurring in nature that says "Made by God." But if there were such a message, it would cry out for a final-cause explanation. The strong version of the anthropic principle, however, comes close to just such a cry. In any case, the credibility of a designing, purposive God and a somehow central and intelligent humanity has regained some of the ground it lost earlier in the century. Both Creator and creature are reasonably open for a compatible acceptance among Christians who honor science but also press for more ultimate meanings.[8]

Closed and Open Dissipative Systems

The change of view since Paley's watchmaker, however, does not end there. It was not clear at the time when and whether the creation, in its watch-analogue form, would ever run down. Had Paley lived into the next century, he would have seen many ingenious attempts to devise successful perpetual motion machines, all of them failures. He was a little too early to know the second law of thermodynamics, which says that mechanisms, including even the universe, expend energy and eventually run down. Everyone knows, for example, that expended gasoline cannot be recovered by pushing a car backward to the place it occupied when the tank was full. This, on a larger scale, was bad news for a happy creation: the prospect that the universe would eventually either lose the energy to keep expanding and implode back into itself or else scatter ever outward and freeze away to nothing in heat death. Such thoughts led Bertrand Russell to counsel an "unyielding despair" over a humanity "beneath the debris of a universe in ruins." Similarly, mathematician Norbert Weiner suggested:

> We are swimming upstream against a great torrent of disorganization, which tends to reduce everything to the heat-death equilibrium and sameness described in the second law of thermodynamics . . . our main obligation is to establish arbitrary enclaves of order and system. These enclaves will not remain indefinitely by any momentum of their own after we have established them. . . . No defeat can deprive us of the success of having existed for some moment of time in a universe that seems indifferent to us.[9]

This pessimism, however, was held captive by the thought of how the second law works inside closed systems. Gas molecules within a closed cylinder, for example, will not naturally cluster over in one corner and leave the rest of the space in vacuum. They will disperse as evenly as possible. When heated, they will move about, colliding with one another, but when heat is withdrawn, this agitation expends itself, and the molecules will once again return to their dispersed state: a spent, but stable equilibrium.

Closed systems, however, are artificial. Paley's watch is a kind of closed system: its works are energized by a spring and operate in an even, regulated way until its energy runs down. But out in the real world, the watch is a poor analogy because nature uses open systems, where something very different occurs. Open systems are not contained: outside energy can pass through them. Instead of an evenly distributed state of equilibrium, open systems can reach what is called "far from equilibrium stabilities." A whirlpool, for example, is a highly unusual state for water to be in, but under the right conditions, and with a stream of energy passing through on the edge to keep it whirling, a whirlpool will remain in its own sort of equilibrium. Its equilibrium is not made up of molecules evenly dispersed and at rest, but clustered into an order suited to utilize the energy that passes through. Hence the term "open dissipative system," and because this order is not one of even dispersion, it is called a "far from equilibrium stability."

Living things tend to be in this kind of stability: promoting a fragile-yet-tough organization of tissue, taking advantage of some flow of energy to maintain themselves in a far-from-equilibrium state. Living things also enhance the toughness of this state by being capable of a measure of self-repair, reproduction, and adaptability. Paley's watch can't do these things. Living things also exist in interdependent communities: a coral reef, for instance, or the canopy of a tropical rain forest. Energy from the sun is stored through the green chlorophyll of plants, making carbohydrates, which are eaten by animals, whose flesh in turn supplies energy for predators and, by decay, puts nutrients into the soil. Similar dependency cycles abound, and the general trend is to utilize available energy with a minimal loss.

The lesson to be learned here is that, while the universe may be running down, degrading its energy, this effect drives life toward greater sophistication.[10] Furthermore, in a closed system, when energy has been expended, as in a cylinder filled with air, every molecule is evenly distributed like a perfect wallpaper pattern. By contrast, in an open, biological system, where some energy—however slight—is passing through and maximally utilized, the configuration will be more like an oil painting than a collection of evenly dispersed dots: a different kind of order that can plausibly be said to carry purpose. In fact, it is difficult to avoid talking about purpose when discussing the various functions of a biological system.

Thus, a biological community is relatively unstable because its equilibrium is so different from the equilibrium of a closed system. But it is also unstable because it is always in flux. A biological community faces the danger of an invasion by a master predator, like a disease or some voracious life form, or the danger of a creeping or abrupt change in the environment, all of which can upset the community's equilibrium. These threats oblige life to be continually experimenting with possible improvements, possible ways to evolve, protect, and adapt. In other words, the equilibrium of life must exist with a toughness rather close to the phase change that would plunge it into an out-of-control chaos.[11] For example, a tree may use some of its nutritional resources to make toxins to fight invading insects instead of using that nutrition to make leaves and capture sunlight. The tree may very well be close to a phase change, a change that could spell disaster by making the wrong toxins, or not enough toxins, or falling below crucial levels of chlorophyll through lack of leaves. One can also imagine a community of coevolving species, interdependently searching for a better state of mutual fitness. It is one of the wonders of nature that these communities seem to cooperate in such a way that a mutually optimal fitness is promoted. They are said to "self-organize" as if guided by an "invisible hand."[12] A theology of nature, however, will say that such organizations are part of the creatio continua, the continuing creativity of God through boundary conditions that maintain stability, but keep that stability near the edge of innovation, or near the edge of what the last chapter called "stretching."

Biological systems are also irreversible. If energy is withdrawn from a closed system, it will be degraded like a film running backward to each earlier state. And if energy is reapplied to a closed system, it will be like running the film forward again. But if some disaster strikes a biological system, as, for example, when a meteorite struck Central America and a great percentage of species became extinct, living things and their communities don't build themselves back up in exactly the same way. On the other hand, there are certain kinds of "congruences," or adaptive measures, that are repeated again and again in evolution. The fossil record seems to indicate, for example, that evolution "invented" wings several times over with a remarkably similar structure each time. The same appears to be true of eyes and other traits held in common. It is not as if each species is an entirely separate and novel creation. Instead, living things are made up of parts held more or less in common. Some of these parts are naturally "invented" time after time because of their fitness.

Open Systems and Chaos

A modern term for the direction creatures and their communities take is the term *attractor*. Switching to an analogy from geography, a lake could be considered an attractor because it forms a basin of attraction for the drainage area that surrounds it. Similarly, out of a number of possible limbs an animal might form, the feasibility involved in the mechanics of flight serve as an attractor for how a wing, out of many possibilities, should be formed.[13]

Attractor is a term for the direction an open system takes, and the process itself falls under the nonlinear mathematical rules, given the somewhat misleading term *chaos*. Paley's watch operates in a linear mode: that is, if the spring energy of the watch can be known together with the resistance of its gears and escapement, then one can determine when the watch will entirely run down, or how much energy will be left for any given moment in the interim. In other words, given the right initial information for a closed system, it is possible to determine its future state for any given moment. Machines work this way, but most of nature is not like a machine but more like an organism.

In open systems, new information is required all along the way. In order to predict weather, for example, new input is required hour by hour, interval by interval, feeding in data to successive weather stations, location by location, each calculation using values derived from the previous location, incorporating variations in pressure, temperature, topography, encounters with other systems, and all the factors that accrue as weather develops. Initial conditions aren't enough. Weather has to be tracked. If plotted on a graph, the weather's progress would be not a smooth line but one with jerks, abrupt turns, and lurches. Hence the term *nonlinear*. Another example: it is possible to plug a nonlinear formula into a computer in such a way that the shape of a fern can be generated on the monitor. Each new iteration of the formula takes the results of the last iteration, uses them in its computation, and passes its results on to the next "crunch" of the formula. Bit by bit a fern appears on the screen.

The same nonlinearity is true of living things individually and in community. Even though nonlinear formulas are classical and seem determinative in principle, from a practical point of view, anything like exact prediction of future states becomes well-nigh impossible. Nonlinear mathematical models are used for this purpose, and—with computers crunching the numbers at a faster rate than would be humanly possible—a considerable number of variables can be put into the mix. But what causal connection these variables may have is not always clear, nor can one be sure that all relevant variables have been inserted. Suppose, for example, that one tried to devise a nonlinear computation model for the effects of introducing a new strain of grass into western rangeland, or a model to predict the better outcome between allowing a tree-killing beetle to have its way in the national forests or subjecting the forest to the effects of a widespread chemical spraying to kill the beetle. These problems not only involve a virtually insuperable complexity but also have to allow the possibility that even the smallest perturbation somewhere along the way can have important effects on the outcome. Precise predictions are out of the question. The ironic upshot is that creation is a place where there is not only considerable freedom but also interdependence: many things are possible and practically everything matters. A communal life system, like that of a tropical coral reef, with its complex interdependencies, stays up on the edge of a "tough" equilibrium by affording each constituent niche sufficient viability so that no constituent or constituent group changes too quickly. It is as if an *attractor* settles ecosystems into a cooperative groove, where each member keeps a stable genetic profile and yet also experiments with a certain amount of genetic change just in case adaptation is needed. Here again, a kind of fine-tuning seems to be built into the order of nature, as ecosystems find their equilibrium on a threshold of innovation just short of falling into disorganization.[14]

But what scientifically plausible way might God use to exercise a continuing creativity? In what way does the protological work of God take place? Some theologians believe that the continuing and innovative action of God in creation ought to occur on a "top-down" basis. On Arthur Peacocke's account, top-down divine action occurs on the analogy of the way human mental decisions can govern bodily physical action. Assuming that the mind, the seat of consciousness, is not reducible to the gray matter of the brain, a mystery remains as to how mental events can govern physical ones, and yet it is intuitively appealing to believe that they do. Peacocke, who suggests that humans are a "psychosomatic unity," believes that God's relation to creation is analogous: self is to body as God is to world.[15] While Peacocke leaves his version of divine action shrouded within this analogy, his contemporary, John Polkinghorne, tries to flesh out a plausible top-down account of divine action by suggesting that divine action occurs through a holistic, nonenergetic information imparted over chaotic systems. An ensemble of possible outcomes might pose themselves in a developing chaotic system, and God influences the actual resolution. But what sort of information this is and how it works are unspecified.[16] The other causal channel suggested for divine action comes in the realm of quantum mechanics.

Quantum Unpredictability

It is difficult to describe phenomena at the quantum level, but consider the following contrast with baseballs. Compared to a baseball, or other ordinary-sized object, the arena of the extremely small is strangely different. A baseball hit or thrown on a baseball field can be seen *realistically* for what it is, having mass, location, and velocity, and, given the dynamic forces that interact with it, its activity can be predicted at any time. But an electron shot from an electron gun will usually constitute a field of its own—not of grass but of probability.

Consider the following. On a baseball field, a pitcher aims to throw at the strike zone, one pitch at a time, one ball at a time. It would be unthinkable to present several fanned-out strike zones facing a pitcher and ask him to hurl *each individual ball at all of them at the same time,* such that each ball would somehow visit all the strike zones but only actually go through one. Such a ball would not behave like a discrete entity. It would be as if the pitcher threw not a ball but an advancing wave of possibilities, exploring openings, as it were, in multiple strike zones but entering only one, though not the same one each time. There would be no telling exactly which zone the ball actually entered, except that in quantum theory, it is possible to indicate some zones as more likely possibilities than others. Hence, a quantum baseball would be more like an advancing probability wave, but at the same time it would seem also to be an object, since it eventually enters only one zone.

The way quantum phenomena behave, however, is influenced by the way a quantum experiment is prepared and observed. Continuing with the baseball analogy, if there is only one strike zone presented for the pitcher to hurl his quantum ball at, then the ball will behave like an ordinary baseball. But if more than one strike zone is presented, then the quantum ball will assume wavelike behavior in its exploration of more than one zone before it actually goes through a specific zone. And the one who prepares this quantum baseball experiment must also observe its resolution; otherwise the resolution of the wave to one zone will be left in probability, its exact resolution indeterminate. Thus, quantum systems are not independent of the observer-preparer.

Another example of inextricable human participation comes in Heisenberg's Indeterminacy Principle. On a baseball field both the position and the momentum of an ordinary baseball can be pinpointed at a given moment. But in the quantum-theoretic field of an atom, if the position of an electron is determined, its momentum smears out; and if the momentum is pinpointed, then the position smears out. Both cannot be determined at the same time.

But if this strange world is what underlies the more familiar world of base-balls, what prevents the ordinary from the same sort of weirdness? The answer is that objects and behaviors in the macro world are huge agglomerations of quantum events averaged out into the regularities one finds, for instance, in watching a baseball game. Only in very peculiar circumstances have quantum effects been manipulated to manifest themselves in the macro world, as, for example, with a superconducting magnetic ring, where many of the electrons in the ring are paired up and cooperate as superlative conductors, rather than compete among themselves. This superconductivity requires a state of quantum coherence not found in ordinary objects like baseballs that are, by contrast, decoherent.[17]

Nevertheless, quantum theory is far from just a curious piece of irrelevance to the ordinary world. Many aspects of the ordinary world depend on these theories. As Ian Barbour explains:

> There seem to be *system laws* that cannot be derived from the laws of components; distinctive explanatory concepts characterize higher organizational levels. Interpenetrating fields and integrated totalities replace self-contained, externally related particles as fundamental images of nature. The being of any entity is constituted by relationships and its participation in more inclusive patterns. Without such holistic quantum phenomena we would not have chemical properties, transistors, superconductors, nuclear power, or indeed life itself.[18]

Theologians find quantum theory attractive because it offers an opening for the sustaining and innovative activity of the Creator. If resolution of quantum wave packets (either singly or in constellations) at the quantum level is open to conscious manipulation, then a causal gap has been discovered in the very makeup of nature, meaning that this gap is ontic rather than epistemic—that is, a gap in the nature of things rather than a gap of knowledge yet to be filled in. If humans can, in prepared experiments, influence the outcome of quantum events, then it is plausible to think that this is the causal juncture where God might also operate. Indeed, since quantum events are thought to be at the bottom-most level of any causal event, it is here that the channel for divine action ought to be placed.[19] This is known as a "bottom-up" version of divine action.

Similarities with Human Communities

The foregoing discusses evidence from nature on the delicate but tough way in which the ecology of communal life finds support in open systems where energy is used efficiently for a fitness that must be conserved but also poised on the edge of innovation. This web of interdependence does not stop with organic life but extends into how the physical realm is fine-tuned to support life. Very much the same situation exists in human cultures, communities, and systems. The infrastructure of an economy provides many niches where various goods and services are offered in order to provide people with livings. But the communities and systems find it necessary to be forever exploring and implementing new options in order to stay viable. Economist Joseph Schumpeter wrote of capitalism that it "is by nature the form of . . . economic change and not only never is, but never can be stationary." It has a competitive process he called "creative destruction," which is its "essential fact."[20] But even during this "creative destruction," the economy has to maintain its strength. Its components cannot innovate wildly and throw it into utter chaos. So here again an accumulation of fine-tuning is required to keep things within the limits of such impositions as fiscal and monetary controls, restrictions on debt, price fixing, monopoly, and protection for labor.

It is because human systems so closely parallel and interweave with natural systems that human work can be called "cocreative." "Creativity" seems to imply or even overstate an activity of making something new and innovative. But, as just noted, if a natural or a human system innovates excessively, it gets out of control, loses its stability, and falls into disarray. The far-from-equilibrium stability in which living systems exist requires that they always be open to innovation in order to survive in a competitive and changing world. But this innovative activity should not be overstated. It is only the cutting edge. A much larger part of the task is the maintenance of what has already been put together.

A manufacturing company, for example, must have an arm devoted to research and development in order to stay healthy in a competitive environment, but it must, even more, be able to maintain in good working order what it already has. Therefore, most of "creation" or "creativity" is given over to preservation, conservation, or what here comes under the general category of "maintenance."

THE CREATOR AS PROTOLOGICAL

In a similar way, an important element in divine creativity can be imagined as maintaining a natural base for any forthcoming innovation. The *creatio,* either *ex nihilo* or *continua,* is protological because is sets the boundary conditions for creativity. It is the seedbed for innovation. The universe is a rational universe, amenable to rational inquiry, scientific laws, and an isotropic uniformity. It is sometimes thought that the initial *ex nihilo* creation is in tension with the continuing, *continua,* creation because if God were obliged to be continually involved with creation, it would belie the quality of what was wrought from the beginning. The situation would be like a car always in for repair because it was poorly made. The analogy is false, however, because the creation is always in process, always evolving. The natural constants and basic natural laws are boundary conditions governing how the evolution takes place, and they are signs of what is protological in creation. But the creation does not stand still. It is not a still life but a growing life, not a set piece but a procession, less like a machine than like an organism; this is another indication of a protological creation.

From the human created cocreator side, it is the area of maintenance where by far most work is done. A great deal of effort is needed simply to keep things from "sliding backward." This is why people pay their bills, hold monthly sales meetings, repair their machinery, audit financial reports, make sure each generation learns to read, carry out the garbage, wash the clothes, protect endangered habitats, plan tomorrow's menu, practice the violin, clean the shop floor, keep an eye on market reports, communicate with field representatives, plan next week's advertisement, and a myriad of other activities. These things are done to maintain a position in the world of work. Only a few workers will be outstanding innovators; the majority will be people who have done their part to maintain what they have been given to do. These are the police officers, firefighters, teachers, social workers, mail clerks, and many others, for practically everyone spends most of his or her working time with issues of maintenance. It may seem humdrum, but it is laudable work.

But part of maintenance is concerned with removal of the obsolete and guarding against harmful consequences of what is new.

Removing What Should Pass Away

Maintenance also requires culling out those things that are no longer useful for the general upkeep of a working endeavor: old machinery, ideas, methods, systems, techniques, structures, or even—regrettably—occupations. It is not thinkable that new things should take hold without the necessity of some old things passing away. Practically every biblical mention of the new things includes "things passing away" as well:

> Remember not the former things,
> Neither consider the things of old.
> Behold, I am doing a new thing. (Isa. 43:18–19a)

Sometimes new things can bring unintended detriment to the creation. The chemical industry may invent new solvents, new medicines, and other new agents, but it also creates pollution problems. New and helpful buildings are erected and roads built, but they also take away farmland. Computer-aided design facilitates the development of new blueprints, but it can throw drafting people out of work. Modern food packaging reduces concern about disease but increases problems of waste disposal.

It seems clear enough in the working world that (1) helpful gains should be held onto so that things do not slide backward; (2) what is old and replaced needs to be discarded; and (3) harmful developments also occur that require considerable attention. Maintenance is the working seedbed where all these issues fall and get mixed together. It should not be surprising, therefore, that—in the human dimension of work—where maintenance is the receiving ground for possible new things, there is a tension about what things will be received or even entertained. Newness, even when it evolves out of the old and is meant to be helpful to creation, is not necessarily accepted. History is replete with instances where prophets of newness of one kind or another went without honor in their home countries because people were biased toward preserving the old and could not cope with the new.

Incorporating the New

The problem here is one of assimilation and exhibits the difficult and challenging side of the work of maintenance. Bernard Lonergan's ideas are helpful at this point. *Insight* is his word for some new idea or innovation that is potentially helpful.

> . . . concrete situations give rise to insights which issue into policies and courses of action. Action transforms the existing situation to give rise to further insights, better policies, more effective courses of action. It follows that if insight occurs, it keeps recurring; and at each recurrence knowledge develops, action increases, and situations improve.

On the other hand,

> . . . flight from understanding blocks the insights that concrete situations demand. There follow unintelligent policies and inept courses of action. The situation deteriorates to demand still further insights and, as they are blocked, policies become more unintelligent and action more inept. What is worse, the

deteriorating situation seems to provide the uncritical, biased mind with factual evidence in which the bias is claimed to be verified. So in ever increasing measure intelligence comes to be regarded as irrelevant to practical living. Human activity settles down to a decadent routine, and initiative becomes the privilege of violence.[21]

Lonergan divides knowledge into several areas, one of which is common sense, which is concerned with short-term practicality: doing, making, eating, sleeping, food, shelter, and the like, and fails to grasp long-term consequences and the deeper sense of responsibility to be drawn from such consequences. There are also aesthetic, religious, and theoretical-scientific senses of knowledge. But the most prolific after common sense is that side of theory expressed in technology. The difficulty with technology is that it proliferates at a geometric rate: one invention begets several others. A new technology spawns a host of supporting elements: new inventions; manufacturing, distribution, and marketing techniques; financial underpinning—all the complexities of industry.

But the supporting theoretical insights of economics, politics, and religion that are needed to cope with a fast-changing world of technology do not readily appeal to common sense the way technology does. Common sense recognizes such deeper coping and adapting needs but is more attracted to immediate and more palpable goods.

> It needs to be guided, but is incompetent to choose its guide. It becomes involved in incoherent enterprises, it is subjected to disasters that no one expects, that remain unexplained even after the occurrence, that can be explained only on the level of scientific or philosophic thought, that even when explained can be prevented from recurring only by subordinating common sense to a higher specialization of human intelligence.[22]

Sin and Malevolence

Thus, the work of maintenance cannot simply be the acquisition, use, and preservation of technology. Much deeper questions abide. Too often these questions are addressed by psychological, social, political, or economic theoreticians who address them as problems that prescind from God in favor of therapy or management solutions. Thus a modern drift occurs toward "social engineering and totalitarian controls."[23] What is needed, according to Lonergan, is not only more and better insight into human nature but also "reverse insight" into the causes and preventions of human perversity, or—in a word— insight into, and acknowledgment of *sin*.[24] A human science, therefore, is incomplete without recognizing the facticity of sin and the need for reintegration into an onward-moving continuing creation. The creation moves on, and the maintenance part of human work is to be able to assimilate that movement wisely.

Maintenance is undoubtedly the most difficult and time-consuming part of human work. The impact of the new on history and its assimilation is far from an ameliorative, smooth upward curve. Time and again, problems of change have displaced people, precipitated wars, and caused economic hardship, unemployment, and other calamities. Sad to say also, the logical space allowing the possibility of new things allows space also for the emergence of evil things, sometimes by happenstance but sometimes by malevolence. As the Lord says to Cain,

> If you do well, you are accepted;
> if not, sin is a demon crouching at the door.
> It shall be eager for you, and you will be mastered by it. (Gen. 4:7)

And similarly, from 1 Peter 5:8–9:

> Awake! be on the alert! Your enemy the devil, like a roaring lion, prowls round looking for someone to devour. Stand up to him, firm in faith, and remember that your brother Christians are going through the same kinds of suffering while they are in the world.

Christ's Participation in Overcoming Sin

It is here that the creative work of Christ takes on a suffering/overcoming role with the Father to redeem the creation from disaster. Part of this role is one of forgiveness and reconciliation, but that aspect is included with the Son's showing a new or (in Paul's expression) a "better way," by which creatures are folded into the Creator's love, opening a metemphatic and constructive way of living. Thus, as the primitive church matured in its retrospective grasp of Christ's significance, the Gospel of John richly expresses a mutual "abiding."

> Anyone who loves me will heed what I say; then my Father will love him, and we will come to him and make our dwelling with him. (John 14:23)

Of course, not all change comes under the category of "new things," and even the new things Jesus brought were, regrettably, received with turmoil. Yet even though—in the interest of a theology of work—the work of the Father is maintenance and the work of the Son is new things, the two interweave, and there is no tension between them. One would wish that humans could cope with creativity in the same harmonious way. In the high priestly prayer used by the Gospel of John to close Jesus' ministry, this desire is expressed:

I glorified you on earth by finishing the work that you gave me to do. So now, Father, glorify me in your own presence with the glory that I had in your presence before the world existed. . . . I have made your name known to those whom you gave me from the world. . . . And now I am no longer in the world, but they are in the world, and I am coming to you. Holy Father, protect them in your name that you have given me, so that they may be one, as we are one. (John 17:4–6a, 11)

The *oneness* between the Father and the Son and those to whom the Son was sent is required if history and the kingdom are to go forward according to the divine promise. Why, then, is there no smooth progress in this direction? Because people can fail to do the maintenance needed to assimilate new things, and because they perversely create things that are evil. As a result, history can regress. Lonergan argues that liberty is required if there is to be insight, the key to human knowing. But liberty allows slack in the order of things, a leeway in nature that can permit history to either advance or slide backward. This means that humans have a considerable share in God's creative work. The twentieth century, with its burgeoning populations, awful instruments of destruction, complicated and interdependent economies, global communications, and complex but shrinking ecosystems, has brought an appreciation of the way human involvement in the natural order makes the creation at once an intricate, interwoven, and fragile environment.

Clearly, the human cocreator, the *homo conservans,* has a freedom to do well or poorly with the creation, implying a weight of considerable responsibility. But what provision is the *homo artifex* and *conservans* given to carry out this responsibility? The creation has its function and boundaries already in place, thanks to the protological work of God, and there is a function of continued maintenance carried on through divine action. The creation can very well exist independently of humans. It is also pulled toward newness out of the eschatological promise of the Christ. And whatever wreckage, failure, and struggle may occur is also offered redemption as a feature of this promise.

But what equipment is the cocreator given for his or her role of working responsibly in this context? The previous chapter argued that humans are unique for having a "phenotypic plasticity," more than any other species able to manipulate the environment to their own uses. They also pull along with them through time an accumulating culture of narrative, history, and learning that gains especially in technical sophistication but tries also to gain in the wisdom needed to be a responsible participant in creation. Further, humans have an intelligence that can be congruent with nature's design and a spirit able to share with God the love and excitement of creativity. They also build complex communal, economic, industrial, and national structures of their own that mimic many of the features found in natural ecological networks. There is good reason, therefore, to underline the divine comment in Genesis that humans are made "in our image" and are given dominion over the creation.

Nevertheless, there is a sense in which all this human accumulation of effort is too inadequate to face the daunting, seemingly overwhelming demand to be responsible as cocreators. What is it that especially encourages and equips the *homo artifex* and *conservans* to be a *homo viator,* someone who feels equipped to take on the work ahead and is on his or her way according to the eschatological promise? The question here becomes a pneumatological question, dealing with gifts of the Holy Spirit.

6

The Spirit, Pneumatology, and Homo Viator

THE ACTIVITIES ASCRIBED TO THE HOLY SPIRIT are very diverse. In the Old Testament, the Spirit is the agent of God during creation (Gen. 1:2; Ps. 33:6), and as *ruach*, "breath," the very force of life itself (Ps. 104:29–30; Ezek. 37:9–14). The Spirit imbues prophets and kings, especially the "servant" of Isaiah 42, with inspiration and power. The Spirit also invigorates community, as in Joel's text, where the Spirit is "poured out on all flesh" so that "old men dream dreams and young men see visions" (2:28–29). In the New Testament, the Spirit comes to Jesus with power (Mark 1:9–11), gives the disciples boldness and clarity of speech (Acts 2; 4:8), and is powerfully associated with baptism and the laying on of hands (Acts 8:15–17; 11:15–16).

More generally, the Spirit molds the Christian experience after the apprehension of who the Son is. Because of linkage with the Holy Spirit, Christians find themselves released from sin (Luke 20:23) and thereby free (2 Cor. 3:17–18), raised to a state of adopted sonship (Rom. 8:14–17), sharing in Christ's destiny in this world and in the world to come. Warrant of the Spirit's efficacious presence comes in the confession of Christ's incarnation and lordship (1 John 4:2). The Paraclete of John, in addition to being "another Comforter," is also the "Spirit of truth," who will keep the followers on the path of righteousness and faithfulness (John 16:7–13). The apostle Paul finds further activity of the Spirit in the *charismata*, "spiritual gifts," exercised in worship, but praises the virtue of love above all and elsewhere (Gal. 5:22) includes love as first among a set of virtues he calls "fruits of the Spirit": "love, joy, peace, patience, kindness, generosity, faithfulness, gentleness, and temperance."

THE SPIRIT AND THE TRINITY

With such a plethora of activity coming from the Spirit, it is ironic that little theological space sometimes seems available to mark off a distinct identity for the Spirit vis-à-vis the other persons of the Trinity. This problem of making room for the Spirit occurs because the role of Christ as mediator, the one who reveals the Father, our *Abba,* to the world, seems to leave nothing left for the Holy Spirit to do. The gap has already been bridged: Jesus accomplishes, in Rowan Williams's words, "a penetration from forecourt to inner chamber." There doesn't seem "any *structural* necessity for second mediatorial presence except as some kind of continuator of the Logos' revealing activity."[1]

But this problem goes away if the sequential assumption of Father-then-Son-then-Holy Spirit is given up. A better beginning intuition of the Trinity is to remember how each witnesses to the other and that it is not possible to think of one without thinking of the others. Thus, for example, the Father sends the Spirit to the Son in whom he is well pleased (Mark 1:10–11), but the Son credits not himself but the Father in heaven in terms of goodness, and credits the Spirit for his ability to cast out demons (Matt. 12:28), and it is the Spirit who accompanies Jesus in the wilderness temptation (Matt. 4:1). For its part, the Spirit is the one who enables a believer to confess faith in the Son (1 John 4:2; 1 Cor. 12:3) and gives access to the Father (Eph. 2:18, 22).

This mutual witnessing can be expressed on the analogy of close human friendship, as developed by Richard of St. Victor in the twelfth century. The relation of love between two persons, he argued, could exclude others, but there is a different and open dynamic in a threesome that is not exclusive but outward-looking and enfolding. Bonaventure called this relation a *circumincessio,* meaning "to move around one another." It is a Latin term for the Greek *perichoresis,* also used to describe the trinitarian relation. Catherine Mowry LaCugna suggests that *perichoresis* be thought of on the analogy of a physical object's length, width, and height.

> It is virtually impossible to separate an object from its dimensionality, though we can say that another object of the same class could be shorter or longer, wider or narrower, deeper, or more shallow. . . . The dimensions are perichoretic in the sense that width implies length, and for physical objects . . . width and length imply height.[2]

But a relation of love also entails the promotion of goodness for the beloved, and neither love nor the goodness love contains is limited; instead they are fecund, desiring an outward expression enfolding others. Both love and goodness wish to communicate themselves. Hence, the language, especially in Johannine texts, of an "abiding in" or "dwelling with" (John 17:11–12, 21; 1 John 3:24), which is meant to include the believer in fellowship with the Trinity and serves also as the model for human interdependence.

Clearly, however, this view of the Trinity depends more on the human apprehension of God on the analogy of personal relations than on a unity of substance that is serially disclosed first as Father, then as Son, and afterward as the Holy Spirit.[3] Indeed, it is important to distinguish between what God may be like *in se*, that is, as an inside essence, on the one hand, and, on the other, according to human experience of God in creation and history—that is, between the *internal structure* of God and the *self-expression* of God. Trinitarian formulae cannot explicate the inner nature of God, nor should they presume to do so. But this caution in no way vitiates an already known and experienced fellowship with the Trinity. As LaCugna puts it,

> God's presence to us does not exhaust without remainder the absolute mystery of God. . . .[But] the life of God is not something that belongs to God alone. *Trinitarian life is also our life.* As soon as we free ourselves from thinking that there are two levels to the Trinity, one *ad intra,* and the other *ad extra,* then we see that there is *one* life of the triune God, a life in which we graciously have been included as partners.[4]

The main concern here, however, is to set out those particular modes of partnership with God that have to do with work. So far the focus for a theology of work has been on the *doing of new things* with Christ, and the *activity of maintenance* with the Mother/Father. The special emphasis for work that is enhanced by the Holy Spirit is twofold: *skill* and *rapport. Skill* has to do with the special abilities people acquire that facilitate their work, and *rapport* is concerned with the quality of mutual support found among people who work together.

SKILL

Skills are like the "fruits of the Spirit" Paul mentions in Galatians 5:22, the virtues of "love, joy, peace, patience, kindness, generosity, faithfulness, gentleness, and temperance." They are virtues, in part, because they are dispositional and are not vices; that is, they are ways people are inclined to behave that promote goodness, creativity, and cooperation. They are also virtues because they are not acquired momentarily, as one might turn on a light or put on a new suit, but they are gained over time through cultivation and self-discipline until one acts out of habit or second nature. For example, the Good Samaritan of Jesus' parable, when we find him, has already developed a disposition to help those in distress. Even when he is confronted by an example of distress without being forewarned, he will act appropriately because he has cultivated an innate disposition to do so. It is a disposition that the priest and the Levite lacked because they saw the man in distress but chose to pass by on the other side of the road. As the saying goes, "It wasn't in them" to be able to help. Similarly the fruits of the Spirit Paul mentions are skills for Christian living that one would hope to possess, though it requires discipline and practice over time to gain such skills.

The notion of a "skill" also provides other openings on what constitutes a virtue. Skill is different from knowledge, where it is possible to articulate how something is done. One may *know* that a person in distress ought to be helped but be awkward or inappropriate in giving that help. What may be the felicitous way to come to the aid of a distressed person can vary in each instance. Yet some people have the knack or skill to be good at helping people in distress. Skill is a matter of what Michael Polanyi calls "personal" or "tacit" knowledge. The rules by which things are done through skill can never be entirely articulated, according to Polanyi. There are rules of thumb and various kinds of advice that can be given, but a skill seems to be, in the last analysis, an ability or a gift that one acquires through practice. Polanyi uses bicycle riding as an example: a rider will turn the handlebars back and forth to keep from falling over, so that the slower one rides, the more the rider will be winding one way and then the other. More exactly, "for a given angle of unbalance the curvature of each winding is inversely proportional to the square of the speed at which the cyclist is proceeding."[5] But the cyclist doesn't compute these relations—plus others—in order to be able to ride. His knowledge of bicycle riding is *tacit* and *personal*. So also with the skills that are indispensable for a given occupation. With practice, a good photographer gains a second sense about the light values and composition required for taking quality pictures. Over time, a baker gets a feel for when bread dough has risen properly. A computer programmer develops a special intuition for searching out program bugs. A personnel manager can acquire a way of assessing a person's employability. A skilled hod carrier makes a great difference to the efforts of the mason he assists:

> A good hod carrier is half your day [says the mason]. He won't work as hard as a poor one. He knows what to do and make every move count makin' the mortar. It has to be so much water, so much sand. His skill is to see that you don't run out of anything. The hod carrier, he's above the laborer. He has a certain amount of prestige.[6]

Furthermore, these and countless other skills, when put to good work, can arguably also be called gifts. They and the aforementioned "fruits" listed in Galatians, are like the virtues: they are developed out of intentional practice, but, once acquired, they become habits or dispositions, something one confidently knows how to do without being able to fully explain it. Further, only a very vain person gives himself sole credit for a skill, because a skill seems so much like a gift—something one feels pleased and fortunate to have. Hence, on the level of ordinary work, skills may be called fruits of the Spirit.[7] Part of the reason skills have this strange combination of cultivated effort and unmerited gift is because they are created out of risk. David Pye's analysis of workmanship is very helpful in this respect. He defines two kinds of workmanship: "workmanship of certainty" and "workmanship of risk." Workmanship of certainty is found in objects that are mass produced, where jigs, molds, numeric controls, robots, assembly lines, and other such devices make it possible for things to be uniformly manufactured. An aluminum beer can, for example, is a delicate and perhaps even an elegant object, but it is produced with a risk-free and boring sameness. By contrast, the risk factor

> means simply workmanship using any kind of technique or apparatus, in which the quality of the result is not predetermined, but depends on the judgment, dexterity and care which the maker exercises as he works. The essential idea is that the quality of the result is continually at risk during the process of making.[8]

Pye uses the example of a rough board being smoothed by hand by means of an adze, a kind of axe but with a cutting surface slightly rounded and turned so that it can be swung between one's legs in a slow arc that will chip away at the surface as one stands on it, making the board flat and smooth but with a rippled effect. A certain dexterity and adroitness in handling are required, plus patience and a good deal of practice. Old-style shipwrights were probably best at this skill, but there are plenty of modern instances of other risk workmanship.

Every setup where a uniform quality of certainty is assured—as with a beer can—requires prior workmanship of risk. Computer programming, for example, closely resembles traditional craftswork. Only after a program's design meets with an assured result can it assure a uniform and relatively risk-free outcome such as numeric controls require in manufacturing. Skilled pattern makers, who engage in one of the most exacting forms of woodworking, are still needed to make the molds necessary to cast many parts for mass-production machinery.[9]

Workmanship of risk usually yields poor or failed results when first attempted, and, indeed, a person may not have the measure of native talent needed, say, to ever be a cellist in a professional symphony. She may instead have a knack for the orderliness of figures, the sort of talent that can make a good accountant.[10] This is why an important ingredient in a working skill is *gifted* despite long hours of practice. But it is of critical importance that everyone have some working skill that is put at jeopardy by risk in order to feel a sense of accomplishment. Dorothee Soelle remarks:

If we understand life as a school, a training ground in which we strive to become something more than we are at present, then work becomes creative praxis. . . . Good work gives the person a chance to utilize and to develop her faculties. . . . There is an element of art in good work. Art, like all good work, enables us to release the power of our imaginations and to become persons as we use this power to come up with an invention, a new solution to a problem, a new way of working. In this sense, the worker-artist collaborates with God in creating, and she or he experiences this labor, praxis, self-activity as pleasure and enjoyment. Art pleases the senses, and so does good work.[11]

The skill required to create something successfully in the face of possible failure or poor results, brings out, when successful, a joy in work, a certain kind of delight that is charged with a metemphatic spirituality. And because there is a creature–Creator cooperation implied by the cultivation of a gift, it is entirely reasonable to say that the Holy Spirit and the human spirit have come together in a creative endeavor. Notice also that skills are communicative to others: they have a centering effect when performed that affirms the worth of the skilled person but also often communicates a gift, service, or a pleasure to others. These kinds of experiences can come in many ways, as when a skillful mediator brings two contentious parties to an agreement, or when a developmentally disabled adult takes third place in a discus throw at a Special Olympics meet, or when somebody's mom once again makes her prize biscuits, or when a fly fisherman successfully casts across a stream into a shaded quiet place where a trout just jumped, or when a crane operator from high above places some steel girder in just the right position for the next phase of construction. These are good working skills, and they should be regarded as fruits of the Spirit.

RAPPORT

The communicative aspect of cocreativity has to do with *rapport*, the second way the Holy Spirit interacts with workers. But instead of launching into an exposition of rapport as a Spirited quality of community relations, it would be better to start by observing the biblical caution to "test the spirits" (1 John 4:1–5), because just as there are bad, false, or lying spirits, the same may be said of the rapport among workers. Some common forms of bad rapport follow.

Harmful Spirits

The first of these harmful spirits comes in a form of worker disrespect. Treating workers like fungible commodities creates an anxiety over job loss, making workers subservient, compliant, but also resentful. In *Death of a Salesman*, when Willy Loman is finally fired by the uncaring son of his old boss after years on the road representing the company, Willy says, "You can't eat the orange and throw the peel away—A man is not a piece of fruit!"[12] In *Downsize This!* Michael Moore writes:

> CEOs of our top 300 companies are earning 212 times what their average worker is earning. As these CEOs fire thousands of employees, they, in turn, become even wealthier. AT&T chairman Robert Allen lays off 40,000 workers while making $16 million. Louis Gerstner of IBM fires 60,000 workers, then takes home $2.6 million. Scott Paper fires 11,000 people, merges with Kimberly-Clark, and CEO Albert Dunlap bags $100 million! . . . Yet, with every round of firings, the societal problems we must deal with rise at a corresponding rate. According to a study conducted by economists at the University of Utah, for every 1 percent rise in the jobless rate, homicides increase by 6.7 percent, violent crimes by 3.4 percent, crimes against property go up 2.4 percent, and deaths by heart disease and stroke rise by 5.6 and 3.1 percent, respectively.[13]

Coupled with the worker-as-expendable-commodity is the way production operators have often been de-skilled so as to perform nothing more than mechanical operations. Ben Hamper's book *Rivethead* is an eloquent tour through the degradation, indifference, and rebellion among assembly line workers. Here, he writes as a young boy, about seeing his father at work for the first time:

> His job was to install windshields using this goofy apparatus with large suction cups that resembled an octopus being crucified. A car would nuzzle up to the old man's work area and he would be waiting for it, a cigarette dangling from his lip, his arms wrapped around the windshield contraption as if it might suddenly rebel and bolt off for the ocean. . . . We stood there for forty minutes or so, a miniature lifetime, and the pattern never changed. Car, windshield. Car, windshield. Drudgery piled atop drudgery. Cigarette to cigarette. Decades rolling through the rafters, bones turning to dust, stubborn clocks gagging down flesh, another windshield, another cigarette . . . NOTHINGNESS. I wanted to shout at my father "Do something else!"[14]

Another form of control has come into being through the kind of "big-brother-is-watching-you" technology made available through sophisticated communication equipment. Many members of the American Trucking Association, for example, now have trip recorders installed in their trucks with satellite transmitting capability that enables a central office to monitor driving performance.[15] This sort of computer control is a form of "lashing," reminiscent of how gangs of oarsmen were kept under control when boats were powered by their efforts. Technological oversight might also come under the name of "panopticon," a kind of all-seeing ability to garner knowledge about worker performance.[16] It not only extends a system of discipline and control of employees by means of surveillance, but it compiles the information in a central place.

Another major debilitating factor in workplace spirit comes from an old American sacred cow: the belief that the best work comes out of a competitive workplace. This is a belief that permeates the educational system as well. Alfie Kohn writes about "structural competition" and what it logically implies: "mutually exclusive goal attainment": some must lose in order that others can win. It is assumed that competition brings forth one's best effort, but there is a basic confusion here: beating someone else is not the same as one's best effort. Those who are beaten tend to become society's throwaways, underachievers, welfare recipients, or prison inmates. Competition probably comes from the idea that only individuals exist, not groups, and that evolution makes it only natural that individuals compete. But Adam Smith was wrong in thinking that everyone necessarily benefits when people struggle against one another, and Herbert Spencer was wrong in his mean-spirited adaptation of Darwin, where humans are naturally pitted against one another for a "survival of the fittest." These ideas are only social constructions, the way in which society has decided to organize itself and give meaning to its life. It is as if society has decided that if everyone stands on tip-toe they will be able to see better, or as if, in a burning theater, it will expedite escape if each person struggles to be first out the door. Structural competition, so pervasive and second-nature to American culture, is often blind to the possibility of structural cooperation, the possibility that, rather than each person "going it alone," it makes better sense to utilize the collective talents of a team of people.[17]

Yet another harmful spirit often found in workplaces is fear, which is a natural companion of powerlessness and occurs in the company of job insecurity and the kind of poor communication that fosters suspicion and secrecy. Daniel Oestreich gives the following illustrative case study.

An executive team for a large government division is beset by communication problems. People do not trust the recently appointed manager of the Division—his agenda seems very different from the past incumbent. The manager, in turn, does not trust the team. He feels they will give lip-service to his new directions but go right ahead with their own agendas based on allegiance to the past manager and their own bureaucratic fiefdoms. The manager has wondered to some of his political friends in Washington, DC whether he should fire or transfer one or two of the executive team members as a way to "send a message" that he won't tolerate any "funny business." This word has gotten back to the team, confirming their worst suspicions that he is a "loose cannon." As a result people are keeping their heads down and going along, being very careful what they say and covering up any possible problem area that would give the manager an excuse to exercise his termination authority.[18]

Symptoms of fear include a perceived need for secrecy on both employee and management levels, accompanied by an active rumor mill, a lack of candor about past mistakes or problems, worry about reprisals, difficult customer relations, and a list of "undiscussables" needed to clear the air but never raised at meetings. Relations between employees can become strained, with "us–them" tensions, cynicism, excuses, undermining, and blaming.[19] All these behaviors indicate a harmful working spirit.

Part of the reason harmful working spirits arise comes from Frederick Taylor's methods of rationalizing work, resulting over the years in a great boom in consumer goods but also in considerable de-skilling, equating humans with the machines they operate. At the basis of virtually all forms of harmful spirits is the assumption of a *master–slave relationship*. But it should be appreciated that this relationship is not as asymmetrical as it might seem. While the master may have power, fear and general unhappiness can nevertheless afflict both parties. A manager, after all, has her own set of worries: there are undisciplined and poor workers, production schedules, absentee problems, machinery breakdowns—all of these requiring measurements of control.

Three Methods of Labor Control

Richard Edwards gives the most comprehensive review of labor control with his three divisions of "simple," "technical," and "bureaucratic" control. *Simple control* has its classic expression in the "straw boss," someone immediately at hand who supervises workers and has enough power to fire, degrade, or demerit those under his supervision so that his authority must be obeyed. The difficulty with this sort of control is not only the resentment and antagonism it causes but its inefficiency in organizations of any size, since one person can only directly supervise a small number of workers. Simple control also causes complex hierarchies, since shop floor supervisors must be answerable to the next echelon up, and the command structure requires an organizational pyramid. This sort of centralization has required an increasing number of white-collar laborers: engineers, personnel specialists, accountants, planning and promotion people, market researchers, and the like, plus the various secretarial people who support them. In 1910, only 15 percent of the work force was white collar, but by 1960, it was one-third, and 40 percent by 1975, and 50 percent by 1979.[20]

The second means of labor control is *technical*. Classically, this is represented by Taylor's de-skilling and rationalization of crafts production, or again, by Henry Ford's moving chain assembly line, where speed-ups could be managed by simply increasing the speed of the chain. Computer surveillance offers a new and extensively used method of technical control. The difficulty of trying to control machine operators who work on assembly lines was first demonstrated during the 1930s with sit-down strikes. Computer monitoring likely also has its countermeasures, with viruses, falsified feedback, and the like. But regardless of how workers might resist these forms of control, the main issue is that the control tends to foster antagonism.

Bureaucratic control is the new and most complicated of labor control methods. It is constituted by a very complex web of work rules, incentives, penalties, ranks, and procedures, making possible a faceless and depersonalized way of ensuring worker performance. Edwards uses the example of Polaroid in the late 1970s. The basic strategy is divide and conquer. Of the eight thousand employees, "there were eighteen different job grades, not to mention a dichotomy between salaried and hourly workers. . . ." In addition, each niche was "further positioned along the pay scale so that for any given job, seven distinct pay steps were possible. . . ."[21] Any kind of old-time notion of solidarity is set aside, and workers have the impression they have only to compete against themselves for advancement, only themselves to blame if they fail to advance. But there is also a great bloat in administrative personnel. The downsizing of the 1980s and 1990s has been, in part, the substitution of computers to gather the supervisory information middle management once gathered.[22]

In terms of testing the spirits, simple and technological control can lead to an adversarial relation between labor and management, such as that depicted in the highly cynical antics of assembly line workers in *Rivethead*, struggling to keep their sanity. Bureaucratic control brings an inflexibility and sluggishness to a corporation, stultifying innovation. All three kinds of control can create a spirit of powerlessness and fear among workers. A company organized into an intricate bureaucracy tends to look like a meritocracy, where some people get ahead and others don't, based on individual achievement. Failure to advance invites self-blame, even when that failure is in the face of the company's tight control and high demand. Research shows that such conditions produce worker stress and keep people from performing at their potential. Workers set in competitive channels with little freedom for creativity have a higher incidence of absenteeism, heart attacks, and depression. Michael Lerner's blanket term for this situation is "surplus powerlessness," because the lack of democracy in the workplace is often reinforced by a similar resigned helplessness in the economic and political areas of life.[23]

There is a tendency especially in Protestantism to see all spiritual estrangement as a matter of moral sin. Jürgen Moltmann argues that this generaliza-
tion does not hold up in light of the Gospels, in which, he writes,

> There are the outcasts, the poor and the homeless, who cannot keep God's law
> and are therefore outside the law, and without any rights. The parables in the
> synoptics show that the situations into which Jesus enters are always situations
> in which there is human conflict—between the healthy and the sick, the rich and
> the poor, men and women, Pharisees and tax collectors, the good and the
> wicked, the evil-doers and their victims . . . .

These distinctions are all distinctions of power rather than willfulness.[24]

Honor and Shame

Similar issues lie within the distinction between honor and shame. These are
symbolic qualities conferred on a person in terms of "having the right stuff"
for a given role. Honor is a mark of both personal self-esteem and societal
sanction not necessarily connected to any scheme of moral entitlement. People are often obliged to take jobs (in Terkel's words) "too small for their spirits," or sometimes, as when supervisors rise beyond their level of competence,
people are given undeserved honors. Slavery comes to mind as an example of
someone's spirit being broken into subservience, but the effort to remove
honor from people who take orders from their "superiors" is common in
many laboring contexts. It is also not unusual to find persons hiding behind
pretensions of honor, using it as a tool for authority. It is well to remember that
God sent his Son into a context fraught with this tension on a mission that cul-
minated in great social dishonor to himself. His controversies with authority
were often aimed at those with self-conferred honors, while keeping an
identity with lepers, tax collectors, prostitutes, and peasants so as to invest column 2 existence with dignity.[25]

A Spirit of Holiness

The Holy Spirit is often associated with mountaintop ecstatic experiences that
a genuinely "spirit-filled" person should be able to exhibit. Speaking in
tongues and high-voltage worship experiences have their place but can dangerously misdirect the believer into thinking he or she is getting a glimmer of
life in column 1 (as described in chapter 4 above). The Holy Spirit is also com-
monly thought of as the ambience possessed by a church on analogy with the
atmosphere in a restaurant. The discussion here, however, has to do with an
ambience among people in secular settings. It assumes that there is a secular

reservoir of experience able to recognize a holiness of rapport when it occurs in workplaces. Quoting from Moltmann's *Spirit of Life:*

> It would seem as if the Spirit of God is simply and solely the Spirit of the Church, and the Spirit of faith. But this would restrict 'the fellowship of the Holy Spirit,' and make it impossible for the church to communicate its experience of the Spirit to the world.
>
> . . . the possibility of perceiving God in all things, and all things in God is grounded theologically on an understanding of the Spirit of God as the power of creation and the wellspring of life.
>
> It is in Augustine that we find the theological and anthropological basis for Western spirituality. The concentration of his theology on 'God and the soul' leads to a devaluation of the body and nature, to a preference for inward, direct self-experience as a way to God and to a neglect of sensuous experience of sociality and nature.[26]

By contrast, life in the Spirit is an enfolding or abiding experience where one begins to share the concerns of God. And these concerns are marked by the decision not to turn away from column 2 existence but to embrace the bounds of a creation that possesses a generous amount of freedom and potential for fruitfulness and good even if one can be exposed to hurt and risk. An important part of this divine decision is the renunciation of a magical (column 1) deliverance. The Trinity is not passively disengaged from a creation that "groans in all its parts as if in the pangs of childbirth" (Rom. 8:22). Consequently, sharing the concerns of God can mean sharing the dismay of God as well as the love and encouragement of God. Such love is a powerful anchor to persevere in the faith, but hardly has its hallmark in column 1 ecstasy. When, as Paul says, "through our inarticulate groans the Spirit himself is pleading for us" (Rom. 8:26), it is like laughing or crying, an emotional overflow that surpasses verbal outlet. By contrast, the abiding quality of the Spirit is more like a steady hope, the energy of an envisioned destination. As a shared workplace energy, this Spirit has many manifestations in secular settings. An example from the working world would be the Edison lab's arduous search for an efficient filament for the vacuum light bulb, or the communal strength of struggling dust-bowl emigrants as described in John Steinbeck's *Grapes of Wrath.* In many working occupations, there is an infectious hardiness that is spirited by a longing that is holy but not ecstatic.

Master–Slave, Teacher–Disciple

The master–slave paradigm pervades philosophical literature as the only realistic way to describe how humans relate to one another. It assumes that every relationship carries an implicit contest of power, a scramble to establish a pecking order, some subtle or overt way to determine dominance and submission. The master–slave tradition stretches from Callicles in Plato's *Republic*, to Machiavelli's *Prince*, to Schopenhauer's "will to power," to Nietzsche's "superman," to Hegel's *Phenomenology of Mind*, to Marx's understanding of class warfare, and is certainly an important basis for much of management theory. There supposedly has to be somebody in charge and somebody to take orders: the arrangement of work requires some form of subjugation of the inferior by the superior. If the Spirit of God were like the spirit of a remote CEO or a *paterfamilias,* or an aloof judge, then the ordering among humans that is encouraged by the Spirit would fit well with this master–slave paradigm.

But the divine decision is to abide with the *homo viator* in a column 2 world, along with the divine vulnerability that entails. Jesus works by a different paradigm. Instead of master–slave, his relational model is that of teacher to disciple or, in workplace parlance, *journeyman* to *apprentice*. In this case, the teacher cares about the disciple and gauges his success by how well the disciple learns, growing to a maturity of equal or better standing with the teacher, and similarly with the journeyman, whose goal is to raise the apprentice to equal or better status. Jesus reflects this relationship when he says "a disciple is not superior to his teacher, but everyone, when his training is complete, will reach the level of his teacher" (Luke 6:40). And again, "In truth . . . I tell you, he who has faith in me will do what I am doing; and he will do greater things still because I am going to the Father" (John 14:12). He also sometimes turns the master–slave paradigm inside out to indicate a preference for a servant–servant situation—that is, a mutual obligation among equals (Luke 22:26–27).

It is the *journeyman–apprentice* or the mutuality of *journeyman–journeyman* relation that correctly reflects a holy workplace rapport. A fruitful exposition of this relationship can be found in the work of French philosophers Emmanuel Levinas and Paul Ricoeur.

Emmanuel Levinas and Being for Others

Levinas belongs in that tradition of European philosophers who have developed the prereflective dynamics of encounters between persons, those forces and feelings that come nakedly to consciousness before they can be overlaid with any rationales, excuses, or pretenses. One can imagine, for example, very young children battling to possess the same toy. Each gains a distinct intuition that the other has its own center of purposive possessiveness. Each child is what Jean Paul Sartre calls a "for-itself," very different from the toy, which is an innate "in-itself." A very large aspect of growing up comes in the stark realization that there are other people in the world and that one will always be reck-oning with other for-itselves. Put in Martin Buber's language, the difference is between the way an "I" relates to an "it," compared with how an "I" must take into account a "thou."

For Levinas, the prereflective encounter is a face-to-face coming into con-tact with another human, where the raw apprehension is an obligation to respond to that person in order for the "I" to become anything. As Levinas expresses it, ". . . with the appearance of the human—and this is my entire phi-losophy—there is something more important than my life, and that is the life of the other."[27] The being of the other always surpasses oneself in such a way that using, abusing, or somehow appropriating another person diminishes oneself. Consequently, the "I" of oneself only flourishes with the promotion of goodness toward the other.

> This human inversion of the . . . for-itself (of "every man for himself") into an ethical self, into a priority of the for-the-other . . . unique because of its chosen-ness for a responsibility for the other. In meeting with the face, . . . he takes precedence over me from the start; I am under allegiance to him.[28]

Thus, Levinas sees the structure of relationships as one of an open vulner-ability put in trust of the well-being of the other. An other-regarding ethic thus grows out of one's need not just for self-respect but, even more basically, for self-identity. This self-identity has two phases: a sense of self-worth arising out of reliability toward others, and, second, a maintenance or fidelity to oneself. Levinas's philosophy can be more quickly and easily understood by appreciat-ing that his views were forged during the Second World War in France, where Jews, once relatively separate from one another, found themselves called to solidarity over the need to be reliable in maintaining a mutual integrity and welfare in the face of persecution.[29] Paul Ricoeur adds the obvious insight that if the "I" of oneself is contingent on reliability toward the other, then there is a sense of being needed and an other who is needy.[30] People thus come to maturity through opportunities to share mutual needs. The dynamic is like Jesus' observation that we must lose ourselves for the sake of others if we are to gain ourselves. And it is this interdependence that is nourished by a Holy Spirit.

The Practical Insights of Edwards Deming

Such a Spirit in the workplace, where people are mutually needed, is a coop-erative venture, maintained by a common purpose, good communication, and information sharing. The insights of Edwards Deming echo another dimen-sion of Levinas's obligation toward the other, but on more of a community or management level than the strictly interpersonal scale. In any working group, some performance is bound to be above average, some below, according to Deming. The performance does not necessarily track with the people; that is, it is not necessarily the same people whose performance is above or below average. Improving productivity is rarely accomplished by instilling fear, competition, or eliminating people. Instead, it is almost always the system that is at fault: the way the work is being done.[31]

Deming's arguments are interesting because they provide a secular expression for structuring a workplace community with attributes conducive to a holy rapport. In doing so, however, he resorts to deep changes in traditional assumptions about human nature and the working spirit. His main theoretical purchase lies in "statistical process control," a means of continually upgrading product quality. The process requires a strong feedback loop from rank-and-file employees—the people who are on the production line, who drive the trucks, who handle sales, who do the shipping, and so on. They are kept informed and given a strong hand in every phase of the company because their cooperation and input are vital. This practice implements the Roman Catholic social teaching of "subsidiarity," where responsible participation devolves as much as possible to a common working level so that empowerment is spread around rather than kept at the top.[32]

Deming's scheme, first introduced in Japan and then adopted by a number of major companies in the United States, is known as "Total Quality Management" and is different from the traditional "economic model of the firm" with its hierarchical command structure chasing stockholder profits.[33] In Deming's "Fourteen Points," number 12 reads like something from an evangelist: "Drive Out Fear." And numbers 13 and 14 follow: "Break Down Barriers Between Staff Areas," and "Eliminate Slogans, Exhortations, and Targets for the Workforce."[34]

A Christian layman, Deming's influence reflects a movement similar to that described by Michael Welker in his portrayal of the biblical Spirit:

> The action of the Spirit rescues people both out of deficient self-respect and out of the overestimation of self. It restores their capacity to give and to receive respect in sensitive and subtle ways that correspond to the diversity of life as it is really lived. The same thing is accomplished through the Spirit as that which imperialistic monocultures seek in vain to secure in their one-sided, ideological way. . . . The complex interconnections of self-respect, respect for others, and respect from others are renewed and cultivated. People are freed from entrapments—both from those for which they bear the blame and from those of which they are innocent. They experience the lifting up of other people and the renewal of their worth, and are simultaneously given a part in this process.[35]

Frederick Herzberg's Theory of Job Satisfaction

One other secularly expressed insight that is useful for understanding how it is that a holy rapport helps workers comes in Frederick Herzberg's "motivator-hygiene" theory of job satisfaction. His theory is disarmingly simple. It has always been assumed that the range between dissatisfaction and satisfaction at work is on a single continuum. Abraham Maslow's hierarchy of needs, for example, assumes that when material goods are satisfied, then people seek the higher satisfactions of social prestige and, finally, self-realization. But Herzberg observed that the lower parts of this supposed continuum do not necessarily have much to do with the higher parts: people can work under rather poor conditions (low pay, poor lighting, dirty working environment, disregard for safety, etc.) and yet find great excitement and reward in their efforts. Conversely, people can find themselves in ideal working surroundings and yet be unhappy. Accordingly, Herzberg argues that there is no continuum between basic working conditions (what he called "hygiene") and job satisfaction ("motivation"). Each is unipolar, neither necessarily having to do with the other. This means that if an employer provides a clean, well-appointed, safe workplace with good rest rooms, good pay, and good benefits (as one might expect in a bureaucratically controlled workplace), there is no reason to expect that workers will have good rapport or thrive in both satisfaction and productivity because good rapport, satisfaction, and productivity are on a different continuum and do not naturally follow. The motivators Herzberg found important were "achievement," including personal involvement in decisions directly affecting one's work; "recognition" for those achievements; the value of the "work itself," and a sense of personal "responsibility" for what was done.[36]

This hygiene-motivator theory has been confirmed numerous times by further testing[37] and has a clear spiritual analogue in the theological relation between law and grace. As Paul expresses it, efforts to follow the law strictly only lead to an overbearing conscience. The operation of grace is on an entirely different continuum. Similarly, when the "fruit of the Spirit" is mentioned in Galations, this fruit is much more than just abstinence from "works of the flesh." So also with a holy rapport: something more and different is required than the provision of material surroundings and rewards. There must be an open interdependence of need and a metemphatic enthusiasm for the work to be done.

Democratic and Undemocratic Workplaces

Ironically, workplace systems are often very undemocratic, even in a nation like the United States, where freedom and democracy are highly prized. The ratio of supervisors to line workers is higher in America than in any other developed free-market country, and there is also proportionately less cooperation sought between the two. Nations with top-heavy bureaucracies and top-down command structures also have the most conflicted labor–management relations.[38] As an article in *Sloan Management Review* remarks, change to "a new landscape where authority, decisions, and innovation are much more widely shared, " is not easy.

> The management problem with [instituting] TQM is analogous to the problems associated with introducing representative democracy into former autocracies and introducing equal rights into racially segregated societies.[39]

The principles of self-management and participative decision making such as the Total Quality Movement requires, however, work for a more hygienic or holy workplace rapport. Companies that have thoroughly adopted this form of management tend to produce a higher quality product with a much more copacetic workforce. Consider the experience of Janbridge.

Janbridge, Inc., a company that makes circuit boards, changed to a participative work culture. The following remarks from their employees provide an insight into the kind of rapport they enjoy.

From one of their line workers:

> You used to come up with an idea and they'd say we'll check into it, and we'd never hear anything about it. Today nobody comes running down saying "You do this. You do that." They *ask* you to do it. "Can you do this?" It's a lot better way. The greatest reward is to let management know what we're doing down here and that we're not kids. We do give a damn. We do care. Just trying to do it right, that's all. I don't like rework, and I don't like returns from customers.

From the general manager:

> For my part, I think it has helped me tremendously. People respond without having to go back over things several times. They've picked up the responsibilities. That's the relief I personally get out of it. That, and the fact that we're able to service the customers with a quality product with on-time delivery to meet their needs.

From the head of engineering:

> I was of the old school: a boss is a boss is a boss. . . . "Do it my way, or this is it." I've found it's a much easier life for me to share responsibility. People know more than we give them credit for. You can listen to them. It's strange at first. . . . But then you can concentrate more on the planning stages. Before, you were tied up with all the little things going on.

From the director of technical services:

> Now that the day-to-day processes are under control, we can plan where we want to be twelve or eighteen months from now.

And from the CEO:

> I think there's a trust now between everyone. . . . I think they believe in us and we believe in them. It's not "us" and "them" anymore, it's a "we."[40]

Holiness as a Force Field

One final heuristic for describing a holy rapport is the analogy of the Holy Spirit as a "force field."[41] This concept was first used by Michael Faraday to describe action at a distance in the relation between a magnet and a wire coil. When a coil is passed between the poles of a magnet, an electrical current is generated, even though the coil never touches the magnet. Faraday reasoned that there must be something in that space that causes this curious interaction, and he called it a "force field." Something like it describes the cloudy quantum behavior of atoms as well as the way gravity is set into a geometric grid by Einstein's field equations. In Einstein's case, gravity is arrayed into a field in order to describe how bodies can affect one another when they are at a distance—the way, for example, the moon affects the tides on earth, or the astral bodies bend light rays traveling by from the stars. A force field suggests that the space between certain objects gains a pattern of power capable of having an ordering effect on those objects and what passes between them, as, for example, the way iron filings get arrayed around the poles of a magnet. But it is the mystery that needs to be appreciated: How is it possible that things never touching one another can still have an effect? And just as intriguing, when objects (like a magnet and a coil of wire) are prepared in a certain way, something else comes into existence—electricity.

In an analogous manner, if social contexts are prepared in certain ways, a spirit will emerge. The Nazis, for example, looking for a scapegoat for the loss of a war and the inflation that followed, seized upon and cultivated anti-Jewish activities that, in turn, led to a maelstrom of anti-Semitic spirit. A "force field" was set up that helped identify a pervasive enemy and galvanize a people into industry and patriotism. Joan Williams uses the analogy of the "force field" to describe how men tend to be pulled into "ideal worker" roles, while the force field of domesticity is the most likely role for women.

Thankfully, the Holy Spirit is an even more powerful force field, transforming people for good expressions of themselves and their work. And this force field is available not just for churches but for workplaces as well. Not to say that the Holy Spirit can be invoked, or manipulated, or made present for selfish ends, but the structure of human relations can be instituted that will make this Spirit welcome. People can come within its influence as "bearers and as borne, as constituting and as constituted."[42]

The fruit of the Holy Spirit is never private, and love is chief among the virtues or skills because it is guided by a sensitivity to suffering and isolation and has the power to impart both freedom and inclusion. But all the skills imparted as fruit of the Spirit are meant for a mutual upbuilding, and as they are shared with a holy rapport, they powerfully reflect a holiness that can be found in the atmosphere or ambience of a grocery store, an accounting firm, a construction site, or a manufacturing plant. Churches don't own an exclusive franchise on the Holy Spirit. A spirited kind of holiness can be powerfully present anywhere "two or three are gathered together" in Christ's name to do good work whether explicitly or implicitly.

This chapter began by noting how the creative energy of the Trinity, driven by a love and fecundity that cannot be self-contained, reaches out to bring human cocreators into the joy, freedom, and risk of a beloved creation made metemphatically available. But humans cannot appreciate this fecundity nor grasp its love unless they themselves possess some free measure of participative creativity and risk. But where does this creativity find its excitement? Where is the lynchpin, the innate yearning in the human heart that makes contact with the divine? There are a variety of answers: prayer, of course, is one; meditation and worship also count, as do others; but ordinary work must also be included in the mix. Where is the enthusiasm (*en Theo*) provided by work?

The dream and excitement are most perspicuous in doing something new, whether it be some great accomplishment like the World Wide Web, or a restorative act like cleaning up the Cuyahoga River, or some small event like reaching a better understanding with a heretofore estranged co-worker. New things are especially exemplified by Christ and have a special human yearning because people want to "make their mark" or be remembered for having made a contribution.

But if doing new things is the high and less frequent flame of excitement, the element that gives lasting satisfaction can be found in *maintenance,* the routine and by far the largest share of work. This facet of laboring life is invested in "keepings": as in keeping it together, or keeping things from sliding backward, or simply keeping on keeping on. For a student it means taking the required courses; for a bricklayer and his assistant, it means cleaning up the tools and the mess at the end of the day and checking on supplies for the next day; for the house framer, it means checking one more time to see that the walls are plumb; for the homemaker, it means deciding what to cook for supper. People don't always enjoy maintenance work at the time, but there is a retrospective satisfaction in knowing that it has been accomplished.

Finally, the Holy Spirit comes to working people with the twofold gifts of *skill* and *rapport*. Skill brings together the complexity of a native talent—a gift—that has been cultivated by discipline into an artful ability to work well at one or more aspects of one's occupation. As such, a skill is a working extension of a virtue or fruit of the Spirit. Skills are found in the way a wood carver can discern how the grain flows in a piece of wood and make her cuts to the best advantage. Skills are found in the knack a cook has of mixing ingredients properly without slavish dependence on measuring cups and spoons. Skill is found among airline pilots who can stay cool and rational in dangerous situations. A holy rapport comes into existence when people devote themselves to a teacher–disciple relational paradigm, rather than one of master–slave, and look forward to a relation of respectful and mutual servanthood, where quality of product and honor of worker share the "bottom line" that makes profits possible. Into such a working arrangement the Holy Spirit comes like a force field, giving energy and life to a working community.

7

Good and Godly Work

VIRTUALLY EVERY OCCUPATION has its own standards of conduct. Business ethics and management theory, for example, recommend moral codes within their appropriate sweep of work. There are professional rules for lawyers and other rules for journalists, for those in the construction trades, and certainly for educators, plus a large body of literature dealing with medical ethics. Furthermore, at the cutting edge of every field of endeavor are moral dilemmas and controversies. Those who work in genetics are perplexed by questions regarding cloning; teachers struggle with the demand for competence testing; stock analysts are caught up in problems of how to manage and disclose information; developers find themselves dealing with the need for environmental mitigation; and baseball players are having trouble with performance-enhancing drugs. Small wonder, then, that the manifold paths taken in human occupations require a large and purpose-driven study of ethics.

Small wonder also that discussions about work often become discussions of moral conduct at work. And there are Christian writers making significant contributions to work ethics, especially in the area of business ethics and management. Their efforts exploring specific issues are far more comprehensive than what will be found here.[1]

In keeping with this book's overall purpose of staying as much as possible within theology and touching only minimally on spirituality and ethics, the aim here is more foundational. This foundational interest also affords a time to cover an overdue explanation. References have been made to "good and godly work" as if the meaning of such things can be assumed. They cannot. This chapter will try to draw out a meaning for what constitutes goodness with respect to work, workers, and how this goodness might also be godly. Explicating the concept of "good" in these contexts serves as a possible propaedeutic for a Christian ethics of work and also—because goodness carries its own spiritual charge—an underpinning for the spirituality of work.

Finally, the chapter closes with how work ought to find expression in the liturgy of the Eucharist.

GOOD WORK

Good work can be constituted by an artifact like a painting, a dovetail joint, a cost-benefit analysis, a news article, or any number of other products of human effort where something tangible remains. But good work can also cover activities such as a ballet performance, a sales presentation, an arrest, a counseling session, a speech, a liturgy, or some other occasion of purposive activity, even when what is done is invested in the activity itself and leaves behind no physically tangible result. In addition, sometimes good work is entirely conceptual, so that there is only a web of ideas coming forth, ideas that can become publicly transferred, often suggesting further extrapolation, as with an architectural concept, a teaching technique, a proof in mathematics, the well-tempered scale, or so-called fuzzy logic.

But these descriptions do not say what is *good* about good work. Finding the "good" in good work is helped by accumulating some notions that demarcate good from bad or indifferent work. The first of these notions comes by revisiting the metemphatic quality of good work. *Metemphatic* was used earlier as an adjective to describe those objects, acts, or events that possess an inherent property such that they can be valued for what they are rather than symbolically pointing beyond themselves or denying themselves in favor of something greater. The term was coined to provide a separate category of spirituality from the "kataphatic," in which something (an object, act, or event) plays a symbolic role as a vehicle pointing to a deeper meaning. The simple outline of a fish, for example, was used by the early church to symbolize its faith because the Greek words for "fish" also serves as an acronym for a simple confession of faith.[2] The other traditional category of spirituality is the "apophatic," in which something is valued only for contrast as a means to say that God is wholly other or beyond that thing. For example, Psalm 147:11–12 says of God:

> He is not impressed by the might of a horse;
> he has no pleasure in the strength of a man;
> But the Lord has pleasure in those who fear him,
> in those who await his gracious favor.

By contrast, a metemphatic value occurs when God and the believer come together because something has an inherent value in itself that evokes a mutual love, admiration, or fellowship. When Jesus bids little children to come to him, or expresses admiration for a childlike faith, he is evoking a metemphatic value. Similarly, when he teaches the value of lilies of the field or birds of the air, he is evoking a love for objects that allow God and the believer to come together because both admire that object for the value it has in itself.

Alasdair MacIntyre has a useful illustration for what may be taken as a metemphatic value. The coming together of people in mutual fellowship occurs frequently where some skill is involved, and as they exercise the skill they enjoy a metemphatic experience with one another because they are both focused on that skill. MacIntyre's example imagines a chess player trying to imbue a child with the love of the skill required for playing good chess. The chess player bribes the child by promising a certain amount of candy if they can go through a series of games together as an exercise that is repeated over reasonably spaced periods of time. The chess player's hope, of course, is that the child will eventually find value in the inherent charm and challenge of the game itself and dissociate that inherent value from the external incentive of the candy. The point of MacIntyre's example is that there are many skills or "practices" that possess what he calls an "internal good." In the case of chess, the skill of chess playing is an internal good, while the candy is external. He goes on to argue that internal goods may be called "internal" because the relation of means to end in such goods cannot be entirely separated. Means and end are internally related when one necessarily affects the other. A child playing an indifferent game of chess only for the sake of sweets, shows no internal relation to the game: other things might just as well be done to obtain the candy. But a skillful chess player executing, say, a two-knights defense, has devised a way to pursue standards that can approach an excellence within the game itself.[3]

The inherent or metemphatic value of a skill like chess playing and its internal means–end relation to the game, also has the feature of nonscarcity; that is, if the child acquires the skill of playing chess, it is not the case that this skill is decreased, leaving one less skill available in the world of chess. The skill cannot be sold or traded, nor, upon death, can it be inherited. It is not a commodity subject to ordinary mechanisms of the market. Therefore, as a metemphatic good, it is in a different category from what are referred to as "goods and services" in a market economy.

Another way of noting good work can be seen in David Pye's separation of those kinds of occupational skills and products that involve "workmanship of risk."[4] Executing a relief carving by hand is different from duplicating one with a numerically controlled laser beam. There is no sure guarantee about the first, because there is risk; but the second is merely a matter of "workmanship of certainty." If there is an element of uncertainty about some task involving skill, then clearly the execution will be internally related to the result because one will affect the other.

What is meant by "good" in "good work" might also be subject to the fact/value distinction, where "value judgments" are taken to be distinct from facts. According to this line of thinking, facts can be agreed upon as objective realities, but value judgments are subjective. On some occasions, this is the case, especially cutting-edge issues where a given occupation struggles to find a morally acceptable solution and different and contrary views are expressed. Journalism, for example, has conflicts over whether stories should be reported because they are newsworthy or because they enhance commercial interest. "If it bleeds, it leads" is sometimes used as a derisive slogan for the ten o'clock news.

On the other hand, when one looks away from cutting-edge controversies and back at the history of a given occupation, there are usually well-established standards for what constitutes good practice. The art of bricklaying, for example, has standards of layout, pointing, leveling, and truing that require considerable skill.[5] These standards will demarcate good work from bad work, and the standards are reasonably objective and certainly beyond mere taste and subjective or emotive scales.

While the various skills and vocational practices always face difficult moral dilemmas and perplexities that are sometimes persistent and sometimes new in their development, vocations nevertheless create a historical record of relatively settled moral issues that are generally received within a given occupation. Usually there is an accepted terminology that gives moral guidance, and this moral guidance is meant to prevent instances of *akrasia*, or wrongful use of a skill. Bankers and bookkeepers have a fairly clear idea of what *embezzlement* means, while politicians and administrators have a notion of *malfeasance*, and writers know about *plagiarism*. *Police brutality* and *planting evidence* are moral terms within law enforcement, and *shoddy work* or *cutting corners* have clear implications for the carpentry trade. These terms tend to be "thick"; that is, they carry both a descriptive and a moral connotation. They are "thick" because they contain fact and value as unified objective elements. "Embezzlement" carries a connotation that describes a certain kind of activity, but it also connotes a wrongful act. It is not necessary to say, "and by the way, embezzlement is wrong," because the word carries that meaning as well.[6]

The thickness of words capable of encompassing both fact and value also has another revealing characteristic: the great majority of them deal with an activity that is bad. Consider, for instance, the thick terms involved with stealing. For bookkeepers, stealing is known as "cooking the books"; for longshoremen, stealing is "pilfering"; for cattlemen, stealing is "rustling"; while insurance agents can steal by "defrauding," and public officials do virtually the same through "bribery." These job-specific terms complement "embezzling" by bankers and others who handle money. There are no specific thick terms, however, that would fall on the good side of moral behavior in specific opposition to these bad terms. There is no word for "not pilfering," for "not rustling," for "not defrauding," and so forth.

The reason for this lack of opposing terms for goodness is at least twofold. One reason is that, to the general language-speaking public, "defrauding" is more interesting than "not defrauding." No newspaper is going to carry a story covering all the instances of "not defrauding" on the previous day. This is the reason for saying that "no news is good news." The second reason thick terms for bad behavior lack equally specific terms for good behavior is that good behavior in these circumstances is not exactly defined. "Not defrauding" clients, or "not rustling" cattle, or "not pilfering" cargo simply indicates the run of normal activity for a given vocation. The various instances of stealing are not part of ordinary conduct but are out of the ordinary. Consequently, a major aspect of goodness is simply invested in the way things are supposed to occur ordinarily.

For a theology of work, especially as described in chapter 5, this aspect of good work is mostly that cocreative activity involved with *maintenance,* where attention is given to avoidance of whatever actions might lead to bad results, including those actions deemed morally bad. This notion of goodness has a strong and illuminating analogue to health.[7] There are a multitude of terms to indicate the many ways one can fall into ill health, and very few of these terms have equally specific good-health terminology. Good health is simply the norm from which ill health deviates. Hence, *goodness* is often equated with *flourishing,* a notion closely connected to good health.

Good work also requires skill, and skill, as discussed in the previous chapter, is analogous to the traditional "fruits of the Spirit" (Gal. 5:22) because a skill has the double-sided nature. A skill is like a virtue or good character trait because it takes discipline to acquire and maintain to the point where it becomes a disposition, allowing one to act in a certain way when need arises. On the other hand, a skill is also a gift, a fruit indeed of the Spirit because one feels gifted to have the skill and, indeed, it is not unusual to call a working skill a "gift."

In summary, goodness and good work, as theological themes, have metemphatic value. What God declares "'good" about creation is also valued by the cocreator and is a means of coming together in fellowship the way two people might come together over something their work has faithfully produced.

Implied in the skill and satisfaction of good work is the possibility of a workmanship of risk, where success is not guaranteed. The result of good work, whether it be some physical thing, event, or idea, also involves the application of skills, and when these skills are internally related to the end result, they also have a metemphatic quality. Furthermore, these qualities are not subject to market scarcity. Possession does not decrease the availability to others. One may own a beautiful and expensive painting, but there is no way to purchase the ability to discern its beauty. Such skills are gained not by luck but by discipline and practice, and yet not without a gifted aspect. Some would call it "luck," but the believer should credit the Holy Spirit.

A perennial problem of skills and the knowledge required to produce good work is the problem of *akrasia*, the possibility that what equips a person for good results can just as well lead to evil deeds. Safe cracking, for example, is a skill, and con artists are often very skillful people, as are the schemes involved with terrorism. Goodness seems to be turned upside down when people speak of "a good con game," a "good scheme for a robbery," a "good way to cheat," or "the perfect murder." *Akrasia* is a trait of the *vices*, counterposed to the moral *virtues*, and it is through the virtues that the good worker should be sought.

GOOD WORKERS

Obviously a good worker is someone who engages in those traits just mentioned above; that is, a good worker is someone who does *good* work. But "good work" has two rather different senses: one moral and one nonmoral. The moral sense is implied when people speak of good work as a "good deed." The nonmoral sense occurs when goodness is merely instrumental, as with a "good knife" or a "good legal brief." Regardless of their gifted aspect, skills can be nonmoral and instrumental because they can be turned to morally good or bad use. A person who is clever at number theory might be morally helpful at computer logic, or morally harmful when applying his skill to computer hacking.

So what is it that makes a good worker morally good? The virtues. A virtue may be defined as an intentionally acquired habit or disposition that enables a person to act in a way that promotes goodness. Thus, a person who has cultivated the virtue of courage, when confronted with a situation requiring courage, will be predisposed to act appropriately. A person disciplined to temperance habitually never drinks to excess. Someone who is truthful may be said to possess truthfulness even while asleep, because if awakened and tempted to be deceitful, that person will not lie.

Virtues and skills tend to foster one another. Children learning to read or play a musical instrument, for example, also develop corresponding character traits needed to pursue those abilities. Indeed, MacIntyre defines virtue as "an acquired human quality the possession and exercise of which tends to enable us to achieve those goods which are internal to practices and the lack of which effectively prevents us from achieving any such goods."[8] One cannot become, for example, a good surgeon without patience and a good deal of practice that requires perseverance. Since skills involve the risk of failure, a measure of courage is needed. Similar arguments can be made for prudence or practical thinking, and temperance. All these could be employed, however, by someone who wishes to become a good confidence man, a forger, or somone intent on developing any of a number of the other artful vices.

How does the problem of *akrasia* get solved? Generally, the Greeks, who first thought of the virtues, dealt with the problem by aspiring to higher traits of character. For them, the best sort of person was the moral hero who equipped his character to excel at war, in Homeric terms, or sought after an all-encompassing harmony and goodness, in Plato's terms, or thrived in the life of the *polis*, the city-state, in Aristotelian terms.[9] But there is a strong patrician exclusivity to this model because its requirement of leisure puts ordinary working people hopelessly below.

It is Aquinas's efforts that recast the Greek virtues by refining them into four "cardinal virtues," prudence, justice, temperance, and fortitude.[10] And he caps them following St. Paul (1 Cor. 13) with the "theological" virtues of faith, hope, and love,[11] where love, the highest of the virtues, issues from friendship with God in the context of acceptance, grace, and peace, rather than the heroic striving or conflict model that undergirds the Greek virtues. For Aristotle, the virtuous man is self-contained, at home as master to slave, reserving friendship only among equals. But the theological virtues require a relational giving that replenishes itself in the giving rather than in the besting. A person of charity can be virtuous even in weakness or poverty, uneducated or lacking sophistication—quite the opposite of the patrician tone that Aristotle implies for a virtuous man. There is also provision for forgiveness in the outgoing and overcoming love of God and the grace that is infused thereby. Thus, Thomas's use of the theological virtues turns the classical virtues in a very different direction.[12]

Aquinas does, however, attribute the highest calling to the contemplative life of either the religious or the priesthood, with no mention of the laity. People of his time accepted "the great chain of being" as part of the created order, where ordinary workers were relegated to the bottom link. The *opus Dei* (worship and contemplation of God) leaves little room for the *opus manum* (work of the hands).

There is also a problem of pushing perfection too far into the virtues. In her article "Moral Saints," Susan Wolf writes:

> I believe that moral perfection, in the sense of moral saintliness, does not constitute a model of personal well-being towards which it would be particularly rational or good or desirable for a human being to strive. . . . One prefers the blunt, tactless, and opinionated Betsy Trotwood to the unfailingly kind and patient Agnes Copperfield; one prefers the mischievousness and sense of irony in Chesterton's Father Brown to the innocence and undiscriminating love of St. Francis.[13]

And indeed, there can be an unhealthy naïveté involved in promoting and pursuing the virtues toward a never-attainable perfection. The priesthood can be easily susceptible to this trap, especially when someone taking up the counsels of perfection is revered and assumed somewhere near perfection by an admiring laity. Christ sent his disciples out as "sheep among wolves," but advised them to "be wise as serpents" even if "innocent as doves." And there are many people who lead virtuous lives without pretending to perfection.

So what is it that instills virtues of goodness in people? Whether or not virtue can be taught is a question as old as Plato's *Meno*. Christian ethicist James Gustafson remarks that "distinctive characters are best shaped by relatively closed communities with strong ideological or religious and moral beliefs. Such conditions do not today prevail for most persons."[14] E. F. Schumacher, in his little classic *Good Work,* also says that smaller communities of work are better. He favors "human scale technology" rather than the "economies of scale" that run toward increasing size and complexity.[15] There are good reasons to believe that many rank-and-file people get lost in big corporations, being used as fungible instruments, where the very bigness begets a kind of faceless anonymity and inefficiency.[16]

There are, however, examples of small-scale industries in central Italy, Japan, and Taiwan, where there are numerous "job shops" contracting for specialty items. Such "flexible specialization" has become increasingly valuable, because many products have shorter life cycles and because computer-aided design and small shops tend to be more efficient and flexible. Mini-steel mills are an example. Located close together, such shops can also take on the look of interdependent regional conglomerates. Construction industries in U.S. cities are sometimes like this, as is the garment district in New York City. Michael Piore and Charles Sabel write of the garment district as a community that nurtures the virtues:

> the community has been based primarily on ethnic ties—first among Jews and Italians, more recently among Chinese and Hispanic groups. Both the employ-

ers' associations and the unions are active in their members' ethnic communities. Thus, Jews attend and contribute to fund drives for Italian orphanages, and Italians help out with the United Jewish Appeal; such activities reinforce the cohesion of the community in which the industry is rooted. Similarly, ethnically oriented family occasions—weddings, christenings, bar mitzvahs, funerals—provide further opportunities to assert the unity of the community and its identity with the industry. This effort for the greater community tempers competition within the community: manufacturers and union leaders are always present at public rituals in the families of their competitors, as well as their colleagues. This carefully nurtured solidarity also makes possible—and is reinforced by—institutions that serve the whole industry: for example, the Liberal Party, the Fashion Institute of Technology (a public school that trains designers for the multitude of small firms), and the zoning regulations protecting the manufacturers' loft spaces from residential and commercial competition.[17]

The idea of relatively small working groups is promoted also in Catholic social teaching under the principle of "subsidiarity," with the idea that "people do better at tasks they themselves plan and control."[18] One excellent example of subsidiarity in action occurs in so-called base communities spawned by Latin American liberation theology, where people at the grass-roots parish level meet for Bible study, incorporated with practical community problem solving that issues in action at the community level. A similar notion of responsibility appears in different form with Walter Shewhart and Edwards Deming's Statistical Quality Control, where quality control is removed from management and given to the line workers directly involved. If more than one working group is involved in sequencing a product, then each group treats the successor group as if its customer satisfaction must be met.[19]

An earlier chapter discussed the question of *what there is to be* as a prior question to *what there is to do*, and portrayed four people, some from history, some from fiction, who were exemplary in one way or another. It is their exemplary nature that stirs others to admire and become like them. This is especially true when they are blended into the purposive narrative of a community that is small and articulate enough to guide character formation. The church, as a participant in the kingdom of God, is meant to do this. But it is far from alone in mediating this formative power. Not only small working units are capable of influencing character formation, but also athletic teams, schools, and academic disciplines, among others.

But the influence is not necessarily always good. Robert K. Massie, Jr., an Episcopal priest who attended Harvard Business School in the 1980s, wrote of some sixteen hundred other MBA students that

Privately and personally [they] were warm human beings, but publicly many adopted aggressive, cynical, and callous styles. In the fall we saw a movie on the coal miners' strike in Harlan County, Kentucky, and the sight of the over-weight miners' wives brought wave after wave of cackling derision. When, in discussion of textile workers in England, it was revealed that a woman who had sewed for 12 years for $100 a week might lose her job, the class was almost unanimous in the feeling that she deserved to be laid off, since she was being paid too much.

Moreover, all day long the students talked about money. Discussions about money [in classes] had a clinical quality, as though money were a force with its own properties and principles, like electricity. At meals, though, the conversation would turn to money as something to be pursued for the freedom and pleasure it gave. People would talk about how much a person used to make, or how much someone had inherited, or how much they would earn. . . I asked one student what he most wanted to do in life. "What I most want to do is make a great deal of money," he said amiably.

The first article of faith in the HBS doctrine was an unquestioning conviction concerning the economic and moral superiority of large-scale corporate capitalism. The basic justice and integrity of current economic arrangements were never publicly challenged. There were many corollary tenets to this central creed, notably that:

- Competition is always the most efficient means of distributing resources.

- Government is always inefficient and something to be reduced, controlled, and mocked.

- Monopolies are bad if you are on the buying end, but good if you can achieve them in your own industries (this is called building market share).

- American workers are fat, slow, and inefficient, and labor unions are a destructive force.

- Poverty and unemployment are the result of inefficiency and primarily the fault of the poor and the unemployed.

- Almost any marketing or promotional campaign can be justified on the grounds that if a consumer actually buys the product, it must be to fulfill some "need."

- Individual greed always aggregates to a larger good, therefore the rabid pursuit of materialism is only a good thing.[20]

Clearly, this indicates a climate for bad character formation and may account for some of the current chicanery among those at high corporate levels. But it also indicates a society where there are competing life narratives and purposes, conflicting paths open to the formation of moral disposition.

This effort to define a good worker has concentrated on the virtues and skills. A good worker will possess at least some virtues because they occur necessarily alongside the development of skills. Furthermore, they are nurtured by the example of people held in esteem, especially in the environment of small working groups. But none of these processes ensures a morally good worker. To assure virtues that possess moral goodness, the Greeks vaunted a heroic model, forged either in conflict or in a thirst for goods not only higher in quality but also higher in moral perfection.

Thus, in trying to solve the problem of *akrasia*—skills and virtues gone bad—it becomes obvious that some capstone principle or reality must be invoked to align the virtues toward moral goodness. For Plato, this reality is some essence of beauty, harmony, or goodness itself. For Aristotle, all virtues are drawn to their purposive goodness by a magnetic god. Aquinas revolutionizes this scheme with a Christian God and, following St. Paul, uses heretofore not-listed virtues, beckoning humans to follow not as heroic strugglers but as redeemed creatures, beckoned forward by the nurturing love of God.

Acknowledging the need for a capstone force that aligns the virtues toward moral goodness, and holding in mind the contribution Thomas has made in this light, it will be useful now to offer a fresher and less patrician account of this force for goodness. For Christians, the account of what makes a good worker will remain incomplete until this divine force for goodness is brought to bear on the issue.

GODLY WORK

It is tempting to give an idealistic exposition of what godly work might be, but the context of human cocreative work is always a column 2 affair (see chapter 4 above), with compromise efforts often prevailing over any ideal aspirations. Already those elements of work that run cooperatively with the Trinity have been mentioned and qualify as godly work: maintenance, new things, skill, and rapport. The question to be asked here is whether that context of column 2 existence called "the market economy" can afford room for godliness in terms of the virtues. In some ways the market is an incredible engine of commerce, and in other ways it is, as has been said of democracy, the best of a number of poor alternatives.

An interesting champion of market forces is Friedrich A. Hayek. In a way similar to how Charles Darwin managed to account for speciation without resorting to a theological doctrine of special creation, others have attempted (much less successfully) to derive the common good and the moral virtues from commerce alone. Hayek's conception of the common good employs only the invisible hand of market synergism with no divine role at all. A freely functioning market and price system automatically coordinates the vast disparity of ingredients and interests required to serve the common good. People enter into this system in a manner analogous to acquiring a language. With no grasp of the immense complexity involved, a child simply begins to speak and gains linguistic ability with little or no knowledge about such a richly rule-governed activity. In like manner, people participate in the market to the well-being of all without the necessity of thoroughly understanding how the market coordinates the wide mix of forces and interests that are poured into it. Over time, a liberal government will discern whatever rules seem to be especially important to preserving this market and will enforce those rules that allow the market to operate freely.

The price system of a free market, as Hayek sees it, comes about by a similar spontaneous generation. There may be some trial and error involved in the evolution of the market mechanism, but as people participate, it will grow itself. There is no primordial "state of nature," where fair-minded persons sit down and discuss how they wish to arrange their common life to yield a common good. Instead it just happens, as the market is allowed to evolve unencumbered by artificial restrictions. Nor is there any point to something like the Catholic principle of subsidiarity that will encourage the common good, because reasoned debate, political participation, and grass-roots citizen activity will not help the nomological ordering of a free market.[21] Instead, rational self-interest is sufficient. Charles Schultze, of the Brookings Institution, former economic advisor to the president, expressed a similar view:

> Market-like arrangements . . . reduce the need for compassion, patriotism, brotherly love, and cultural solidarity as motivating forces behind social improvement. . . . Harnessing the "base" motive of material self-interest to promote the common good is perhaps the most important social invention mankind has achieved.[22]

This attempt to have the market blandly swallow up all issues of common good entirely omits two critically important goods: public goods and so-called externalities. Public goods are those goods where the value is publicly shared, as with parks, information, highways, schools, or police protection. The economic term *externalities* covers indirect costs of production that are not brought to market but adversely affect the common good. Black lung disease among coal miners, for example, is an externality, as is industrial air and water pollution, diseases caused by tobacco, the denuding of forests, or the displacement of people, goods, and services during an economic downturn. Free-market theory has no way to account for such "downstream" costs. They may argue that black lung and other harmful human effects can always be avoided because workers could just as well find other employment, but this argument presupposes a perfectly free and efficient market, rich in job opportunities, but such conditions hardly ever exist. External costs can be made up by compensating insurances, taxes, rules, and penalties, but these are brought about politically rather than economically, and often at public expense rather than that of whatever industry incurs the cost.

Economic theory commits a category mistake by including land and human work under the heading of manufactured commodities: all for sale and possession. With regard to land as property, the owner is given too much license to ignore ecological and social responsibilities inherent in land. For example, it is permissible for a stand of redwoods in northern California to be bought and logged off in order to service the junk bonds used to acquire a company in some other part of the United States. With work as a commodity, the human performer is somehow distanced from her work by a scale of indifferent necessity. That segment of labor used more purely in this way is migrant agricultural labor, long recognized as America's "harvest of shame."

Hayek, of course, has no recourse to theology, but his confidence in the market engenders a pedestrian theology by default. The view of land and labor would presuppose a god that is something like a self-contained emperor who makes things in order to own them, smiling down on humans insofar as they can wrest and win their own property, much as Prometheus stole fire from the gods. Nothing should be easy, and, once acquired, complete control is an entitlement.[23] The image of a god who helps only those who help themselves carries with it a certain self-justification along the lines of "nothing succeeds like success." But for those without property, a measure of freedom is lost inasmuch as they "own" only their own labor. This too may be understood as personal property, but without any other kind of property (e.g., land or capital), a worker's choices are limited to whatever work can be had. At worst, this is a laissez-faire situation, played to a stern or whimsical god or, somewhat better, a *paterfamilias* who, like the ancient gods of Greece and Babylon, does not work but is meant to be served.[24]

These grasping qualities don't quite fit the American spirit. MacIntyre has found an example of the kind of virtues that attach to free-market theory in those given by Benjamin Franklin. A reading of *Poor Richard's Almanac* will yield a strong sense of what it takes to thrive in an atomistic competition for wealth and security. Among Franklin's virtues are industry, diligence, self-reliance, thrift, and abstemious behavior, plus an acumen for the competitive acquisition of wealth. These virtues are very little different from the "Protestant work ethic" and render a kind of advice that many people of faith find helpful.

But a better fit for those who work in a market economy but wish to cultivate godly virtues comes from an analogy of God promoted by Douglas Meeks. Attention is given to God as the *oikos*, in the Greek sense of manager of a household, expressed by Paul in Galatians 6:10 and Ephesians 2:19. Both passages describe a community formed around purposeful narrative:

> . . . let us work for the good of all, especially members of the household of faith.

> You are no longer strangers and sojourners, but fellow citizens with the saints and members of the household of God.

The "household of God" connotes a covenantal bond and relationship of management and caring of God toward her people by creating, maintaining, reconciling, and equipping. There are useful paronyms for *oik-* found in modern language, especially "economy" and "ecology." Thus the analogy opens on economic theory and also the praxis of working conditions as they fold into the creation.

If labor is a Franklinesque self-possessed right, then there is little room for self-giving service; but it is exactly this sort of service that is the special and peculiar mark of the work of God, who comes, in Christ, as a servant. The creation, a continuing work, is a liberating act, one which, among other things, equips humans with the wherewithal necessary to exercise fruitful work. "The mystery of work," writes Meeks, "is the power given to the human being to love God by serving life in God's creation."[25]

That all is not well in the capitalist system is made obvious by how the incentive to work must be supplemented by ideologies. The chief carrot on this stick is a hyper-stimulated desire to consume under the assumption that human wants are insatiable. This changes the scheme of life into a matter of getting and maximizing rather than giving oneself in servanthood and cultivating the virtues. It is based on the premise of *scarcity*. By contrast, God expresses a *plēroma*, a fullness, rather than a scarcity.[26] A Christian perspective ought to see that there is enough of what is required for life and that no one should be in want while another has too much. Scarcity and insatiable wants are social constructions rather than timeless truths.[27] Helen J. Alford and Michael J. Naughton remark:

> Native Americans expected their white visitors to give back their gifts so as to keep them moving. This idea of setting gifts in motion equally baffled westerners, who coined the pejorative phrase, "Indian givers." What Native Americans understood, and what we should take heed of, is that when a gift is not shared, it corrupts the holder. The one who makes the gift an occasion for self-

ish hoarding, rather than keeping the gift in motion, becomes corrupted by the gift itself. . . . St. Augustine pointed out that the word *private* comes from "privation," signifying a certain loss of meaning or substance. To understand property *only* in private terms is to refuse to recognize its inherent "giftedness."[28]

The chief fault in Franklin's virtues is the implication that success is measured by personal acquisition of scarce goods. Instead, the secret to godly work comes in finding where the Householder's *plēroma* lies. What is it that others have that one can also have that is not subject to laws of scarcity? The answer lies with the skills and virtues required to carry on one's life and work. As argued earlier, skills and virtues are internally related to the results they produce such that means and ends cannot be disconnected. A farmer may profit from his labor and acquire yet more barns and storehouses, but these acquisitions are not internally related to the health of his soul. What is internally related is his skill as a steward of his land, so that it is not degraded. Similarly his other-regarding respect for his employees, his way of sharing with his community of farmers, his care toward his family, and other similar traits. He is also served well, of course, if he has a good sense of farm markets, crop gestation, fertilizers, and has the sort of working diligence that Franklin would admire. None of these traits is necessarily subject to scarcity. There is no master–slave dynamic behind them, no possessor–dispossessed syndrome, no best–bested exchange, no richer–poorer mechanism. In fact, just the opposite occurs. Like a teacher to a disciple, the teacher is enhanced when the disciple becomes the teacher's equal, and the dynamic becomes even richer when these skills and virtues are engendered within a community and the community's narrative.

"Take heed," Jesus says in Luke's Gospel (12:15), "and beware of all covetousness; for a man's life does not consist in the abundance of his possessions." When the life of another is assessed, it is in terms of the virtues and skills that person developed. And these are *internally* related, as means to ends, to whatever accomplishments are achieved. If a person is skillful at public speaking and uses that skill to accomplish some public good, then her skill is internally related to that good because each has an effect on the other. But if she is paid money for her efforts, or somehow rewarded with material goods, those results are only *externally* related because they do not affect the quality of the act or its accomplishment. Such rewards are also subject to scarcity. But the internally related factors are not subject to scarcity in the sense that to possess a virtue or a skill does not mean there is one less on the market. There is still a fullness of possible acquisition for others.

Thus, if work is good, done by a good worker, and godly, it will be ennobled by a divine *plēroma* that breaks through ordinary barter and exchange. It does not follow, however, that ordinary market economies are bad. Perfectly free markets don't exist. All markets have some intervening laws to compensate for cases where the "invisible hand" brings bad results. Vast numbers of Christians find honorable callings within these markets. There are numerous books, including significant ones by Christians, dealing with the dangers of capitalism and ways to improve it.[29] There is not space for such a critique here.

In summary, the problem of skills and virtues going bad (*akrasia*) cannot be solved by automatic mechanisms of the market, nor, for Christians, by a god who encourages striving for acquisitions. Some overarching power for moral goodness is needed, and, in this context, the idea of "godly work" seems best explicated on the analogy of God as "householder." This analogy implies a just allocation of goods needed for flourishing of life, but also points to a divine *plēroma* that is not subject to scarcity, and it is here that the virtues and skills promoting goodness are encouraged.

But the training ground for virtues occurs mostly within occupational communities and whatever divine effect the Holy Spirit implicitly has there. If the occupational virtues are going to be consciously connected to godly work, then the churches must come awake to Christian expressions that cultivate the workday week. The last section deals with how daily work can connect with the Eucharist.

EUCHARISTIC LITURGY AND WORK OF THE PEOPLE

From the beginning of the book and scattered throughout are complaints about the gulf that exists between the Sunday expression of the faithful and how little connection that has to the devotion these same people give their weekday work. There exist a number of practical and useful suggestions for the many ways this gulf can be overcome.[30] But once again, the purpose here is foundational in suggesting a theological connection between the Eucharist and the work of the people.

The meaning of "work of the people" is a symptom of the problem. The expression clearly ought to refer to the workaday lives of the people, how they earn their livings; how they serve the economy, the common good, the creation, and their families; and whence comes the money that supports the local institutional church. But "work of the people" is also the literal meaning of the Greek *leitourgia*, borrowed from the language of that culture to express a reciprocal action between God and humankind that occurs in the Eucharist.

The most important part of this action comes from God. The Eucharist is a powerful recollection of the gift of God's Son, even unto death on the cross.

God's action at the Eucharist transsignifies the bread and wine to the body and blood of Christ as a powerful means of grace and renewal for the faithful. Aidan Kavanagh writes:

> The liturgy, the dwelling place of present and remembered encounter with the living God, itself begins to think and speak for the assembly and turns wholly into music, not in the sense of outward, audible sounds, but by virtue of the power and momentum of its inward flow. Then, like the current of a mighty river polishing stones and turning wheels by its very movement, the flow of liturgical worship creates in passing, and by the force of its own laws, cadence and rhythm and countless other forms and formations. . . . What results from a liturgical act is not only "meaning," but an ecclesial transaction with reality, a transaction whose ramifications escape over the horizon of the present, beyond the act itself, to overflow even the confines of the local assembly into universality.[31]

A piece of music such as one by J. S. Bach is so rich that it can be played again and again without losing its power and newness. The Eucharist is like that but even more so. Its rhythm and cadence, its conceptual flow and mystery always possess a depth of freshness coming from God. And it is fundamental to the catholic faith that God's action at the Eucharist always happens.

But what is the human side of the Eucharist? Søren Kierkegaard has an especially perspicuous way of capturing the meaning of "liturgy" as "work of the people" in his rough but useful analogy between church worship and the theater.[32] This analogy takes three roles from each activity and asks how they would best be paired in order to capture what is meant in worship. In worship, the three roles are God, congregation, and officiant (priest or minister). In the theater, the roles are actor (or actress), prompter, and audience. At first glance, it seems obvious that the congregation is going to be the audience, leaving the priest or minister in the role of actor, and God doing the prompting. But this alignment has the obvious fault of nonparticipative worship, where the burden of success or failure is on the priest or minister. Indeed, in nonliturgical settings, the quality of worship often hinges on the quality of a rather lengthy sermon and pastoral prayer, both done by the minister. At worst, the role of the people-as-audience amounts to coming to church to watch Rev. Jones worship. Anytime people participate *solely as an audience*, they are entitled to say "I got something out of the performance," or "I didn't get anything out of the performance" the way one might when leaving the theater. On the other hand, if the roles are paired differently, then the congregation becomes the actor, the priest or minister a prompter, and God can be the audience. The virtue of this combination is that the quality of worship depends on the *acting* or *work of the people*. They are no longer entitled to say simply "I got something out of it," or "I didn't get anything out of it." Instead they must preface whatever they say with a personal evaluation: "I performed well and got something out of it," or "I performed poorly and didn't get anything out of it." Kierkegaard's little analogy thus has the merit of focusing a significant part of the burden on the people who come to worship God.

But what is this burden the people bear as their active and contributive part to liturgical worship? An excellent purchase on the answer lies in how the Greeks used the word and why Christians used it also as a term to describe their worship. In Greek culture, *leitourgia* primarily connotes an act of public service done without pay by one or more individuals as a contribution to the common good; then, derivatively, the word was used for public worship.[33] Thus, the idea of a public service or "work" was closely tied to public worship as a "work of the people."

If the challenge is to overcome the Sunday/weekday schizophrenia, then the question is how to link the Sunday eucharistic work of the people to their weekday work in the world, when the Sunday action carries, in some sense, a service done without pay that originates in their occupations. There are several theological answers to this question and also a practical one. First, there is the *plēroma* of God toward creation and the cocreator, a fullness not subject to scarcity. Working people find its manifold in the undercurrent of sustenance that supports their efforts, in the Sabbath grace that precedes, in the ever-developing promise of new things proleptically prefigured by God's Son and dramatized in the Great Thanksgiving of the Eucharist. There is also the rapport of the Holy Spirit spread like a net over the people. Thus, the *plēroma* of God comes "in good measure, pressed down, shaken together, and running over."

But the people also bring their own (God-given) *plēroma* of nonscarcity to the Eucharist. First, they reflect a means of serving others beyond themselves because their work—if it is morally good—serves a common good toward others well beyond themselves. This willingness to serve, even sacrificially, can go far beyond the rewards of salary, as was exemplified recently by New York firefighters and police, who gave their lives as part of what was required of them in the service of the common good. Second, the laity, in all their various occupations, embody a multitude of working skills that are richly available for serving others, and yet their possession does not deny that others can have those skills. This pleroma of the people is especially expressed because, as the body of Christ, they represent a powerful aspect of the real presence of Christ at the Eucharist. And this body "has many parts": an internist's skill for diagnosing the sick, an architect's skill for creating living space, a teacher's sensitivity for motivating students, a dietician's knowledge of healthy food, a parent's passionate but tough love for children, a mechanic's intuition toward faulty engines, and many more, expressing a vast plenitude of working know-how.

The practical side of the question asks what provision is available in the eucharistic drama for the laity to act out their apostolic (worldly) calling? The role of the priest as presider is plain enough, and likewise the deacon, lectors, lay eucharistic ministers, and others who assist. But where do the laypeople fit in? How is the work of the people expressed? This is a practical problem, because the liturgy is a drama with design features that are meant to express essential elements needed for the overall action. In liturgical action, there is always a danger that some important phase will be glossed over, lose its power, and be forgotten. The "kiss of peace," for example, was revived so that all participants would, after the confession, be obliged to symbolize that they are at peace with one another in the spirit of Jesus' admonition:

> If, when you are bringing your gift to the altar, you suddenly remember that your brother has a grievance against you, leave your gift where it is before the altar. First go and make your peace with your brother, and only then come back and offer your gift. (Matt. 5:23–24)

This quotation is also apt because the best opportunity uniquely to express the work of the people as laity should occur in offering a gift. In the Eucharist, the Offertory occurs when the alms (money) and oblations (bread and wine) are brought forward, the latter to be consecrated, transsignified, into the body and blood of Christ. But if the Offertory is conceived theologically, then it incorporates a much larger phase of the Eucharist than just the alms and oblations. It incorporates the confession, but especially the "prayers of the faithful" or prayers of the people. This prayer, in its various forms, is now usually said standing, the posture for offering, and attempts to collect a wide variety of concerns: for peace, for care of the earth, for the sick and the dying, for families, for enemies, for those in authority, and, *sometimes even for daily life and work*. One could say that God already knows these things, but they should be said nonetheless. There is a peculiar kind of estrangement that occurs when a parent knows what is in the heart of a child but the child remains bottled up and won't express it. So also when the cocreator doesn't offer his or her concerns to God.

Just as the kiss of peace obliges people to greet one another to exemplify their reconciliation, so also the liturgy ought pointedly to oblige people to express their worldly occupational offerings and concerns. This can happen by rewriting the prayers of the faithful so that such expressions are more explicit. It can also happen when people are encouraged to offer aloud their own prayerful occupational issues during appropriate pauses in this prayer. On occasion, various instruments can be offered with the alms and brought to the altar or table: an accountant's spreadsheet, a carpenter's nail gun, a chef's hat, a musician's instrument, a chemist's beaker, and so on. In addition, the laity ought to have regular opportunities to preach or give talks relevant to their occupations. It is far too easy to make the laypeople merely passive participants, whose liturgical "work" is confined to singing hymns, reciting a psalm or two, putting money in the offering plate, and partaking of the sacraments when their turn comes. This degrades the eucharistic drama and focuses far too much on a showy clerical side. If anything, the laity ought to have a more primary place of dignity as actors in the Eucharist. They are, after all, the principal part of the body of Christ.

The purpose of this chapter was to flesh out the heretofore assumed meaning of "good and godly work." *Good work* focused on those products or acts of work having metemphatic value; that is, value whose realization brings both a divine and human satisfaction. As occupations gain in history, they accrue standards, codes, and a "thick" vocabulary of what constitutes good and bad work. They also face into a cutting edge of newness where what constitutes goodness has yet to be settled. Generally, however, the "good" of good work is conceptually analogous to the "good" or "flourishing" of good health.

A good worker is defined by the possession of skills that are, in their way, very much like the *charismata* of 1 Corinthians 12; they are developed gifts. As such, skills tend to be instrumental rather than moral goods. But they are guided toward good (rather than bad) work by the virtues, where "virtue" receives its conceptual development by the Christian tradition of divine grace rather than the Greek tradition of a competitive or combative quest toward perfection. The Christian graceful cultivation of virtue occurs especially in communal experience, as it might be found, for example, on a shop floor, but it is also (or should be) perspicuous in liturgical expression.

Godly work reflects the householding side of divine activity, guiding human cocreators toward a metaemphasis on maintenance and the doing of new things. This divine activity also operates in an economy of *plēroma* rather than scarcity, since the gifted skills and metemphatic satisfaction arising from the joint work of Creator and cocreators is immune to market pressure: possession by one does not necessitate deprivation to another. Anyone who develops sensitivity can rejoice over the birds of the air or the lilies of the field, can appreciate and develop virtues cited in the wisdom literature, or can develop some collection of the manifold ways that "a teacher of the law has become a learner in the kingdom of heaven, . . . like a householder who can produce from his store both the new and the old" (Matt. 13:52).

8

Tying Themes Together

CONSIDER ONCE AGAIN the opening question of this book: What typically happens with Christians after Sunday? How are they supposed to carry their faith out the church door and into the coming work week? Also consider once again Barbara Zikmund's answer as quoted in the introduction:

> The four ways we tell serious Christians to live out their vocation are either simplistic and shallow, or they are so demanding that people pale at the task. At the risk of caricature, we insist that an authentic understanding of Christian vocation: (1) has little to do with our jobs, (2) has something to do with all jobs, (3) has more to do with certain jobs, (4) or has everything to do with on-the-job and off-the-job existence. No wonder good Christians get confused.

Taking these in order, when laity are told that their Christian vocation (1) has little to do with their jobs, usually a strictly personal pietism is assumed that only glosses superficially over daily work as a matter of being kind to others, offering a "ministry of presence," keeping the Ten Commandments, and finding time for private meditation and prayer as needed.

If people are told (2) that a Christian vocation has something to do with all jobs, then almost always this "something" is tied into one's job as a means to serve others. The Christian aspect of being an auto mechanic, for example, occurs in such things as doing free work for someone in financial distress, giving equal courtesy to black customers as to white, taking extra time for the handicapped, finding time to coach a little league team, and—aside from being competent—*nothing to do with fixing cars.*

If a Christian vocation has (3) more to do with certain jobs, then these are always people-helping jobs like counseling, teaching, doctoring, or working with personnel. Unlike the auto mechanic, who helps cars and only indirectly gets a chance to help people, the foregoing have the good fortune of dealing directly with people. Lurking behind this view is the tacit assumption clergy often promote that only people matter, not things. Upon reflection, however, much of thinghood and personhood go together: the oceans matter, the weather matters, other life forms matter, the doctor's kit of instruments matters, and so do the mechanic's tools. Extending this line of thought, practically everything matters so long as one is not in the business of pornography, trading on illicit political connections, scheming to fleece consumers with frivolous or faulty merchandise, making fraudulent insurance claims, skimming mutual fund fees, taking contract kickbacks, recommending bad stocks to support investment banking fees, exploiting conflicts of interest, or engaging in numerous other kinds of chicanery.

Thus, given the caveat that there are immoral kinds of work that must be disallowed, one seems led otherwise to "cover all the bases" by saying that (4) Christian vocation "has everything to do with on-the-job and off-the-job existence." This conclusion, though driven by the necessity of reason, nevertheless brings people to a place, as Zikmund says, "so demanding that people pale at the task."

The purpose of this book has been to articulate that task (so far as work is concerned), with the hope that, once the task is taken apart and examined, people won't "pale" at it, but will find those elements of their work *they already know* to be exciting, fulfilling, and dutiful as ones that can be claimed to be part of a godly vocation. The assumption here is like that of the apostle Paul, who, when preaching to the Athenians, assumed that they implicitly already knew of the God he proposed to make articulate to them. Just as Paul sought to evoke within Greek experience an articulation of the "unknown God" the Greeks somehow felt the need to honor, so the effort of this book has been to evoke the neglected God whom people implicitly already know as the divine who can, and does, come to life in their daily work.

As advertised in the beginning, the book is meant to avoid sliding off right away into a spirituality of work or into work ethics, in the belief that a theology of work can be expressed at a more fundamental level than these topics. This theology should serve as a propaedeutic, logically prior to and supportive of an ethic or spirituality. Consequently, theology of work has been the primary interest, but along the way foundational questions about spirituality and ethics have come up.

The book's presentation, however, has been scattered to fit a range of topic headings. This chapter will pull the various themes together more systematically, starting with barriers that must be changed in order for a work theology to have the logical space it requires. Second will come what has been the theological heart of the book, having to do with the work of the Trinity and how creaturely work falls into a complementary mode. Third, a propaedeutic for spirituality is made more apparent by pulling a number of themes together, followed by a similar but modest effort for ethics.

BARRIERS IN THE WAY

There are barriers standing in the way. Some of these are merely habits of mind that are common assumptions among clergy and churches and church people, but they get in the way of honoring daily work. In other cases, the barriers come from deeper theological categories that need to be changed.

One of the deeper theological barriers concerns the concept of perfection, a notion that appears in many guises.[1] The Catholic tradition has the "counsels of perfection," elevating celibacy and the contemplative life above ordinary working life, assuming that Mary always chooses the better portion and Martha the lesser one. There are also Protestant efforts to restore the church to a primitive and therefore (it is supposed) to a perfectly pristine, uncorrupted status, or else to find the power of Christ's atonement so strong that "being saved" elevates one above sin. In the working world, perfectionism is somewhat admired, but eventually disdained because perfectionists are too brittle, unable to tolerate criticism or failure. It is ironic, then, that among many people, fulfillment of Christian life is supposed to aspire toward perfection, and Christ is often thought to "restore" humanity to an Edenic perfection through the atonement and eventually bring all things to a perfect end. But behind all these notions of perfection is the old Greek idea of paradigmatic perfection, something only roughly imitated on earth but found perfected in heaven. The contrary argument given here is that the biblical use of "perfect" would be better translated as "mature" or "open-hearted," and that perfectionist expectations about daily life tend to be the enemy of the good and the excellent. Furthermore, Christ neither leads nor restores humans to the idyllic perfection of Eden, but leads instead toward new things.

Second, traditional guides for communing with God are the kataphatic and apophatic paths. The kataphatic uses some earthly situation or object metaphorically. In Paul Tillich's language, a symbol is "broken" in order to "point beyond itself" to God.[2] An example would be "As the deer longs for the water brooks, so longs my soul for you, O God" (Ps. 42:1). This metaphor has value because it denies itself in order to carry its thought toward God. The apophatic path uses comparisons to clear the way to God not by saying what God is like, but by saying what God is not, as in Isaiah 45:20–21:

> . . . you fools who carry your wooden idols in procession
> and pray to a god that cannot save you . . .
> there is no god other than I, victorious and able to save.

While useful, these should not be the only paths for communing toward God, because both denigrate earthly things and the objects of human work.

Such things are "broken" and denied an inherent value. People commune with God just as often—if not more often—through a mutual excitement over the inherent value of some object or situation, as when the shepherd rejoices together with the heavens over a lost sheep now found, or when God closes each phase of creation by declaring it "good."

Coming together with others and with God in this third way is coined as "metemphatic," meaning an *appearing* or *emphasis* that occurs *with* that situation or object. Thus the metemphatic spiritual path allows an appreciation for the efforts of daily work. It could occur with a well-sharpened hand plane or a well-played violin sonata. In any case, the tools and accomplishments of good labor are deserving of divine and human appreciation in their own right for what they are.[3]

A third barrier is the firewall Augustine and Luther put up against any ultimate value for work. Wanting to hand everything over to God's saving grace, Augustine leans toward a doctrine that those to be saved are predestined to that outcome. But if Augustine's firewall is grace, Luther strengthens it by his two-kingdoms doctrine. There is a kingdom of life on earth, where humankind is charged with mutual service after the example of Christ. But none of that matters in the heavenly kingdom, where the only thing that counts is the saving grace given through faith. Whatever "works righteousness" one might accumulate in the earthly kingdom has no value.

These firewalls carry great wisdom but, when taken simplistically, disallow a rightful honor and meaning that work should have. The argument for getting around these firewalls can be encapsulated in Jesus' saying, "By their fruits you shall know them" (Matt. 7:20), and by the distinction between internal and external relations. When Jesus says that a good tree bears good fruit, he is speaking of an internal relation, where one thing necessarily affects the other. It is not just the fruit that is good but the fruit and the tree. By contrast, an external connection occurs in the relation between the fruit and the money the farmer gets for his crop. The fruit might be very good, but the price is only externally related. Its dependence is on market forces of a given time. Similarly, good work necessarily crafts goodness within the person performing that work. But the accumulation of riches or status has no relation to that goodness. It is the latter misplaced hope of riches and status that counts for nothing in the scheme of salvation and deserves the firewall rather than the goodness of good work or its product.[4]

A fourth barrier has been the neglect of natural theology and theology of culture. Even though Galileo began to upset the medieval worldview, where science was required to conform to theology, the harmony of natural theology with revelation was still healthy in Newton's time, when scientists thought that unlocking the secrets of nature also disclosed something about the mind of

God. Since Darwin, however, natural knowledge has increasingly gone its own way, while theology showed signs of an inward spiritual search, as with Friedrich Schleiermacher's "feeling of absolute dependence," or Adolf Harnack's internalization of the kingdom of God. Proofs for the existence of God, unaided by revealed knowledge, have been the traditional hallmark of natural theology, but the powerful skepticism of David Hume and Immanuel Kant's argument that nature, by itself, cannot be known, also had a powerful effect on the involuted form taken by theology toward idealism and romanticism.

Other influences also played a role, separating not only knowledge of nature but also culture, away from theology. In America, disappointment over the sanguine but naïve aspects of the social gospel movement were reflected in Reinhold Niebuhr's doubts regarding a this-world kingdom. An even more powerful influence came from Karl Barth's neo-orthodoxy, a complete denial of natural theology and an equally complete dependence on the revelation of God through Christ. Pressure to sanction Nazi culture as something folded into the Christian promise led to Barth's participation in the Barmen Declaration and influenced his renunciation of any place for culture within the scope of Christian belief.

Not until the latter part of the twentieth century has the grip of these influences been released and a reopening for natural theology occurred. There are now studies of natural theology within the Bible itself,[5] and new openings toward dialogues with culture.[6] A variety of institutes and conferences have sprung up around the country fostering dialogues between science and religion. Traditional proofs for the existence of God in natural theology have been replaced by studies in which the interface between science and theology reaches a "consonance" of interest.[7]

A theology of work requires a strong immersion in both culture and knowledge of nature. These interests dialogue with the revealed knowledge of a believer, because a confessing believer uses her revealed belief to interpret and make sense of her working world. The combination of culture, nature, and revelation falls well within Paul's speech to the Greek's unknown-but-implicitly-worshiped God: "What you worship but do not know I now proclaim" (Acts 17:23). And it also chimes with Paul's argument in Romans, that "God himself has disclosed his invisible attributes; that is to say, his everlasting power and deity have been visible ever since the world began to the eye of reason in the things he has made" (Rom. 1:19–20).[8]

A fifth barrier occurs in the tacit assumption that the kingdom of God is coextensive with the church.[9] It is a "tacit assumption" because, upon reflection, few people would say that God is not active in nature or in the affairs of history, both of which have a broader reach than that of the church. Nevertheless, a good deal of current language assumes that the church is God's enclave into an otherwise godless world. People are asked, for example, to go out and "spread the kingdom into the world," or to "work for the furtherance of the kingdom." This assumption makes henotheists out of Christians, who must serve other gods out in the world if the kingdom has no scope or power there. Sometimes the kingdom is idealized to the extent that the troubles and compromises of this world betray the presence of a kingdom now. It can only be hoped for among the last things at the end of time. This view also leaves the working world bereft of any divine activity. If the kingdom is merely within the hearts or spirits of individual Christians, then once again the work of God is stunted to what might be accomplished within the believer. There is no divine *creatio continua*, no way that God continues to guide and care about the creation except through the hands, hearts, and voices of believers.

The kingdom of God has to be the reign of God, not just over the flock of believers set on a small planet in one solar system, within the arm of a single galaxy, among billions of others, but it must have a broad hand in nature, in the many forms of life, in the vast expanse and every corner of creation. True, it is tied to the eschaton and to the hope of wider fulfillment, but as an already-but-not-yet-entirely phenomenon. The doctrine of Christ's preexistent participation in creation, of the ongoing sustenance of the Father/Mother, of the life-giving energy of the Holy Spirit, speaks of a creation that is yeasty with divine things happening quite independent of humans, perhaps most of the time, but also possibilities set in the paths of believers and others to find and bring into participation.

The equivocation and ambiguity of the church's teaching and preaching about the location, timeliness, and activity of the kingdom make the whole doctrine hazy and cloud the vision of what might otherwise be a more active apostolate in the world of work.

Accompanying this cloudiness and making matters worse is the tacit pietism the church tends to teach and preach. This is the sixth barrier. Among the churches, it is often the clergy who alone are "licensed" to preach as professionally trained messengers of the faith. Their training, however, mostly involves biblical interpretation, a run-through in theology, and an acquaintance with personal spirituality, usually as found in the trove of popular autobiographies and testimonies and in their own personal devotions. The result is a repeated message that promotes the Christian life as a matter of personal piety sometimes enhanced by an urging of kindness toward other people. But little else. Good as this message may be, it leaves little or no guidance regarding the work week, the quality of an electrician's code compliance, the safekeeping of a company's pension funds, the virtues and vices of a trade union, the techniques for annealing glass, the way God might be working in quantum physics, and the myriad of other worldly topics that occupy the hearts and minds of many Christians.

The consequence of this stunted message being purveyed by the church is that the kingdom of God does not get the opening it should have for a lively faith as the kingdom is found available and waiting in a secular world. Furthermore, the secular world is not structured in a pietistic way, as if existence were constituted of hermetically sealed private people bumping into one another through life. Instead, people are molded by the "force fields" of many different structural interests: consumerism, professional demeanor, competitive contests within careers or companies, management by fear, "keeping up with the Joneses," among many others. The kingdom of God, by contrast, is not a human or societal invention but the force field of God contending among these other interests. And the scope of this contention is not merely within private lives. It contends "not against flesh and blood," as Paul says, "but against principalities and powers, and spiritual hosts of wickedness in heavenly places." The working world is an arena of contending kingdoms, and the pietistically equipped Christian is poorly clothed with the armor she needs for participating in this world.[10]

Going hand in hand with pietism's failure to recognize "principalities and powers" is its preference for a substitutionary theory of the atonement, a seventh barrier. Among this theory's unhappy features is the preference for a personal savior who redeems individuals but not the products of corporate human effort. A pietistic atonement has nothing to do with the structures and systems of an ordinary worker's environment, no effect on the contending kingdoms that make up part of the occupational milieu, at least not until the end of time. The Christus Victor theory is a far more adequate atonement theory. It allows space not just for individuals but also for the principalities and powers that contend with working people. It could be city hall, or economic inflation, labor relations, the pall of tyrannical management, an inefficient labor force, or a crop infestation. All such conditions must be within the redeeming or resolving power of Christ's atonement.[11]

An eighth barrier concerns the position of the laity and its consequent influence on the nature of the church. The situation here is like that of the kingdom of God: one theory is espoused, while a different theory is practiced. The laity are acknowledged to be at the core of the church, rather than the clerical hierarchy, but in actual practice, the laity are the clientele of the ordained. They are people who need to be nurtured and assisted into a spiritual mode at worship, a social and supportive ecclesiastical mode, and ushered toward heaven in the mode of a flock. The result is a church that is mostly self-absorbed with its own activity, an easy pitfall, because the demands and needs of church people can often put the clergy in the position of professional-to-client. If the church manages to break out of self-absorption and move outward toward the world, it usually does so with social, counseling, and health efforts. These are very laudable measures, but, alas, little or nothing is left for an energy that might cultivate Christianity in the arena of secular occupations. Yet this is precisely where the most unique gift lies among the laity. If the church is to look outward toward the world, then this unique gift must be given a place of honor and articulated in the church to better equip its people to perceive and exploit the yeasty opportunities and insights the kingdom affords in the world.[12]

Finally, as a ninth barrier, the chief mission of the laity is often styled after wishes of the clergy—that is, to serve the church, to bear witness to Christ, and to work for world reconciliation. The job description is laudable but has little to do with an auto mechanic's obligation to fix cars, or the farmer's duty to raise corn, or the homemaker's duty to bake bread. The chief duty of every Christian, especially the laity, ought to be cocreativity. As a genus term to cover Christian activity, *cocreativity* can include ordinary secular occupations within its scope. Bearing witness to Christ, serving the church, and working for reconciliation can also fall under this wider heading.[13]

How does the modification of these barriers assist in making space for a theology of work? In quick review, making room for a theology of work requires replacing various notions of perfection with concepts like maturity that do not imply a paradigmatic ideal but instead imply growth toward whatever potential goodness there might be in a person, thing, or event. Perfection also looms as a potential misconstrual of the incarnation. The temptation in the wilderness should be seen as a renunciation of any sort of magic or restoration to perfection involved in Jesus' vocation. Instead of demonstrating the possibility of a perfect life, Jesus exemplifies the possibility of new life. This possibility is implicit not just in Jesus' earthly ministry but in nature itself and in the fabric of human social, political, and economic structures, such that the newness Christ exemplifies and holds out as his promise cannot be encompassed theologically without a natural theology and a theology of culture.

The kingdom of God must also be part of this wider expanse so that divine creativity comprehends not just the church but the natural and cultural worlds as well. Furthermore, this wider scope of divine participation means that a Christus Victor atonement is more adequate to the message of salvation because it provides the power to contend with the natural and human structural forces where people work rather than settle simply for saving individual souls as a substitutionary atonement would have it. Therefore, while reconciliation is part of the salvation story, it folds within the larger drama of God's creativity with Christ as the leading edge of that ongoing divine activity. It follows that the calling of humans, as those made in the image of God, should be a mission of cocreativity. This shift of emphasis does not preclude reconciliation or redemption, but does put these roles within the larger genus of creation.

As a context for human work, the creation deserves a certain divine–human fellowship and delight over whatever might come to a good result. Hence a metemphatic kind of spiritual access should be recognized as a godly side of work satisfaction. There is not only a divine–human appreciation involved but also an internal relation between a good work and the worker who wrought that work, such that the goodness of one enhances the goodness of the other in the same sense that a good tree bears good fruit, a good carpenter builds square walls, or a good painter makes the best use of color values. This sort of good work escapes the problem of an externally related works righteousness. Herein also lies the *plēroma*, the fullness of God that defies any rules of economic scarcity, because the mutual love, gift, and talent of good work does not lead to anyone's deprivation. Finally, since it is principally the laity who serve the creation in the richest and most manifold ways, it is they, rather than the clerical hierarchy, who should constitute the primary identity of the church.

Having listed the important barriers that get in the way of a theology of work, a more positive section can go forward. The thesis here is that the work of humanity is cocreative and finds its meaning by accompanying the creative work of God.

THE WORK OF GOD AS TRINITY

God the Father/Mother

The experience of women in the workplace and the resultant changes occurring in work environments closely parallel the feminist movement and the changing image or doctrine of God promoted by feminist theologians.[14] The aseity of God as a self-contained, self-sufficient being wholly other from the creation forms an image of God as an aloof monarch, closed away from the ordinary bustle of creation. If there is any divine act of goodness, any gesture of love or caring toward creation, it takes nothing away from the absolute nature of this monarch, depriving the divine being in no way. There is a strong note of self-reliance in this image; it comports well with the masculine ideal worker image of someone able to go anywhere and undertake any task, unperturbed by any demands that are needed by his dependents, always aloof, secretive, but also always right, risking nothing.

In contrast, a woman worker should not be "unbent" from her gender obligations, should not be unperturbedly expected to go anywhere or do anything, if she wishes to have strong commitments and family ties to children and household. As more women are obliged to join the work force to help support their families, so also their mates should share in household domestic obligations. These gender obligations are not signs of weakness, but come from a vast reservoir of strength that can be spent, of love that can be invested, of creative enthusiasm that can run over the top. Workplaces and work rules can be restructured to make room for women who can be effective both at work and at home.

The resultant feminine image of God implies a strong mothering role of creative involvement, of nurturing in the hope that what is created will share in the excitement of creativity. There is nothing aloof to this divine image, because a mothering role always involves risk that the effort and love invested might turn sour, might fail, or might lead to other unhappy consequences. The expectation of love puts the lover at risk of dismay, on the one hand, but in hope of joy, on the other. Feminist theology, however, does not portray a God who is at risk to fail utterly. A hope in the ultimate success of God's purposes is not strictly a masculine kind of expectation. The mother image can keep this hope just as steadily and well. Indeed, the mystery of God's power made mature through weakness comports well with this more feminist side of God.

The Work of the Father/Mother as Maintenance

A parenting image of God is a good key to the work of God when that work is inferred from nature, but it is also useful to add the image of oeconomus, or householder. The cosmos is an exceedingly fine-tuned and evolving phenomenon that, to the believer, can imply a designing intelligence. Although it yields no proof, it is not unreasonable to think of God as the necessary being that sustains the delicately balanced contingency of creation.[15] A microcosm showing the dynamism of this contingency is especially perspicuous in ecological fitness landscapes. Life in a coral reef, a rain forest, a wetland, or in the arctic tundra is a delicate community of interdependence between the living and nonliving. The watchword is not "survival of the fittest" so much as a well-honed and tested communal interdependence. But the interdependence is never static. A disease may come along, a new predator, a change of climate. The fitness of a given landscape must rely on adaptive change to conditions requiring maintenance above all, but also an ever-probing cutting edge of newness that promotes vigor and thriving. Over time, for example, trees "learn" to combat invasive beetles by signaling one another of danger and including repellent ingredients in their sap. Beetles, however, are great waste managers, helping return organic material to the earth, and many other creatures depend on an enriched earth. An "arms race"[16] might seem like the best strategy for each species to adopt, but the purpose of an arms race is mastery and elimination. If some member of the community becomes extinct, others may follow and even set up an avalanche of extinctions. Chaos would ensue. After all, of the totality of species ever in existence, 99 percent have gone the way of the trilobites and the tyrannosauruses. So an optimal condition might seem to be reached when all denizens of a landscape are at their respective fitness peaks, as one finds, for example, in a mature old growth forest. There is a certain protection each offers the other, where the species population exists almost entirely as a regime tuned to minimize the rate of extinction.

Therefore, the chief work of God as Father/Mother is like an "invisible hand" set into the dynamism of nature that ensures the synergy of an individual, but communal *maintenance*. And the same may be said of human endeavor: the occupation of humanity is mainly to keep things from sliding backward, to ensure a stability in what has already been reached. When a nurse autoclaves surgical instruments, when a janitor cleans the school hallways, when a road crew patches a pothole, or when an airline crew carries out a safety inspection, the task is one of maintenance. It is by far the largest aspect of work. Maintenance also involves keeping bad things at bay as when a night watchman makes his rounds, a misbehaving child is sent to the principal, drinking water is checked for mercury content, or firemen answer an alarm. Maintenance work also occurs with work of both preservation and disposal. Photos, letters, seeds, and butterflies are archived; libraries enhance their collections and discard out-of-date literature; factories that make buggy whips and horse-drawn wagons close. All these activities stand in relation to the work of God the Father/Mother, who watches over the coordination of complex events like a householder. Maintenance is the chief part of the householding of God and also the chief occupation of humans as cocreators.[17] God is the *protological one* who sets things going and continues to sustain them.

The Son as Exemplifier and Guarantor of New Things

Mature, old-growth forests and other instances of stable evolutionary landscapes do not exist in a changeless stasis. Nature seems always to probe for something new. Even, for example, when animals have plentiful foraging territories, they will still be on the lookout for new ones. Genetic variation seems to speed up when a form of life faces new challenges. It is good that this is so because most landscapes are under conditions of flux, the possibility of some threat, some change in climate, some disease, or perhaps some new predator. Hence, landscapes thrive best if they maintain an interdependent stability that is on the cusp of innovation without falling into the chaos of a competitive "war of all against all."

If the Father/Mother role of the Trinity can be conceived as one of nurturing householder, chiefly concerned with maintenance, then that of the Son lives on this cusp of new development. This may seem a strange interpretation of Christ's mission, usually thought to be one of reconciliation, but the role of reconciliation can be seen as part of this cusp of new things. Jesus' earthly ministry, after all, is an exemplification of new possibilities: his teaching turns old received truths in fruitful new directions; his way of seeking out the lost and dispossessed enlists them with realistic new hope; his healing and miracles issue a promise that lifts new life out of despair; his gift of himself to seemingly shameful execution opens new vistas on the overreaching love of God; and his resurrection breathes new life into all these dimensions. Furthermore, the doctrine of the preexistent Christ as one who collaborates with the Father/Mother in creation expresses the fact that newness is a built-in factor of the creation itself. A newness on the cusp of an evolving nature is always a realistic presence. It comes not by magic but by transformation of what is already there. Neither does it come by a restoration to some Edenic state, because its direction is always toward the new.

The same promise occurs in the work environment of human affairs. Everyone spends most of his or her life in worthy works of maintenance. But people especially respond with life dedication to visions that venture into new development. Grameen microbanking, for example, is making small entrepreneurial efforts possible among women in third world countries like Bangladesh and has since spread to many other places. In nano-optics, new ways are being developed to bend light rays in structures smaller than the wave length of light sources, leading to improvements in filters, wave guides, and laser components. Unlocking genes and proteins opens the possibility of new tests for genetic predisposition to and therapy for, or even prevention of, cancer. In aerospace, tiny rocket engines capable of emitting large amounts of thrust may allow small aircraft to fly higher into the atmosphere. In cities, novel forms of public transportation could make life free of traffic snarls and help the mobility of the disabled. The medical mission Doctors Without Borders works in Africa to make antiretroviral drugs and treatments affordable and available to populations infected with HIV.[18] According to a theology of work, these and many other visions express the Christ as exemplifier and guarantor for the possibility of new things both in nature and in human affairs.

While technological progress is not necessarily synonymous with human progress, and while it is true that bad and destructive new developments also appear, there is much that is commendable and necessary about the promise of new things when they promote goodness. Whether in technological, social, economic, or some other occupational field, working people are especially blessed when they can attach their life strivings to the promise of new things that promote the common good. This should be acknowledged as the promise and exemplification of Christ as the *eschatological one*.[19]

Finding the Holy Spirit in Skill and Rapport

The Holy Spirit as the "giver of life" or energy, that necessary confidence and excitement needed to perform quality work, is found first in the various requisite occupational skills. Skills are a mystery. Despite the efforts of Frederick Taylor's rationalization efforts and many other programs aimed at making skills entirely explicit, they can't be exhaustively formalized. In a pattern-maker's shop, for example, one skilled workman with a box of tools can build the same object as many men can accomplish with purpose-built machines. Skills involve a workmanship of risk that entails not just success but also a learning history of failures in such a way that success includes an element of luck, and repeated success can never be a matter of self-congratulation, but instead is always considered a gift. Cooks who are successful at devising their own recipes have a culinary gift. House framers who can quickly cut accurate miters with skill-saws have developed a knack for judging angles. Mothers who can detect the moods of their teenage children possess an intuitive insight. There is no reason why these skills should not be part of the Holy Spirit's charismata. They are the equipment necessary for successful work.

The second aspect of the Spirit relevant to work is found in the working spirit of people singly, but especially in groups. If people have caught a vision of some newness to express, or are well attuned to the importance of some maintenance they are doing, they usually have a holiness of spirit. Scripture suggests that the authenticity of a given activity can be determined by "testing the spirit." The implication is that there are many spirits that may pervade a workplace, not just the Holy Spirit. A spirit of lifeless ennui can infect people, leaving them with no motivation. A spirit of oppression can occur under a supervisor who tends to be a petty despot. A rankling spirit of distrust will take place when the rumor mill suggests that management is secretly manipulating affairs to the detriment of workers. A spirit of shame can occur if a company is knowingly bilking its customers. And greed can take the upper hand if a company is hollowed out or bought out in order to strip away its value. There is also a spirit of despair when employees are thrown out of work with little prospect that they will be brought back.

By contrast, a Holy Spirit pervades a workplace when communication is open, when people feel that they are valued, skillful, and engaged in useful employment, when they serve a worthwhile vision, offer a quality product, and are given tasks that don't amount to repetitive drudgery. Like a fitness landscape, a workplace functions best when all its parts are at fitness peaks but still evolving toward newness.

The Holy Spirit, therefore, is the *pneumatological one*, enlivening all the aspects of the work of the Trinity as they come to realization in human communities.[20]

A PROPAEDEUTIC FOR THE SPIRITUALITY OF WORK

Spirituality connects the human spirit to the Spirit of God in a companionate way through time and narrative of life. A spirituality of work comes prereflectively in the "feel" of holiness people have when they work, provided the Holy Spirit is present where they work—as described above—and not some rival spirit like that of greed, fear, oppression, or ennui. This prereflective spirituality accompanies the *vita activa* rather than the *vita contemplativa*.

A reflective component occurs from time to time when people stop to think back and review their work experience outside the activity itself. In terms of Christian formation, this "review" will be an existential narrative, concerned with what there is to become and be. It amounts to a coming to awareness of the persistent and pervasive invasion of God into one's working life. There is no uniform sequence to the stages of this awareness nor formula as to exactly how they occur; nor is it necessary that a person be able to articulate them all, because intelligence or refinement of learning is not required. Therefore, what is listed here is simply one way to provoke or evoke a narrative of spiritual formation as it pertains to work.

One of the stages is an awareness of a world where there is both a freedom to accomplish things and an obligation—one has to make a living—work has elements of responsibility with both irksome and joyful aspects. Hence, work is an ambivalent but necessary undertaking, where one must fight through the irksome aspects to find the joy. A discipline therefore comes about, a certain toughness or persistence of character that includes a sense of responsibility coupled with a feeling of personal value.

Personal value is ordered according to priorities and functions analogous to a "religious operating system" (a ROS) a *de facto* or default religion, as when a working person judges his success and personal worth in terms of his possessions, under a grasping religion of consumerism and wealth. Here examples of others come into play in terms of *what there is to be*, because one can observe the formation of other people's ROSes and make judgments about how adequate they are to reality. Someone whose being has formed into drug addiction is obviously and dangerously out of accord with reality, while a person styled on consumer display of wealth attracts imitation even if it is a hollow form of being. Reality stands over against ROSes of self-aggrandizement and exploitation, causing a restlessness that is estranged from the proper way to live with creation.

It is not possible, however, simply to make God a top-priority concern through an act of will. The divine preference seems to be one of molding people to become concerned about the things that are concerns of God. There are obvious issues of concern to God like losing oneself in the love, respect, and care of other people, of the church, and of social institutions that promote the common good. People are also becoming increasingly aware of the importance of and our dependence on ecology. All of these things tie work into the household and nurture of God. *It has been the thesis of this book, however, that common efforts of good work also share equally with the concerns of God.* There is not one kind of vocation that is a priori better than another.

It is this invasion of God into one's personal ROS that especially focuses the life of prayer as in the spirit of the Psalm 139:1–2, 5:

> Lord, you have searched me out and known me;
> you know my sitting down and my rising up;
> you discern my thoughts from afar.
> . . . .
> You press upon me behind and before.

It is the insistence of God asking each person to share in divine concerns as they are suited to a given vocation that leads to prayerful quarrels and protests, to moments of illumination, setbacks, requests for help to move forward, to shared joys and frustrations, to hopes for a steadier course and a larger vision. The spiritual narrative, therefore, tends to be dynamic, seeking, searching, and somewhat restless, or without rest, as it strives toward an accord where personal concerns and divine concerns are in agreement. St. Paul, for example, speaks of his spiritual condition on the athletic analogy of a "race" that he has not yet finished, and he worries that he might not adequately follow the preaching he has imparted to others (1 Cor. 9:24–27). This issue of keeping attuned to the godly things is matter of *maintenance.*

Another aspect of this spiritual struggle is the need to truly grasp the import of the incarnation and how it points one's destiny in a different direction from any yearning for fulfillment in a paradigmatic perfection. Here the existential narrative really takes hold, requiring the sojourning soul to give up any sought-after perfection and, instead to accept his or her own column 2 existence as something beloved by God and as a beckoning instead toward the excitement of doing *new things.*

This spiritual pilgrimage is reinforced also by a divine–human pleasure over accomplishments at work. When the designing engineer and workmen, for example, survey the arched enforcing structure of a completed bridge, there is, indeed, a deep spiritual pleasure with its spectacle in which God also takes part, even as a parent finds pleasure in the creations a pleased child might bring for shared pleasure and approval. These spiritually charged experiences are *metemphatic.*

The gradual adjustment of one's ROS to harmonize in some particular way with the concerns of God also brings one into the "force field" of the Holy Spirit, and a joy and confidence ensue, where one feels gifted with *skills,* satisfied to do whatever maintenance work is required, able to endure setbacks and fatigue, devoted to visions of new things as they appear in the scope of one's calling. When all this can occur in the company of co-workers, then a Holy Spirit can very well preside over a workplace where the *rapport* of the Spirit has a catching, invigorating, and cumulative power.

A PROPAEDEUTIC FOR THE ETHICS OF WORK

If work is under the aegis of the nurturing household of God, given the promise of new things according to the promise of Christ, and within the force field of the Holy Spirit, one must assume that it is good and godly work.[21] "Good work" divides into two categories: instrumental and moral. A "good knife" is an instrumental goodness, while a "good deed" is a moral goodness.

Instrumental goodness takes its character from several factors: first, it conforms to received standards, the rules, codes, and methods of a given trade or profession as these have accrued over years of experience. When an electrician wires a house, codes must be followed; when a new drug is tested, certain protocols apply. Second, skill is involved in good work, especially in workmanship of risk, where a successful outcome is not guaranteed but achieved nonetheless. A finely made quilt is never an assured result, but when achieved, it reflects the skill of its maker because there is an internal relation between that skill and its product. One necessarily reflects the other in a way that external relations cannot define. The externally related price for the Dover edition of a literary classic is very low, even though the quality of the writing and the skill of its author may be high on the scale of goodness. For that matter, the skill in its making and the appreciation of the result are not subject to scarcity such that if one person has more someone else necessarily has less. Finally, instrumental goodness has metemphatic value, the sort of value that joins both divine and human together in its appreciation. When God ends each day of creation with the declaration of its goodness, humans can appreciate that goodness. There is no reason why the same should not occur when good music is well performed, or when a child makes a loving Christmas card for a grandparent. Why shouldn't God join in the appreciation of such things?

In the case of a working context for moral goodness, once again the trades and professions have built up their codes of conduct, making it clear when wrongdoing occurs. Reporters, lawyers, and clergy, for example, obey codes of confidentiality; physicians are required to "do no harm," police must not "plant evidence" or make unwarranted searches. These occupationally specific moral codes tend to be conceptually "thick," because they encompass both a moral judgment and a state of affairs where that judgment applies. The "thickness" is constituted by joining fact and value together. There are, however, always new circumstances and situations where moral questions are yet to be settled and old circumstances need reinterpretation. The term "miscegenation," referring to marriages between the races, seems to have gone out of style because it connoted something bad, and people no longer hold that view. But stem cell therapy is something new and, as yet, morally ambiguous.

Generally, the codes and terms used for moral guidance tend to be negative, with no counterpart on the positive side. This imbalance of descriptors for badness over those for a countering goodness indicates that moral goodness lies in the range of normal work in much the same way that good health is simply normal functioning and has no specific descriptors to counterbalance all the ways that sickness can occur.

But sickness does occur and so does bad work. Just as there are skills developed for doing good work, there are also skills for bad work. Hot-wiring and stealing cars, for example, is not something anyone can do. Hence, to assure good work rather than the work of criminals, virtues are necessary, that is, ingrained dispositions to behave temperately, honestly, justly, and so forth. These qualities may seem to spring naturally from the general marketplace of human interaction in much the same way that the manifold niches for species in a fitness landscape get along best when a creaturely cooperative interdependence is achieved. An ecological balance of living things can't get along well if they are always in an "arms race," with one another, or in a "war of all against all." People like F. A. Hayek think that in a laissez-faire economy virtues are instilled simply because the fair exchange required in a free market will automatically generate good deeds along with good work and good products.

While the synergism of free-market systems can help generate good and fruitful human interaction, markets do not embrace everything that needs to be considered, notably externalities and public goods,[22] nor does it entirely prevent the generation of those dispositions that are the opposite of the virtues, namely, the vices. It follows that some external governance is needed in market economies, such as the Securities and Exchange Commission is supposed to provide for the stock market.

From a theological point of view, the missing consideration is that of God as householder, where the work of the Trinity interacts with the creation and where the fullness of God escapes any notion of scarcity. That fullness is made obvious in the wonder of creation itself, and in the way virtues and skills are made available to daily work. A novelist, for example, who writes a well-crafted best-seller may buy himself a sports car and an upscale home, but his real riches are invested in his talent as a stylist, and only in the continued hard work of writing will his satisfaction be truly found. Without the *creatio continua* of God active in people's lives, history and the purpose of creation have no backbone. Humans, that aspect of creation most free and given cocreative responsibility, are good for being created in God's image, but they are also terribly fallible. They seem to need a special looking-after that can be seen in the theological virtues of faith, hope, and love that St. Thomas adds to the traditional cardinal virtues.

WHERE FROM HERE?

There are strong pockets of interest in various church traditions that recognize and promote secular work as a Christian vocation. On the evangelical side, the InterVarsity organization and its press have maintained a continuing dialogue under the title of Marketplace Ministries.[23] Within the Catholic tradition, the University of Notre Dame Press has a long history of publications giving Christian views on work, and the lay publication *Initiatives,* coming out of the National Center for the Laity, is the best periodical for keeping up on events and publications having to do with work. These are isolated islands, however, in a sea of ecclesiastical indifference.

There are also visionary expressions of what the laity might become if they could reach more fully into an authentic ecclesiastical recognition for who they are as people with worldly vocations. This lay expression is especially strong in Roman Catholicism, where it appears likely that laypeople will come more to the core of the church and conform to the delayed promise of Vatican II.[24] And, of course, an emphasis on the laity is always nascent in the Protestant tradition's priesthood of all believers. There are also commissions, publications, and occasional studies carried out by churches at national and international levels, but these come and go without ever breaking through to a wider, more thoroughgoing awareness meant to give Christian meaning to the work weeks of its people.

The contention of this book has been that there are some deep-rooted theological reasons why work remains a stepchild, a poor relation never fully adopted. Secular work as a full and genuine Christian vocation cannot be taken in because the theological space just isn't available to accommodate it. Part of this space problem is merely the institutional church's need to concentrate on itself, its budget, its meetings, its Sunday gatherings, its various committees, and its internal duties, which focus the membership's attention too narrowly. It is important for the church to be a sanctuary of rest and reflection, of respite from a teeming world. Where the concerns of work often generate the most pressure, it is the church that offers the most rest and relief. The theme of respite from the outside world, however, has been taken too far, because church people tend to be church people just on Sundays and to serve other kingdoms, other gods during the week. Moreover, this book has tried to make the case for fulfillment in knowing that honorable work is important and has many dimensions of divine participation.

As mentioned in the introduction, theology of work is a ragged area of inquiry, touched upon from time to time but never taken up and studied with the persistence given patristics or various areas of biblical study, church history, or the lately blooming area of science and religion. But surely theological inquiry into daily work is deserving of a great deal more attention. This plea is made not just to people who are training professional clergy, but also with the hope that it will reach the laity, those especially adept *because the topic is especially theirs.*

Theology of work has a peculiar bridge to cross. It requires a measure of theological sophistication but also familiarity with those forces that uphold and drive the laboring world, forces like economics, management, and occupations such as farming, nursing, carpentry, teaching, merchandising, homemaking, and the many other specific ways that people make their livings. It is not enough to create an occasional conference, commission, or study for this needed branch of theology. More should be done on a sustained basis. The theology of work offers a unique chance for church and secular world to come together as equal partners, each able to enlighten the other because there is a great deal of divine activity and energy not just in the church but in the secular world as well.

> How can they have faith in one they have never heard of? And how hear without someone to spread the news? And how could anyone spread the news without a commission to do so? (Rom. 10:14-15a)

Notes

INTRODUCTION

1. According to a U.S. labor force Economic Values Survey used by Robert Wuthnow, "82 percent of those currently working say their work is "very meaningful," 80 percent say it is "absolutely essential" or "very important" to their basic sense of worth as a person, and 71 percent say they are "very interested' in doing well in their job" (Robert Wuthnow, *God and Mammon in America* [New York: Free Press, 1994], 41).

2. George Herbert was a seventeenth-century Anglican priest, known as an outstanding religious poet, author of *The Temple* (New York: Paulist Press, 1981). George Sturt was a wagon maker and outstanding expositor of his trade and the life of tradespeople in England. He is author of *The Wheelwright's Shop* (Cambridge: Cambridge University Press, 1993).

3. Usage of "church" throughout, unless specifically noted otherwise, will refer broadly to mainline Christian denominations, because all of them pay little heed to whatever theology may be implicitly "out there" in the working world of the laity.

4. Some examples: Mark Gibbs writes: "There are many useful books on lay ministries in church work and committees, a good many on personal and caring ministries in local neighborhoods and involuntary organizations, and not a few on involvement in radical causes and movements; but there is much less available to help either laity or clergy think through some of the hard questions of lay involvement in the secular structures of today's world. Indeed in recent years some church trainers and enablers have seemed to consider such secularly involved laity either as helpless zombies fatally entangled in corrupting and demonic "powers" and structures, or else as hypocritical Christians paying lip service to the gospel on Sundays" (*Christians with Secular Power* [Philadelphia: Fortress Press, 1981], vii). William Diehl writes: "When my church preaches about the ministry of the laity, it speaks in broad idealistic terms; but when it comes down to reality, my church sees lay ministry purely in terms of service to the institutional church" (*Christianity and Real Life* [Philadelphia: Fortress Press, 1976], vii–viii). Patricia Garrett Drake writes: "It is no wonder . . . that we do not feel successful in 'bridging the gap between theory and practice.' We have identified the congregation rather than the world as the arena for 'practice' and the clergy rather than the 'whole people of God' as the principal practitioner. If one footing of the span, the

bridge, is our Judeo-Christian heritage . . . we have ignored the other footing—the world—in our attempt to bridge theory and practice, have effectively created a cantilevered structure—a span connected and supported at only one end—a kind of spiritual diving board, because connection at the other end is seldom correctly identified, much less analyzed" (*The Calling of the Laity,* ed. Verna Dozier [Washington: Alban Institute, 1988], 108). Gregory F. Pierce writes "As I suspect is true in your denomination, the problem in the Roman Catholic Church is not a lack of statements on the subject nor even a faulty theology. The problem is in the execution of those statements and theology in the day-to-day lives of most believers and the activities of most of our parishes. The fact is that our church is an institution, and like all institutions it tends to become engrossed in its own internal affairs to the detriment of carrying out its basic mission in the world" (from a speech given in 1991 to a conference sponsored by the Evangelical Lutheran Church in America).

5. Quotation taken from *Initiatives: In Support of Christians in the World* 122 (April 2002): 1.

6. Typically, theologies have taken *praxis* to be essentially intellectual, moral, or spiritual qualities mixed with relations to oneself, one's neighbor, and God. But liberation theology seizes on work as the heart of praxis. Work—understood as the care of creation and the building of institutions that permit free expression and full life—mediates all relations: to oneself, to neighbor, to social and economic structures, and to God. In liberation theology, Jesus presents an irony: not a Che Guevara, but a quiescent revolutionary, a divinity given to servitude, a penetrating but nondogmatic teacher of truth, a man open to all people but taking his cue from the neglected, a strength choosing the vocation of weakness. The practical expression of this theology comes in base communities, practicing the principle of "subsidiarity," or organized action at the grass-roots level, where people of a parish meet regularly for study, prayer, and discussion leading to joint working groups for common weal. See Gustavo Gutiérrez, *A Theology of Liberation,* trans. Caridad Inda and John Eagleson (Maryknoll, N.Y.: Orbis Books, 1973), 29; José Míguez Bonino, *Doing Theology in a Revolutionary Situation* (Philadelphia: Fortress Press, 1975), 108.

7. For a recent discussion, see Norvene Vest, *Friend of the Soul: A Benedictine Spirituality of Work* (Cambridge, Mass.: Cowley Publications, 1996).

8. Max Weber, *The Protestant Ethic and the Spirit of Capitalism,* 2nd ed., trans. Talcott Parsons (London: Allen & Unwin, 1976); Weber's strong thesis (that industrial capitalism owes its initial spiritual power to Calvinism) has been questioned by many scholars. H. R. Trevor-Roper, for example, argues that the guiding lights of the early industrial revolution were mostly immigrants coming out of the Netherlands, "a Flemish dispersion" of capitalists out to seek their fortune. They were mostly Calvinists, but some were Jews, some Lutherans. They did not practice a strict lifestyle of frugality or thrift, but seem to have come out of an ethos and locality where early capitalism was especially successful and understood. Otherwise this impetus would have originated equally from Calvinist strongholds like Scotland, Geneva, or the Palatinate. Nevertheless, Trevor-Roper adds that "there is a solid, if elusive, core of truth in Weber's thesis"

(see H. R. Trevor-Roper, "The Reformation and Economic Change," in *Capitalism and the Reformation*, ed. M. J. Kitch [London: Longmans, Green, and Co., 1967], 24–36). What "Protestant work ethic" might mean today is discussed by sociologist Adrian Furnham in *The Protestant Work Ethic: The Psychology of Work-Related Beliefs and Behaviours* (London: Routledge, 1990), 15.

9. Barbara Brown Zikmund, "Christian Vocation—In Context," *Theology Today* 36, no. 3 (October 1979): 328. A similar comment from another source says, "We cling to an idea that ordinary work is either indifferent to the Christian enterprise or—at best—it must be somehow *sacralized*. That is, the so-called *secular* might have religious value, but only if incorporated into the institutional Church. Thus in August many parishes bless teachers, but only those employed by the Church. A parish might commission a young nurse who begins a two-year stint in the missions but neglects to bless the nurse who is hurrying out of Mass for her shift. A diocesan peace and justice office might praise those who lobby through a Church affiliated program but never given an elevating word to the civil servant who bangs out the details of a more just social policy" (*Initiatives: In Support of Christians in the World* 121 [February 2002]: 2).

10. For example, William Diehl, *Christianity and Real Life* (Philadelphia: Fortress Press, 1976); idem, *Thank God It's Monday* (Philadelphia: Fortress Press, 1982); Mark Gibbs, *Christians with Secular Power* (Philadelphia: Fortress Press, 1981); Graham Tucker, *The Faith-Work Connection* (Toronto: Anglican Book Center, 1987); Robert J. Banks, *Faith Goes to Work* (Washington, D.C.: Alban Institute, 1993); Robert E. Slocum, *Ordinary Christians in a High Tech World* (Waco: Word Books, 1986); David A. Krueger, *Keeping Faith at Work* (Nashville: Abingdon Press, 1994); Vocation and Work Task Force, Presbyterian Church (USA), *Vocation and Work: Challenges in the Workplace* (Louisville: Dept. of Denominational Resources, 1990); Stephen R. Graves and Thomas G. Addington, *The Fourth Frontier* (Nashville: Word Publishing, 2000); O. Guinness, *The Call: Finding and Fulfilling the Central Purpose of Your Life* (Nashville: Word Publishing, 1998).

11. John Paul II, *Laborem exercens*, in *The Papal Encyclicals, 1958–1981*, comp. Claudia Carlen (Raleigh: McGrath Publishing, 1981); Emmanuel Mounier, *Personalism*, trans. Philip Mairet (Notre Dame, Ind.: University of Notre Dame Press, 1952); Jacques Maritain, *The Person and the Common Good*, trans. John J. Fitzgerald (Notre Dame, Ind.: University of Notre Dame Press, 1952); Karol Wojtyla [Pope John Paul II], *The Acting Person*, ed. Anna-Teresa Tymieniecka, trans. Anizel Potocki (Boston: D. Reidel, 1979).

12. Robert L. Calhoun, *God and the Common Life* (New York: Charles Scribner's Sons, 1935).

13. J. H. Oldham, *Work in Modern Society* (New York: Morehouse Gorham, 1950); M. D. Chenu, *The Theology of Work*, trans. Lilian Soiron (Chicago: Henry Regnery, 1966); Edwin G. Kaiser, *Theology of Work* (Westminster, Md.: Newman Press, 1966).

14. While there is, recently, a plethora of popular efforts, more thorough theologies of work known to me include Thomas L. Shaffer, *Faith and the Professions* (Provo: Brigham Young University, 1987); M. Douglas Meeks, *God the Economist: The Doctrine*

of God and Political Economy (Minneapolis: Fortress Press, 1989); Dorothee Soelle and Shirley A. Cloyes, *To Work and to Love: A Theology of Creation* (Philadelphia: Fortress Press, 1984); John C. Haughey, *Converting Nine to Five: A Spirituality of Daily Work* (New York: Crossroad, 1989); Lee Hardy, *The Fabric of This World: Inquiries into Calling, Career Choice, and the Design of Human Work* (Grand Rapids: Eerdmans, 1990); Miroslav Volf, *Work in the Spirit: Toward a Theology of Work* (New York: Oxford University Press, 1991).

15. For example, B. Briner, *The Management Method of Jesus: Ancient Wisdom for Modern Business* (Nashville: Thomas Nelson, 1996); J. Canfield et al., *Chicken Soup for the Soul at Work* (Deerfield Beach, Fl.: Health Communications, 1996); D. Chopra, *The Seven Spiritual Laws of Success: A Practical Guide to the Fulfillment of Your Dreams* (San Rafael: Amber-Allen, 1994); idem, *How to Know God: The Soul's Journey into the Mystery of Mysteries* (New York: Crown, 2000); Lama Surya Das, *Awakening the Buddha Within: Tibetan Wisdom for the Western World* (New York: Broadway Books, 1997); Charles Handy, *The Hungry Spirit* (New York: Broadway Books, 1998); Michael Harner, *The Way of the Shaman* (San Francisco: HarperSan Francisco, 1990); G. Hendricks and K. Ludeman, *The Corporate Mystic: A Guidebook for Visionaries with Their Feet on the Ground* (New York: Bantam, 1997); K. Inamori, *A Passion for Success: Practical, Inspirational, and Spiritual Insight from Japan's Leading Entrepreneur* (New York: McGraw-Hill, 1995); L. B. Jones, *Jesus CEO: Using Ancient Wisdom for Visionary Leadership* (New York: Hyperion, 1995); D. Whyte, *The Heart Aroused: Poetry and the Preservation of the Soul* (New York: Currency/Doubleday, 1994); etc. Titles taken from Laura Nash and Scotty McLennan, *Church on Sunday, Work on Monday: The Challenge of Fusing Christian Values with Business Life* (San Francisco: Jossey-Bass, 2001).

16. Nash and McLennan, *Church on Sunday, Work on Monday*, 16, 41, 289.

17. For an extensive study of this problem, see ibid.

18. Robert Wuthnow, *The Crisis in the Churches: Spiritual Malaise, Fiscal Woe* (Oxford: Oxford University Press, 1997), ch. 5.

19. Wuthnow, *God and Mammon in America*, 77.

20. Volf, *Work in the Spirit*, 101–2.

21. There is, admittedly, very little ecclesiology in this book. It seemed better to craft a book that would speak to work issues in a wide spectrum of churches rather than recommend any specific ecclesiology.

1. WORK AND THE IMAGE OF GOD

1. *Webster's Third New International Dictionary of the English Language*, s.v. *labor*, *travail*. *The American Heritage Dictionary of the English Language*, s.v. *robot*. Henry George Liddell and Robert Scott, *A Greek-English Lexicon*, rev. Henry Stuart Jones, 9th ed. (Oxford: Clarendon Press, 1940), s.v., *banausos*.

2. Aristotle, *The Politics*, trans. H. Rackham (New York: G. P. Putnam's Sons, 1932), 1258b35.

3. Plato, *Gorgias*, trans. W. R. M. Lamb (New York: G. P. Putnam's Sons, 1932), 512b.

4. Göran Agrell, *Work, Toil, and Sustenance: An Examination of the View of Work in the New Testament, Taking into Consideration Views Found in Old Testament, Intertestamental, and Early Rabbinic Writings*, trans. Stephen Westerholm (Lund: Verbum H. Ohlsson, 1976), 7–13.

5. Compare Isa. 10:15; 15:16; 28:23–29; Pss. 65:10–13; 147:7; Job 5:8–26; Prov. 10:22; Eccl. 2:24–26.

6. Dorothy Soelle with Shirley A. Cloyes, *To Work and to Love: A Theology of Creation* (Philadelphia: Fortress Press, 1984), 11–12.

7. Doreen Kimura, "Sex Differences in the Brain," *Scientific American* 267, no. 3 (September 1992): 120–21. Research into sexual orientation has yielded more subtle differences, traditionally associated with masculinity and femininity. These are thought to come about because of hormonal influence on neural organization during gestation. "CAH females," for example, are girls exposed to too much androgen in utero; sometimes they require hormonal treatment after birth in order to correct ambiguous genitalia and to assure breast development at puberty. These females were inclined to be "tomboys," given to vigorous outdoor activity, with less interest in playing with dolls and in baby care. Yet they gave no evidence of long-term difficulty in becoming mothers and marital partners, even if they are physically tough, athletic females. Even if the sciences of genetics and endocrinology are young, it is not unreasonable to suspect that a great many subtle variations from the average masculine and feminine characteristics could be influenced by prenatal hormonal influences. Such influences, of course, would not prevent the great plasticity both sexes show with respect to how they can be molded by society and by their own interests. See Lee Ellis and M. Ashley Ames, "Neurohormonal Functioning and Sexual Orientation: A Theory of Homosexuality-Heterosexuality," *Psychological Bulletin* 101, no. 2 (1987): 248; see also Bernice Lott, *Women's Lives: Themes and Variations in Gender Learning* (Monterey: Brooks/Cole, 1987), 19–21.

8. Carol Gilligan, *In a Different Voice: Psychological Theory and Women's Development* (Cambridge, Mass.: Harvard University Press, 1982), 11–13.

9. Quoted from Barbara Drygulski Wright, "Introduction to Part I," in *Women, Work, and Technology: Transformations*, ed. Barbara Drygulski Wright, Myra Marx Ferree, et al. (Ann Arbor: University of Michigan Press, 1987), 3.

10. Quoted from Joan Williams, *Unbending Gender: Why Family and Work Conflict and What To Do About It* (Oxford: Oxford University Press, 2000), 43.

11. The proportion of women in the wage labor force has grown in the United States from 14 percent in 1901 to 28 percent in 1947, to 38 percent in 1985, and 45 percent in 1990, increasing to 46 percent in recent figures (Harriet Bradley, *Men's Work, Women's Work* [Minneapolis: University of Minnesota Press, 1989], 16; Williams, *Unbending Gender*, 67). But the segmented structure of employment among women is obvious both in occupational roles and pay. Women are mostly concentrated in jobs traditionally thought to be "women's work": teaching, nursing, secretarial and other office work, store clerking, and routine assembly line jobs. According to 1982 statistics,

96 percent of typists were women, 93 percent of bank tellers, and 92 percent of telephone operators, 80 percent of clerical workers, and 71 percent of retail workers. More recently, 99 percent of those typing at computers, 90 percent of bank tellers, 79 percent of clerical workers, and 70 percent of retail workers are women (U.S. Department of Labor, Bureau of Statistics, *Employment and Earnings* [selected years and January 1993]). Figured at a median real hourly wage, in 1973 women were paid 37 percent less than men. In 1997 this figure improved to 21 percent less. But this reflects a slight decrease in men's real earnings over that period and does not take into consideration the wages of women in part-time work, a labor force that has increased nearly fourfold during the same period (Lawrence Mishel, Jared Bernstein, and John Schmitt, *The State of Working America, 1998-99*, Economic Policy Institute [Ithaca, N.Y.: ILR Press, 1999], 134–35, 245). Thus, equal pay continues to be a problem for all working women despite the Equal Pay Act of 1963. Within the same profession, among men, lawyers earn a median income of $300 per week more than their female counterparts. A similar $100 per week disparity exists for secretaries. For doctors, women earn $500 dollars less per week, and among the 95 percent of nurses who are women, they still earn $30 less per week than the 5 percent who are men. Female professors have a median pay of $170 per week less than male professors, and for female elementary school teachers, the disparity is $70 per week less (National Committee on Pay Equity, AFL-CIO using Household Data Annual Averages, Bureau of Labor Statistics at www.aflcio.org/women/eqp_occ.htm).

12. There is ample evidence of glass ceilings. Among law firms, by 1990, women held half of the entry-level positions, but only 11 percent will become partners. Between 1979 and 1994 only two women became CEOs of Fortune 500 companies. Top partners on Wall Street are 99 percent male, and only 5.6 percent of partners in national accounting firms are women. In academia things changed little from 1920 to 1995 for women in full-time faculty positions: 26 percent to 31 percent. On the other hand, an increasing number of women have found places in areas previously thought to be male bastions and have thereby managed to discredit some old gender distinctions. There are, for example, about three thousand female coal miners who accept the same dirty, demanding entry-level positions as their male counterparts (Ulku Bates, Florence Denmark, et al., *Women's Realities, Women's Choices* [New York: Oxford University Press, 1995], 468). Women have taken up many roles previously reserved for men in the armed services. In 1990, 21 percent of lawyers and judges were women, compared with 5 percent in 1970. Similarly, 19 percent of physicians were women compared with only 9 percent in 1970. Engineers give the poorest showing, with 8 percent women in 1990 compared with 1.6 percent in 1970 (U.S. Department of Labor, Bureau of Labor Statistics, *Employment and Earnings* [selected years]). If the level of education between men and women is any indicator, it appears likely that women will make further inroads into traditionally male occupations. During the same span of time (1970 to 1990), women were awarded 43 percent of the bachelor's degrees in 1970, compared with 52 percent twenty years later; similarly 40 percent of the master's degrees compared to 52 percent in 1990, and 36 percent of doctorates in 1970, com-

pared with about 40 percent in 1990 (Christina Hoff Sommers, *Who Stole Feminism? How Women Have Betrayed Women* [New York: Simon & Schuster, 1994], 160).

13. An example Gilligan uses comes from Lawrence Kohlberg's theory of moral development tested on two sixth-grade youngsters, Amy and Jake. Both bright and articulate, they are asked to puzzle out one of Kohlberg's moral dilemmas in which a man seems obliged to steal a drug (too expensive to buy) in order to save the life of his wife. Jake works through the dilemma in a reasonable, calculating way, identifying with the man as one who stands alone, takes on responsibility, and makes a rationally justifiable decision to steal the drug. He approaches the issue like a math problem, weighing out the advantages and disadvantages of various alternatives to arrive at the best solution. Amy, on the other hand, can't seem to make a decision within the parameters of the dilemma. She sees the problem as "a narrative of relationships that extends over time." Perhaps the druggist can be persuaded to lower his price, perhaps the wife's health will improve over time, or maybe a third party can be found to pay for the medicine. By Kohlberg's standards, Amy is a stage lower in maturity than Jake because "her responses seem to reveal a feeling of powerlessness in the world, an inability to think systematically about the concepts of morality or law, a reluctance to challenge authority or to examine the logic of received moral truths, a failure even to conceive of acting directly to save a life or to consider that such action, if taken, could possibly have an effect." The fault, Gilligan argues, is in how the dilemma is constructed: its theme is masculine from the beginning. Amy's solution is different, but that doesn't make it any less worthy. Amy sees morality in the context of relationships and believes that communication is the best method of conflict resolution, especially when the dilemma is conveyed in a compelling way to those whose sympathy can be enlisted for help (Gilligan, *In a Different Voice,* 25–32).

14. Louise A. Tilly and Joan W. Scott, *Women, Work, and Family* (New York: Holt, Rinehart & Winston, 1978), 232.

15. Nancy Cott quotes the following from an "Essay on Marriage" from *The Universalist and Ladies Repository* of *1834*: "O! what a hallowed place home is when lit by the smile of such a being; and enviably happy the man who is the lord of such a paradise. . . . When he struggles on the path of duty, the thought that it is for *her* in part he toils will sweeten his labors. . . . Should he meet dark clouds and storms abroad, yet sunshine and peace await him at home; and when his proud heart would resent the language of petty tyrants, 'dressed in a little brief authority,' from whom he receives the scanty remuneration for his daily labors, the thought that she perhaps may suffer thereby, will calm the tumult of his passions and bid him struggle on, and find his reward in her sweet tones, and soothing kindness, and that the bliss of home is thereby made more apparent" (Nancy F. Cott, *The Bonds of Womanhood: "Women's Sphere" in New England, 1780–1835* [New Haven: Yale University Press, 1977], 58, 69–70).

16. See, e.g., Elizabeth Perle McKenna, *When Work Doesn't Work Anymore: Women, Work, and Identity* (New York: Delacorte Press, 1997); or Deborah Fallows, *A Mother's Work* (Boston: Houghton Mifflin, 1985).

17. Rosalind C. Barnett and Caryl Rivers, *She Works/He Works: How Two-Income*

Families Are Happier, Healthier, and Better Off (San Francisco: HarperSanFrancisco, 1996).

18. Williams, *Unbending Gender*, 60.

19. Arlie Hochschild with Anne Machung, *The Second Shift* (New York: Viking, 1989).

20. Williams, *Unbending Gender*, 234.

21. See n. 11 above. State governments with comparable worth programs include Washington, Oregon, Minnesota, Maine, and Michigan. Most of the Canadian provinces can be included, with Ontario even having a program for private as well as public employment. Thus, in the United States, the struggle for comparable worth has not had much success. See Margaret Hallock, "Pay Equity: Did it Work?" in *Squaring Up: Policy Strategies to Raise Women's Incomes in the United States*, ed. Margaret Hallock (Ann Arbor: University of Michigan Press, 2001), 136–61; National Women's Law Center, www.nwlc.org.

22. Divorce settlements often reveal a strong prejudice toward the husband as ideal worker. If the wife carries the domestic load of family obligation, she is doubly penalized because not only was she marginalized out of a possible career during child-rearing years, but she also gets a smaller share of her husband's income under the rule "he who earns it owns it." Her monetary settlement, when she carries on the domestic role as a single mother, is assessed according to minimal needs rather than income proportion. Consequently, 40 percent of divorced mothers end up in poverty. Overall, 80 percent of those in poverty are women and children (Williams, *Unbending Gender*, 115).

23. Ibid., 88–98.

24. Arlie Russell Hochschild, *The Time Bind* (New York: Henry Holt, 1997), 92.

25. John Chambers of Cisco Systems received a total salary package of $154.3 million (a 32-percent increase) during the last fiscal year even though his company lost $1 billion and suffered a 71-percent drop in stock value. Raymond Gilmartin of Merck also had a pay raise despite a disappointing year, as did Richard Kovacevich of Wells Fargo, whose income was boosted by 73 percent. Some other CEO salaries were reduced as the performance of their companies fell, but even so, their incomes remain huge by any standard (Claudia M. Deutsch, "Trailing the Chief in Pay, Too," in "Executive Pay: A Special Report," *The New York Times*, Sunday, April 7, 2002).

26. Derek Bok, *The Cost of Talent* (New York: Free Press, 1993), 95–96.

27. Ibid., 103.

28. Ibid., 102. See Ken Belson, "Learning How to Talk about Salary in Japan," in "Executive Pay: A Special Report," *The New York Times*, Sunday, April 7, 2002.

29. Williams, *Unbending Gender*, ch. 8.

30. See the summary in Lee Hardy, *The Fabric of This World: Inquiries into Calling, Career Choice, and the Design of Human Work* (Grand Rapids: Eerdmans, 1990), 140–67.

31. William J. Latzko and David M. Saunders, *Four Days with Dr. Deming: A Strategy for Modern Methods of Management* (Reading, Mass.: Addison-Wesley, 1995), 28–32.

32. Sally McFague, *Models of God: Theology for an Ecological, Nuclear Age* (Philadelphia: Fortress Press, 1987), 93.

33. Ibid., 65.

34. Ibid., 113.

35. Ibid., 85.

36. Soelle and Cloyes, *To Work and to Love,* 23–27.

37. Robert H. Nelson, *Economics as Religion: From Samuelson to Chicago and Beyond* (University Park: Pennsylvania State University Press, 2001), ch. 10.

38. E.g., Sally McFague, *The Body of God: An Ecological Theology* (Minneapolis: Fortress Press, 1993), 149–50; Cynthia Rigby, "Free to Be Human, Limits: Possibilities, and the Sovereignty of God," *Theology Today* 53 (April 1966): 1, 47–62; but see also Arthur Peacocke, *Theology for a Scientific Age: Being and Becoming—Natural, Divine, and Human* (Minneapolis: Fortress Press, 1993), 371–72; Marcus J. Borg, *The God We Never Knew: Beyond Dogmatic Religion to a More Authentic Contemporary Faith* (San Francisco: HarperSanFrancisco, 1997), ch. 2.

39. Elizabeth A. Johnson, *She Who Is: The Mystery of God in Feminist Theological Discourse* (New York: Crossroad, 1996), 230.

40. McFague, *Models of God,* 121.

41. Thomas's most useful teaching comes when he is not being elitist: in his discussion of the *vita activa* (active life) and the *vita contemplativa* (contemplative life). This distinction might seem to separate the religious, reputed for their contemplative life, from the rest of the world. But not so. The active and the contemplative are aspects of life common to all humanity. Each person possesses both faculties. The distinction is between the theoretical and practical intellect, between envisioning Christian salvation and living out that calling, between prayer and morals, between speculation and will, between discerning the truth and doing the truth. Therefore the most contemplative monks and the most common of serfs are both obliged to, on the one hand, know the virtues and, on the other hand, cultivate them; or again, to heed the teaching of the apostolate, and to do good to others through acts of mercy and justice (*Summa Theologiae* 2a–2ae, 179–82).

42. Siegfried Wenszel, *The Sin of Sloth: Acedia in Medieval Thought and Literature* (Chapel Hill: University of North Carolina Press, 1960), 30–31.

43. George Ovitt, Jr., *The Restoration of Perfection* (New Brunswick, N.J.: Rutgers University Press, 1987), 104.

44. Jacques Le Goff, *Time, Work, and Culture in the Middle Ages,* trans. Arthur Goldhammer (Chicago: University of Chicago Press, 1980), 50–52, 116.

45. Lewis Mumford, *The Myth of the Machine: Technics and Human Development* (New York: Harcourt, Brace, and World, 1966), 277.

46. Gustav Wingren, *Luther on Vocation,* trans. Carl C. Rasmussen (Philadelphia: Muhlenberg Press, 1957), 5, 9, 18, 21, 25, 27, 30, 33, 34, 57, 64, 76.

47. Jaroslav Pelikan, *The Melody of Theology: A Philosophical Dictionary* (Cambridge, Mass.: Harvard University Press, 1988), 15–16.

48. José Míguez Bonino, *Doing Theology in a Revolutionary Situation* (Philadelphia: Fortress Press, 1975), 108–11.

2. GETTING A FOCUS ON VOCATION

1. See Howard Gardner, Mihaly Csikszentmihalyi, and William Damon, *Good Work: When Excellence and Ethics Meet* (New York: Basic Books, 2001), 163. These authors frame the notion of vocation "through the psychological concept of *moral identity*."

2. I add a caveat. I do not believe that a "call" to a particular job is foreordained. I believe we are free to choose for ourselves, but, once a morally acceptable vocation is chosen, divine help is available to carry out that vocation as one who serves God.

3. Dorothy Emmet, *Function, Purpose, and Powers*, 2nd ed. (London: Macmillan, 1972), 254.

4. Ibid., 239–53.

5. Mark Ledbetter, *Virtuous Intentions: The Religious Dimension of Narrative* (Atlanta: Scholars Press, 1989), 19–33.

6. Studs Terkel, *Working* (New York: Avon Books, 1972), 391, 394–95.

7. Material about Vernon Johns comes from Taylor Branch, *Parting the Waters* (New York: Simon & Schuster, 1988), ch. 1.

8. Paul Tillich, *The Courage to Be* (New Haven: Yale University Press, 1952), ch. 2.

9. Gardner et al., *Good Work*, 127–28.

10. Ibid., 109–13.

11. Ibid., 101.

12. Robert H. Frank and Philip J. Cook, *The Winner-Take-All Society: How More and More Americans Compete for Ever Fewer and Bigger Prizes, Encouraging Economic Waste, Income Inequality, and an Impoverished Cultural Life* (New York: Martin Kessler Books, The Free Press, 1995), 104.

13. Ibid., 78.

14. Robert Bellah, *Beyond Belief: Essays on Religion in a Post Traditional World* (San Francisco: Harper & Row, 1970), 21.

15. The argument here is oversimplified. The ROS of a person who is attuned to the things God cares about can, realistically, have a variety of top-priority concerns depending on occasion and context, and, optimally, all of them can be consonant with divine interests. For a fuller description, see William Droel's *Full-Time Christians: The Real Challenge from Vatican II* (Mystic, Conn.: Twenty-Third Publications, 2002).

16. Reinhold Niebuhr, *The Nature and Destiny of Man*, vol. 1 (New York: Charles Scribner's Sons, 1941), 261, 267–68.

17. Ninian Smart, "History of Mysticism," in *Encyclopedia of Philosophy*, ed. Paul Edwards (New York: Macmillan and Free Press, 1967), 5:425.

18. Mircea Eliade, *Myths, Dreams, and Mysteries*, trans. Philip Maret (New York: Harper & Bros., 1960), 71.

19. Aristotle, *Metaphysics*, bks. 10–14, trans. Hugh Tredennick (Cambridge, Mass.: Harvard University Press, 1932), bk. 12; *Nicomachean Ethics*, trans. H. Rackham (Cambridge, Mass.: Harvard University Press, 1934), 10.7, 8.

20. Thomas Aquinas, *Summa Contra Gentiles*, trans. Vernon J. Bourke (Notre Dame, Ind.: University of Notre Dame Press, 1975) 3.19, 3.69; *Summa Theologiae*, vol.

47 (2a2ae), trans. Jordan Auman (New York: Blackfriars with McGraw Hill Book Co., 1973), 2.2.184; Stanley M. Burgess, "Medieval Models of Perfectionism," in *Reaching Beyond*, ed. Stanley M. Burgess (Peabody, Mass.: Hendrickson, 1986), 164–68. Use of the word "perfect" in liturgical language likely has its roots in medieval theology, but its theological articulation is more sophisticated than most people would grasp when hearing the word used in the liturgy. Aquinas's notion of perfection is strongly dominated by Aristotle's distinction between potential and actual (*Metaphysics* H2 104269-104328), where all things have the potential to actualize whatever proclivity they possess; e.g., acorns become oaks, eggs become birds, etc. For Aquinas, the actuality any particular existent achieves is invested in its aim to fulfill a suitable and divinely constituted potentiality (*Summa Theologiae* 1a.5.2). When this given actuality is thoroughly achieved, then that existent is considered "perfect" (*perficere*, "what is actual and flawless": ibid., 1a.5.1). But there are gradations of perfection because birds are lower than humans, humans lower than angels, etc., God, being the origin of all else and without any defect, is the most perfect by being thoroughly complete and without defect (ibid., 1a.4.a). There must also be degrees of perfection since many existents do not reach their given potential. That given potential, however, must be formally prior to any actualization (ibid., 1a.4.2). In this way the Greek notion of a paradigmatic perfection shows up in Aquinas.

21. James M. Gustafson, *Christ and the Moral Life* (Chicago: University of Chicago Press, 1968), ch. 2.

22. Richard T. Hughes, "Christian Primitivism as Perfectionism: from Anabaptists to Pentecostals," in *Reaching Beyond*, ed. Burgess, 219, 224, 248.

23. W. F. Albright and C. S. Mann, *Matthew* (Garden City, N.Y.: Doubleday, 1971), 71–72.

24. See, e.g., *The Book of Common Prayer* (New York: Church Hymnal Corporation, 1979), 127, 334, 378, 528; Martin Thornton, *The Heart of the Parish* (Cambridge: Cowley Publications, 1989), 83–84, 212, 235, 256; Kenneth Leech, *Soul Friend* (San Francisco: Harper & Row, 1977), 37, 115, 151; John C. Haughey, *Converting Nine to Five: A Spirituality of Daily Work* (New York: Crossroad, 1989), 73, 75, 109; William L. Droel and Gregory F. A. Pierce, *Confident and Competent* (Notre Dame, Ind.: Ave Maria Press, 1987), 44, 93. Alfons Auer, *Open to the World*, trans. Dennis Doherty and Carmel Callaghan (Baltimore: Helicon Press, 1966), 83, 212–16.

25. Steven J. Hendlin, *When Good Enough Is Never Enough: Escaping the Perfection Trap* (New York: G. P. Putnam's Sons, 1992).

26. H. P. Owen, "Perfection," in *Encyclopedia of Philosophy*, ed. Edwards, 6:87.

27. Leonard Doohan, *The Lay-Centered Church: Theology and Spirituality* (Minneapolis: Winston Press, 1984), 97.

28. George Ovitt, Jr., *The Restoration of Perfection* (New Brunswick, N.J.: Rutgers University Press, 1987), 105–6.

29. Thomas Aquinas, *Summa Theologiae*, vol. 47, 2.2.184.7–8.

30. Doohan, *Lay-Centered Church*, 90.

31. Parker J. Palmer, *The Active Life: A Spirituality of Work, Creativity, and Caring*

(San Francisco: Harper & Row, 1990), 2. Palmer oversells his case here. A frenetic pace of work can be counterproductive. Time for reflective contemplation from such a pace can be a fruitful discipline.

32. I do not mean to imply that there is no theological literature on the *vita activa.* See., e.g., ch. 1, n. 41.

33. Katherine Dyckman and L. Patrick Carroll, *Inviting the Mystic, Supporting the Prophet: An Introduction to Spiritual Direction* (New York: Paulist Press, 1981), 79.

34. Auer, *Open to the World,* 76.

35. The spiritual value of the metemphatic path may seem close to what Aquinas has in mind with the *via eminentia* as in *Summa Theologiae* 1.12.12. The *via eminentia* is a way of reasoning about God under the assumption that some creaturely attributes (e.g., goodness, love, reason, righteousness, power, etc.) must exist not partially, but supremely and completely in the Creator. The metemphatic path, however, is intuitive rather than discursive, a feeling of appreciation where Creator and creature have the sense of being confidently or harmoniously bound together over the inherent value of an object, a thought, or an activity. While *via eminentia* presumes attributes held in common between God and creature, whatever is predicated of the creature is denigrated because that predication is supremely present with God and less so in the creature, whereas something holding metemphatic value is not denigrated. If there is something in Aquinas that looks a little like the metemphatic, it would be the *actus purus* of divine regard for creaturely affairs, where the divine enjoys some act, object, or thought of the creation, as, for example, a masterful pianist might enjoy the struggling accomplishment of a student (*Summa contra Gentiles* I.90.753; 102.849) (Norman Kretzmann, *The Metaphysics of Theism: Aquinas's Natural Theology in Summa contra Gentiles I* [Oxford: Clarendon Press, 1977] 235–37). Here again, however, the rational drive to have God completely actualized and without defect, always necessarily invokes only a humble pleasure from the creature because the creature, standing before the divine, is never thoroughly actualized or perfected on the scale of the Creator. The divine regard through *actus purus* and the ability to draw inferences through the *via eminentia* are reasonable paths toward God, but are not the same as the metemphatic path.

36. Auer, *Open to the World,* 83.

37. I am indebted to Douglas Adams, professor of English at the University of Idaho, for this suggestion. The root word for all three of these categories is *phatikos,* meaning "appearing." Instead of *kata,* which means something like "by," or "according to," and instead of *apo,* meaning "separate," or "away from," the *met* in *metemphatic* means "with," or "among."

A passage from Alice Walker's *The Color Purple* (New York: Harcourt Brace Jovanovich, 1982), captures the idea of metaemphasis quite well (p. 191):

... Listen, God love everything you love—and a mess of stuff you don't. But more than anything else, God love admiration.

You say God vain? I ast.

Naw, she say. Not vain, just wanting to share a good thing. I think it pisses God off if you walk by the color purple in a field somewhere and don't notice it.

What it do when it pissed off?

Oh, it make something else. People think pleasing God is all God care about. But any fool living in the world can see it always trying to please us back.

Yeah? I say.

Yeah, she say. It always making little surprises and springing them on us when us least expect.

You mean it want to be loved, just like the bible say.

Yes, Celie, she say. Everything want to be loved.

A similar metemphatic spirituality is often expressed by scientists, especially in their devotion to the elegance of scientific theories. After Arthur Eddington confirmed Einstein's theory of general relativity by demonstrating how starlight bent around the sun, one of Einstein's students asked what would have happened to his theory if Eddington had disconfirmed it. Einstein replied, "Then I would have been sorry for the dear Lord, for the theory *is* correct." What Einstein meant was that general relativity had too much deep inner elegance and power to be passed up by the Creator. Many scientists through the centuries (e.g., Galileo, Kepler, Newton, Hawking) have prized theoretical elegance and simplicity as an inherent value congruent with the mind of God. By reading the book of nature, so to speak, one reads the mind of God. See Brian Greene, *The Elegant Universe: Superstrings, Hidden Dimensions, and the Quest for the Ultimate Theory* (New York: Vantage Books, 1999), 166.

38. Pronounced "Chick-sent-me-high."

39. To add a bit more to the definition, "flow" experiences can happen on the job so long as there are "clear goals, immediate feedback, and a level of challenges matching our skills" (Gardner et al., *Good Work*, 5).

40. Mihaly Csikszentmihalyi, *Flow: The Psychology of Optimal Experience* (New York: Harper Collins, 1991), ch. 7.

41. See p. 10 above.

42. Gardner et al., *Good Work*, 212–19, 232–45.

3. MAKING SPACE FOR A THEOLOGY OF WORK

1. William James, *The Varieties of Religious Experience: A Study in Human Nature* (New York: Modern Library, 1902), 31–32.

2. T. S. Eliot, *Complete Poems and Plays, 1909–1950* (New York: Harcourt, Brace, and Co., 1952), 364.

3. B. F. Skinner, "Operational Analysis of Psychological Terms," in *Readings in the Philosophy of Science*, ed. Herbert Feigl and Mary Brodbeck (New York: Appleton, Century, and Crofts, 1953), 588.

4. Wittgenstein's argument about private language is a powerful antidote to the problem of private access. It does not necessarily defeat the problem so much as render it otiose by piling up the baggage of difficulties that must be assumed along with private access. Briefly, if each person has private and inaccessible mental phenomena, then it would be reasonable to suppose that Jones's mental referent for "orange" could

be very different from Smith's, and similarly for a whole mental storehouse of referents for the meanings of words. If there is such a private storehouse, then it functions like a "private language," like one's own subroutine to translate public language into terms and referents understandable within the private sphere of one's own mind. If the extra baggage of a private language is allowed, there are difficulties imagining how it could plausibly operate. Using a language means engaging in a convention-governed activity, and one of the most important uses requiring consistency is reidentifying words and phrases and using them in the same way. But these conventions require some objective check, and there is no good private way to be sure these rules are followed. There would be no way, for example, that one could be sure that the same private referent for "orange" was being used. Hence, the basic requirement of language as a convention-governed activity is undermined if one holds the private-access view. So there doesn't appear to be a private language carried about by each person. See Ludwig Wittgenstein, *Philosophical Investigations,* trans. G. E. M. Anscombe (New York: Macmillan, 1958), no. 243; see also Saul A. Kripke, *Wittgenstein on Rules and Private Language* (Cambridge, Mass.: Harvard University Press, 1982), 55–113.

5. See, e.g., Michael Lerner, *Surplus Powerlessness: The Psychodynamics of Everyday Life and the Psychology of Individual and Social Transformation* (Atlantic Highlands, N.J.: Humanities Press International, 1991).

6. Maurice Mandlebaum, "Social Facts," in *The Philosophy of Social Explanation,* ed. Alan Ryan (Oxford: Oxford University Press, 1973), 108–10.

7. See, e.g., Ben Hamper, *Rivethead: Tales from the Assembly Line* (New York: Warner Books, 1991); or James O'Toole et al., *Work in America: Report of a Special Task Force to the Secretary of Health, Education, and Welfare* (Cambridge, Mass.: MIT Press, 1981), ch. 2.

8. See Larry May, *The Morality of Groups: Collective Responsibility, Group-Based Harm, and Corporate Rights* (Notre Dame, Ind.: University of Notre Dame Press, 1987); also Thomas L. Shaffer, *Faith and the Professions* (Provo: Brigham Young University, 1987), ch. 3.

9. Walter Wink, *Naming the Powers: The Language of Power in the New Testament* (Philadelphia: Fortress Press, 1984), 5.

10. Gustaf Aulén, *Christus Victor: An Historical Study of the Three Main Types of the Idea of Atonement,* trans. A. G. Hebert (New York: Macmillan, 1969), 4–7, 81–92, 128–33.

11. Quoted from Mary E. Hines, "The Praxis of the Kingdom of God: Ministry," in *The Praxis of Christian Experience: An Introduction to the Theology of Edward Schillebeeckx,* ed. Robert J. Schreiter and Mary Catherine Hilkert (San Francisco: Harper & Row, 1989), 120.

12. Augustine, *City of God,* trans. Marcus Dods (New York: Modern Library, 1950).

13. Albrecht Ritschl, *The Christian Doctrine of Justification and Reconciliation,* trans. H. R. Mackintosh and A. B. Macaulay (Clifton, N.J.: Reference Book Publishers, 1966), 219–26; Wolfhart Pannenberg, *Theology and the Kingdom of God,* ed. Richard John Neuhaus (Philadelphia: Westminster Press, 1975), 58–60, 79, 117–18; Jürgen

Moltmann, *Theology of Hope*, trans. James W. Leitch (New York: Harper & Row, 1975), 224, 329.

14. A. T. Hanson, "Eschatology," *Dictionary of Christian Theology*, ed. Alan R. Richardson (London: SCM Press, 1969), 114.

15. See Edward Schillebeeckx, *Christ*, trans. John Bowden (New York: Crossroad, 1986), 746–62. A particular advocate of salvation history is Oscar Cullmann, *Salvation in History*, trans. Sidney G. Sowers (San Francisco: Harper & Row, 1967), 57–58.

16. E. Frank Tupper, *The Theology of Wolfhart Pannenberg* (Philadelphia: Westminister Press, 1976), 255–57.

17. Norman Perrin, *Jesus and the Language of the Kingdom* (Philadelphia: Fortress Press, 1976), 65–68, 71-80.

18. Ibid., 70–71.

19. Walter Rauschenbusch, *Christianity and the Social Crisis* (New York: Macmillan, 1908), 65.

20. Ralph P. Martin, "The Kingdom of God in Recent Writing," *Christianity Today* 8, no. 8 (January 17, 1964): 5–7. Luke 17:21 is sometimes used as a scriptural reference for this view; that is, "The Kingdom of God is within you." But the translation can just as well read "among you," or "in your midst."

21. Adolph Harnack, *What Is Christianity?* trans. Thomas Bailey Saunders (New York: Harper Torchbooks, 1937), 56.

22. H. Richard Niebuhr, *The Kingdom of God in America* (New York: Harper Torchbooks, 1937), 87.

23. Reinhold Niebuhr, *An Interpretation of Christian Ethics* (New York: Meridian Books, 1956), 60.

24. Howard A. Snyder gives eight models of the kingdom: as future hope, as inner spiritual experience, as mystical communion, as institutional church, as countersystem, as political state, as Christianized culture, and as earthly utopia. While some of these models are at opposite poles, he remarks that usually a belief system will hold strongly to one and less strongly to a few more (*Models of the Kingdom* [Nashville: Abingdon Press, 1991], ch. 1).

25. Thomas Berry, *The Dream of the Earth* (San Francisco: Sierra Club Books, 1988), 126.

26. Dorothy Sayers, *Creed or Chaos?* (London: Methuen, 1947), 58–59.

27. Mark Gibbs, *Christians with Secular Power* (Philadelphia: Fortress Press, 1981), 9.

28. William E. Diehl, *Christianity and Real Life* (Philadelphia: Fortress Press, 1976), v–viii, 1–2.

29. Russell Barta, ed. "The Chicago Declaration of Concern," in *Challenge of the Laity* (Huntington, Ind.: Our Sunday Visitor, 1980), 19–27.

30. For example, the Episcopal *Book of Common Prayer* (New York: Church Hymnal Corp., 1928) listed "orders of ministers . . . in the Church" as bishops, priests, and deacons, omitting laity entirely (p. 294). But the revised prayer book (New York: Church Hymnal Corp., 1979) lists "ministers of the Church" as laity first, then bishops, priests, and deacons (p. 855).

31. I am relying, in part, on distinctions made by Leonard Doohan, *The Lay-Centered Church: Theology and Spirituality* (Minneapolis: Winston Press, 1984), ch. 1.

32. Ives M. J. Congar, *Lay People in the Church*, trans. Donald Attwater (London: Geoffrey Chapman, 1959), 84–87, 128, 143–46, 267, 294, 374.

33. Ibid., 128–36.

34. Aidan Kavanagh, "Christian Ministry and Ministries," *Anglican Theological Review*, 66 Supplementary Series no. 9 (1984): 40.

35. Quoted from Barta, ed., "Chicago Declaration of Concern," 20–21.

36. Gustav Wingren, *Luther on Vocation*, trans. Carl C. Rasmussen (Philadelphia: Muhlenberg Press, 1957), 5, 9, 18, 21, 25, 27, 57, 76.

37. Two things cause difficulties in adapting Luther's thought to a modern theology of work. One stems from a favorite verse (1 Cor. 7:20, "Remain in the vocation to which you were called"), which Luther used to justify the stasis of late medieval class society. To a twentieth-century mind, this would defy the possibility of meaningful work, because the son of a shoemaker must also be a shoemaker. There is no mobility. Second, Luther divides his theological space into two kingdoms: an earthly kingdom and a heavenly one. The first is a kingdom of love and service, where all human work takes place. The second is a kingdom of grace. Since Luther is radically committed to the view that nothing can be gained through work, but only by grace, it follows that there is no ultimate meaning to earthly work.

38. Hendrik Kraemer, *A Theology of the Laity* (Philadelphia: Westminster Press, 1958).

39. Unfortunately, the church at the time of Kraemer's writing (1958) was on a tide of introverted institutional success and was mostly self-congratulatory, self-celebratory, and, consequently, self-serving, calling on and valuing the laity mostly for institutional service. The logical extension of Kraemer's argument would lead to a theology of work, but there is no mention of this, possibly because his notion of the kingdom is unclear. His book does, however, herald an awakening of a servant church and membership such as blossomed in some significant ways in America during the 1960s, when churches effectively addressed a number of worldly issues.

40. I have elaborated a parable originally suggested by N. Patrick Murray, "From a Paper Prepared for a Workshop on Lay Ministry at Christ Church, Little Rock" in *The Calling of the Laity*, ed. Verna Dozier, (Washington: Alban Institute, 1988), 84–85.

41. John A. T. Robinson, *The New Reformation?* (Philadelphia: Westminster Press, 1958), 54–57.

42. James F. Hopewell, "A Congregational Paradigm for Theological Education," in *Beyond Clericalism: The Congregation as a Focus for Theological Education*, ed. Joseph C. Hough, Jr., and Barbara G. Wheeler (Atlanta: Scholars Press, 1988), 1–11.

43. John B. Cobb, Jr., "Ministry to the World: A New Professional Paradigm," in *Beyond Clericalism*, ed. Hough and Wheeler, 28.

44. In fact, this has happened to some extent. A number of lay-authored theological works have appeared, coming from such people as Jacques Maritain, Etienne Gilson, Jacques Ellul, Simone Weil, Dorothy Day, William Stringfellow, Michael

Novak, Mark Gibbs, William Diehl, Dorothy Sayers, Thomas Shaffer, Glenn Tinder, C. S. Lewis, and many others. One would hardly know where to end such a list because theology written by the laity tends to be nonstandard in expression, not fitting neatly into traditional doctrinal categories or modes of expression. Indeed, if one wanted to shade over into literary expression by Christian lay authors such as T. S. Eliot, Graham Greene, Frederick Buechner, or Walker Percy, the list would be almost endless. There are also lay-written volumes dedicated to specific occupations. Shaffer's *Faith and the Professions* deals with lawyers; Parker J. Palmer's *The Courage to Teach: Exploring the Inner Landscape of a Teacher's Life* (San Francisco: Jossey-Bass, 1998) relates to the teaching profession.

45. Edward C. F. A. Schillebeeckx, *The Eucharist*, trans. N. D. Smith (New York: Sheed & Ward, 1968).

46. See Walter Brueggemann, "The Loss and Recovery of Creation in Old Testament Theology," *Theology Today* 53 (July 1996): 177–90; James Barr, *Biblical Faith and Natural Theology* (Oxford: Clarendon Press, 1993), chs. 1, 6.

47. Reinhold Niebuhr, *Moral Man and Immoral Society* (New York: Charles Scribner's Sons, 1932), 60–61, 231–32, 248–65.

48. For an early work in methodology, see Ian G. Barbour, *Myths, Models, and Paradigms: A Comparative Study in Science and Religion* (New York: Harper & Row, 1974). A fuller discussion of the relation between science and religion comes in Barbour's *Religion in an Age of Science* (San Francisco: HarperSanFrancisco, 1990). His latest work is *When Science Meets Religion* (San Francisco: HarperSanFrancisco, 2000). Another noteworthy effort comes in a series of anthologies published through the Center for Theology and the Natural Sciences, the Vatican Observatory and University of Notre Dame Press. These focus on plausible avenues within the various scientific disciplines where "divine action" might occur. Robert John Russell is the general editor; titles are *Physics, Philosophy, and Theology* (1988), *Quantum Cosmology and the Laws of Nature* (1993), *Chaos and Complexity* (1955), *Evolutionary and Molecular Biology* (1998), *Neuroscience and the Person* (1999); Robert John Russell, general editor. Several authors have proposed new schemes to replace the medieval synthesis torn asunder by Galileo, where theology and ethics are once again given an integrated place among the disciplines. See Arthur Peacocke, *Theology for a Scientific Age: Being and Becoming—National, Divine, and Human* (Minneapolis: Fortress Press, 1993); and Nancey Murphy and George F. R. Ellis, *On the Moral Nature of the Universe* (Minneapolis: Fortress Press, 1996).

49. See Murphy and Ellis, *On the Moral Nature of the Universe* (Minneapolis: Fortress Press, 1996), ch. 10. While not denying the need for revelation in theology, they argue that the discipline of theology can be seen as similar to the evaluation of "research programs" in a Lakatosian explanation of how scientific theories stand or fail against rival theories.

50. See, e.g., Paul Davies, "Teleology Without Teleology: Purpose through Emergent Complexity," in *Evolutionary and Molecular Biology*, ed. Robert J. Russell (Notre Dame, Ind.: University of Notre Dame Press, 1998), 151–62.

51. John Hellman, *Emmanuel Mounier and the New Catholic Left 1930–1950* (Toronto: University of Toronto Press, 1981), 191.

52. See Philip Hefner, *The Human Factor: Evolution, Culture, and Religion* (Minneapolis: Fortress Press, 1993), ch. 2.

53. George Sturt, *The Wheelwright's Shop* (Cambridge: Cambridge University Press, Canto edition, 1993), 176.

54. Wendell Berry, *Sabbaths* (San Francisco: North Point Press, 1987), 67.

4. THE ESCHATOLOGICAL CHRIST AND HOMO ARTIFEX

1. Miroslav Volf, *Work in the Spirit: Toward a Theology of Work* (Oxford: Oxford University Press, 1991), 101.

2. Philip Hefner, *The Human Factor: Evolution, Culture, and Religion* (Minneapolis: Fortress Press, 1993).

3. Ibid., 109.

4. Ibid., 42.

5. Ibid., 46.

6. "New creation" and "new thing" are being used synonymously.

7. John C. Haughey, *Converting Nine to Five: A Spirituality of Daily Work* (New York: Crossroad, 1989), 109.

8. M. Douglas Meeks, *Origins of the Theology of Hope* (Philadelphia: Fortress Press, 1974), 108–11.

9. Ibid., 117.

10. Jürgen Moltmann, *Theology of Hope* (San Francisco: HarperCollins, 1991), 105–6.

11. Ibid., 75.

12. Ibid., 203–5, 229.

13. Paul Tillich, *The Shaking of the Foundations* (New York: Charles Scribner's Sons, 1948), 162.

14. Plato, *Theatetus,* trans. Harold N. Fowler (Cambridge: Cambridge University Press, 1977), 146A–147C.

15. See, e.g., Ludwig Wittgenstein, *Philosophical Investigations,* trans. G. E. M. Anscombe (New York: Macmillan, 1958), nos. 66, 67.

16. The argument I use here is similar to the nominalism of William of Ockham, who argued that a universal (i.e., a predicate or property) is just the act of thinking of several similar objects at once. See his *Quodlibets.* For a modern version, see W. V. O. Quine, "On What There Is," in *From a Logical Point of View,* 2nd ed. (New York: Harper & Row, 1962), 10.

17. Steven Hendlin, *When Good Enough Is Never Enough: Escaping the Perfection Trap* (New York: G. P. Putnam's Sons, 1992), 158.

18. Ibid., 158–59. Hendlin's book is a fairly comprehensive study of perfectionism, including perfectionism at work, societal perfection, marital perfection, raising the perfect child, religious pressures to be perfect, and psychological theories about per-

fection. He covers suicide, depression, bulimia, addiction, competitive treadmills, and other disasters that visit people who aspire to perfection.

19. Rom Harre, *Great Scientific Experiments* (Oxford: Phaidon Press, 1981), 112–21.

20. Donald T. Campbell, "The Conflict Between Social and Biological Evolution and the Concept of Original Sin," *Zygon* 10, no. 3 (September 1975): 238.

21. Quoted in Hefner, *Human Factor,* 191.

22. Ibid., 199.

23. Campbell, "Conflict Between Social and Biological Evolution," 243.

24. See Col. 2:9–10: "For it is in Christ that the complete being of the Godhead dwells embodied, and in him you have been brought to completion. Every power and authority in the universe is subject to him as Head."

5. THE PROTOLOGICAL CREATOR AND HOMO CONSERVANS

1. B. J. Carr and J. J. Rees, "The Anthropic Principle and the Structure of the Physical World," *Nature* 278 (1979): 605.

2. Euan Squires, *Conscious Mind in the Physical World* (New York: Adam Hilger, 1990), 97.

3. Again, geometry has been expanded beyond the usual Cartesian coordinates of plus and minus numbers to include numbers in complex space, an ordering that is able to display functions combining both real and imaginary numbers. Iterative logistic formulas in this realm generate a new geometry, called "fractals," having a symmetry of inexact self-similarity. The mathematical rules thus employed can imitate the way natural formations take place, such as snowflakes, leaves, mountainscapes, clouds, or wisps of smoke. See James Gleick, *Chaos* (New York: Penguin Books, 1987), 211–42; also Eugene P. Wigner, "The Unreasonable Effectiveness of Mathematics in the Natural Sciences," *Communications on Pure and Applied Mathematics* 13 (1960): 1–14; Paul Davies, *The Mind of God* (New York: Simon & Schuster, 1992), chs. 4, 5, 6.

4. The anthropic principle gets its strongest case from a notion of the big bang derived when Einstein's field equations for general relativity are "run backward" showing a universe not expanding, but shrinking to a point of mathematical singularity from which—in theory—it originally and explosively came into being. This "big bang" has empirical confirmation in Edwin Hubble's observation that stellar matter continues to recede at accelerating speeds, that there is a background radiation everywhere in space as a cooling remnant of the big bang, and yet some lumpiness to this residue, as observed by the COBE satellite, that would allow astral bodies to coalesce. This "strongest case" is enhanced by the need to explain the evolution of the universe and the elements of the periodic table as they have developed through stellar evolution. It is attractive to theology not just because of design interests but also because it seems to hint at an *ex nihilo* creation. Speculative problems arise, however, because the earliest time spans of the big bang are occupied only by undifferentiated energy, subject to investigation by quantum mechanics; and quantum mechanics has never been theo-

retically reconciled to general relativity. In the quantum area, there are some suggestions that might preclude an *ex nihilo* universe, such as Alan Guth's expansion theory, which suggests that not just one but many universes are around, the Hartle-Hawking suggestion that there was no specifiable beginning to the big bang, or Hugh Everett's hypothesis that there are many universes of any array of complexity occurring all the time. See Steven Weinberg, "Before the Big Bang," *New York Review of Books*, 44, no.10 (June 12, 1997): 16–20. Even if there are ways to undermine theological support for *ex nihilo*, there remains an ontological dependence, enhanced by the delicate seemingly designed element of the anthropic principle, and the fact that these factors don't carry their own ultimate explanation. See Robert J. Russell, "T=0 Is it Theologically Significant?" in *Religion and Science*, ed. W. M. Richardson and W. J. Wildman (New York: Routledge, 1996), 201–24.

5. Quoted in Holmes Rolston III, "Shaken Atheism: A Look at the Fine-Tuned Universe," *Christian Century* 103, no. 37 (December 3, 1986): 1093.

6. Freeman Dyson, "Energy in the Universe," *Scientific American* 224, no. 3 (September 1971): 51–59; John D. Barrow and Frank J. Tipler, *The Anthropic Principle* (Oxford: Clarendon Press, 1986), chs. 5, 7, 8.

7. Paul Davies, "The Anthropic Principle," *Progress in Particle and Nuclear Physics* 10 (1983): 33.

8. For further discussion, see Stephen Meyer, "The Return of the God Hypothesis," *Journal of Interdisciplinary Studies* 11, nos. 1, 2 (1999).

9. Quoted in Arthur Peacocke, *God and the New Biology* (San Francisco: Harper & Row, 1986), 133.

10. Ibid., 141–47.

11. Stuart Kauffman, *At Home in the Universe: The Search for Laws of Self-Organization and Complexity* (Oxford: Oxford University Press, 1995), 223.

12. Ibid., 234.

13. Ibid., 78–79. New arguments are being advanced claiming that some biological assemblages are "irreducibly complex," leaving an opening for debate regarding the plausibility of an intelligent designer. See Michael Behe, *Darwin's Black Box: The Biochemical Challenge to Evolution* (New York: Free Press, 1996).

14. Kauffman, *At Home in the Universe*, ch. 6.

15. Arthur Peacocke, *Theology for a Scientific Age: Being and Becoming—Natural, Divine, and Human* (Minneapolis: Fortress Press, 1993), 163–68.

16. John Polkinghorne, "The Metaphysics of Divine Action," in *Chaos and Complexity: Scientific Perspectives on Divine Action*, ed. Robert J. Russell, Nancey Murphy, and Arthur Peacocke (Vatican City State: Vatican Observatory Publications, 1995), 147–56.

17. David Lindley, *Where Does the Weirdness Go? Why Quantum Mechanics Is Strange, But Not As Strange As You Think* (New York: Basic Books), 177–99.

18. Ian G. Barbour, *Religion in an Age of Science* (San Francisco: HarperCollins, 1990), 105–6.

19. For a summary of this position on divine action, see Dennis Edwards, "The Discovery of Chaos and the Retrieval of the Trinity," in *Chaos and Complexity*, ed. Russell

et al., 157–75. Or see Robert J. Russell, "Does 'The God Who Acts' Really Act?" *Theology Today* 54, no. 1 (April 1997): 43–65; or idem, "Special Providence and Genetic Mutation: A New Defense of Theistic Evolution," in *Evolutionary and Molecular Biology: Scientific Perspectives on Divine Action,* ed. Robert J. Russell et al. (Vatican City State: Vatican Observatory Publications, 1998), 191–224.

20. Joseph Schumpeter, *Capitalism, Socialism, and Democracy* (New York: Harper, 1975), 82–83.

21. Bernard J. F. Lonergan, *Insight: A Study of Human Understanding,* rev. ed. (London: Longmans, Green, 1958), xiv.

22. Ibid., 228.

23. Ibid., 745.

24. Ibid., 628–29.

6. THE SPIRIT, PNEUMATOLOGY, AND HOMO VIATOR

1. Rowan Williams, *On Christian Theology* (Oxford: Blackwell, 2000), 114–15.

2. Catherine Mowry LaCugna, *God for Us: The Trinity and Christian Life* (San Francisco: Harper, 1991), 271.

3. The material on Richard of St. Victor and Bonaventure comes from Denis Edwards, "The Discovery of Chaos and the Retrieval of the Trinity," in *Chaos and Complexity: Scientific Perspectives on Divine Action,* ed. Robert J. Russell, Nancey Murphy, and Arthur R. Peacocke (Vatican City State: Vatican Observatory Publications, 1995), 158–61. See also Jürgen Moltmann, *The Trinity and the Kingdom* (San Francisco: Harper, 1991), 173–76; Elizabeth A. Johnson, *She Who Is: The Mystery of God in Feminist Theological Discourse* (New York: Crossroad, 1996), ch. 10; LaCugna, *God for Us,* chs. 7, 8.

4. LaCugna, *God for Us,* 228. See also Jürgen Moltmann, who states: "The Spirit does not merely bring about fellowship with himself. He himself issues from his fellowship with the Father and the Son, and the fellowship into which he enters with believers corresponds to his fellowship with the Father and the Son, and is therefore a *Trinitarian fellowship.* In the unity of the Father and the Son and the Holy Spirit, the triune God himself is open, inviting fellowship in which the whole creation finds room" (*Trinity and the Kingdom,* 218).

5. Michael Polanyi, *Personal Knowledge: Towards a Post-critical Philosophy* (New York: Harper & Row, 1964), 49–50.

6. Studs Terkel, "The Mason: Carl Murray Bates (An Interview)," in *Work and the Life of the Spirit,* ed. Douglas Thorpe (San Francisco: Mercury House, 1998), 209.

7. A biblical instance: "The Lord spoke to Moses: 'See I have called by name Bezalel son of Uri son of Hur, of the tribe of Judah: and I have filled him with the Spirit of God, with ability, intelligence, and knowledge in every kind of craft, to devise artistic designs, to work in gold, silver, and bronze, in cutting stones for setting, and in carving wood, in every kind of craft'" (Exod. 31:1–2).

8. David Pye, *The Nature and Art of Workmanship* (Cambridge: Cambridge University Press, 1971), 20.

9. Ibid., 34, 52.

10. On the verse, "Everyone as the Lord has assigned to him, everyone as the Lord has called him" (1 Cor. 7:17), Moltmann remarks: "Call and endowment, *klesis* and *charisma*, belong together, and are interchangeable terms. This meant that every Christian is a charismatic, even if many people never live out their gifts. . . . if we ask about the charismata of the Holy Spirit, we mustn't look for things we don't have. We must first of all discern who we are, what we are, and how we are at the point where we feel the touch of God in our lives" (*The Spirit of Life: A Universal Affirmation*, trans. Margaret Kohl [Minneapolis: Fortress, 1993], 180).

11. Dorothee Soelle, "Work as Self-Expression," in *Work and the Life of the Spirit*, ed. Thorpe, 56–57.

12. Arthur Miller, *Death of a Salesman* (New York: Viking Penguin, 1976), 82.

13. Michael Moore, *Downsize This! Random Threats from an Unarmed American* (New York: Harper Perennial, 1997), 13.

14. Ben Hamper, *Rivethead: Tales from the Assembly Line* (New York: Warner Books, 1991), 2–3.

15. Gary Stix, "How's My Driving," *Scientific American* 264, no. 4 (October 1991): 124.

16. The term was coined by Jeremy Bentham as a surveillance scheme for prisons; cited by Stanley Aronowitz and William DiFazio in *The Jobless Future: Sci-tech and the Dogma of Work* (Minneapolis: University of Minnesota Press, 1994), 89.

17. Alfie Kohn, *No Contest: The Case against Competition* (Boston: Houghton Mifflin Co., 1986), 3–5, 45–78.

18. From workshop material given by Daniel K. Oestreich on October 1, 1994.

19. Daniel K. Oestreich and Kathleen D. Ryan, *Driving Fear out of the Workplace: How to Overcome the Invisible Barriers to Quality, Productivity, and Innovation* (San Francisco: Jossey-Bass Publishers, 1991).

20. Richard Edwards, *Contested Terrain: The Transformation of the Workplace in the Twentieth Century* (New York: Basic Books, 1979), 85, 135, 209; Al Gini, *My Job, My Self: Work and the Creation of the Modern Individual* (New York: Routledge, 2001), 33.

21. Ibid., 133–34.

22. David M. Gordon argues that managerial downsizing is really not as true as popularly believed. As a segment of the workforce, the percentage of non-farm managers/supervisors has continued to increase from 12.6 percent in 1989 (when the downsizing supposedly began) to 13.6 percent in 1995 (*Fat and Mean: The Corporate Squeeze of Working Americans and the Myth of Managerial "Downsizing"* [New York: Free Press, 1996], ch. 2).

23. Michael Lerner, *Surplus Powerlessness: The Psychodynamics of Everyday Life and the Psychology of Individual and Social Transformation* (Atlantic Highlands, N.J.: Humanities Press International, 1986), ch. 3.

24. Moltmann, *Spirit of Life*, 125.

25. See Marilyn McCord Adams, *Horrendous Evils and the Goodness of God* (Ithaca, N.Y.: Cornell University Press, 1999), ch. 6.

26. Moltmann, *Spirit of Life*, 8, 34, 90.

27. Quoted in Jeffrey T. Nealon, *Alterity Politics: Ethics and Performative Subjectivity* (Durham, N.C.: Duke University Press, 1998), 36.

28. Emmanuel Levinas, *Entre Nous: Thinking-of-the-Other*, trans. Michael B. Smith and Barbara Harshaw (New York: Columbia University Press, 1998), 202.

29. See Richard Sennett, *The Corrosion of Character: The Personal Consequences of Work in the New Capitalism* (New York: W. W. Norton, 1998), 145.

30. Paul Ricoeur, *Oneself as Another*, trans. Kathleen Blamey (Chicago: University of Chicago Press, 1992), 165.

31. William J. Latzko and David M. Saunders, *Four Days with Dr. Deming: A Strategy for Modern Methods of Management* (Menlo Park: Addison-Wesley, 1995), 71–115.

32. Helen J. Alford and Michael J. Naughton, *Managing as if Faith Mattered: Christian Social Principles in the Modern Organization* (Notre Dame, Ind.: University of Notre Dame Press, 2001), 77–78.

33. Companies that have adopted Deming's methods include Tektronix, Hewlett-Packard, IBM, Ford, Bank of Chicago, Marriott, and Harley Davidson. Peter Drucker believes that the two traditionally antagonistic theories of management, the one favoring "human relations" and the one favoring Taylorist "scientific management" come together with Total Quality Management, because production is still rationalized, but without transforming workers into mere machine operators ("The Emerging Theory of Manufacturing," *Harvard Business Review* [May-June, 1990]: 65–75).

34. W. Edwards Deming, *Out of the Crisis* (Cambridge, Mass.: M.I.T. Press, 1991), ch. 2; Mary Walton, *The Deming Management Method* (New York: Dodd, Mead, & Co., 1986), 72–81.

35. Michael Welker, *God the Spirit*, trans. John F. Hoffmeyer (Minneapolis: Fortress Press, 1994), 157–58.

36. Frederick Herzberg, *Work and the Nature of Man* (Cleveland: World Publishing Company, 1966).

37. V. M. Bockman, "The Herzberg Controversy," *Personnel Psychology* 24 (1971): 155–89.

38. Gordon, *Fat and Mean*, 44, 74.

39. Robert M. Grant, Rami Shani, and R. Krishnan, "TQM's Challenge to Management Theory and Practice," *Sloan Management Review* 35, no.2 (Winter 1994): 34.

40. Walton, *Deming Management Method*, 221.

41. See, e.g., Wolfhart Pannenberg, *Systematic Theology*, vol. 1, trans. G. W. Bromiley (Grand Rapids: Eerdmans, 1991), 382–84; Welker, *God the Spirit*, 120, 227–28, 239, 242; Moltmann, *Spirit of Life*, 195.

42. Welker, *God the Spirit*, 242.

7. GOOD AND GODLY WORK

1. See, e.g., Tom Chappell, *The Soul of a Business: Managing for Profit and the Common Good* (New York: Bantam Books, 1993); Ian I. Mitroff and Elizabeth A. Denton,

A Spiritual Audit of Corporate America (San Francisco: Jossey-Bass, 1999); David Krueger, Donald W. Shriver, Jr., and Laura Nash, *The Business Corporation and Productive Justice* (Nashville: Abingdon Press, 1997); Herman E. Daly and John B. Cobb, Jr., *For the Common Good: Redirecting the Economy toward Community, the Environment, and a Sustainable Future*, 2nd ed. (Boston: Beacon Press, 1994); Helen J. Alford and Michael J. Naughton, *Managing as if Faith Mattered: Christian Social Principles in the Modern Organization* (Notre Dame, Ind.: University of Notre Dame Press, 2001); James M. Childs, Jr., *Ethics in Business: Faith at Work* (Minneapolis: Fortress Press, 1995); Paul Hawken, *The Ecology of Commerce: A Declaration of Sustainability* (New York: Harper Business, 1993).

2. *Icthys* in Greek is taken as an acronym for "Jesus Christ, Son of God Savior."

3. Alasdair MacIntyre, *After Virtue: A Study in Moral Theory*, 2nd ed. (Notre Dame, Ind.: University of Notre Dame Press, 1984), 188.

4. David Pye, *The Nature and Art of Workmanship*, rev. ed. (Cambridge: Cambridge University Press, 1995).

5. MacIntyre doesn't think bricklaying is a rich enough activity to qualify as a "practice," but I believe he is mistaken.

6. The notion and argument for "thick" terms comes from Bernard Williams, *Ethics and the Limits of Philosophy* (Cambridge, Mass.: Harvard University Press, 1985), 129–31, 140–55.

7. See Georg Henrik von Wright, *The Varieties of Goodness* (London: Routledge & Kegan Paul, 1963), 41–62.

8. Aristotle agrees. Aristotle's *Nicomachean Ethics* develops the concept of virtue on the analogy of skills (*technae*) found in the "crafts" (trans. H. Rackham [Cambridge, Mass.: Harvard University Press, 1934], bk 2. 1, 6).

9. See the remarks of John Milbank as reviewed in Stanley Hauerwas and Charles Pinches, *Christians among the Virtues: Theological Conversations with Ancient and Modern Ethics* (Notre Dame, Ind.: University of Notre Dame Press, 1997), 61–69.

10. *Summa Theologica*, vol. 23 (1a2ae 55–67), trans. W. D. Hughes (New York: Blackfriars with McGraw-Hill, 1969), 61–62.

11. Ibid.; see also vol. 31 (2a2ae.1–7), trans. T. C. O'Brien (New York: Blackfriars with McGraw Hill, 1974), 2.2.4; vol. 33 (2a2ae.17–22), trans. W. J. Hill (New York: Blackfriars with McGraw Hill, 1966), 2.2.17.1; vol. 34 (2a2ae.23–33), trans. R. J. Batten (Blackfriars with McGraw Hill, 1975), 2.2.23.3.

12. Hauerwas and Pinches, *Christians among the Virtues*, ch. 4. A good deal of this chapter reflects the thought of John Milbank.

13. Susan Wolf, "Moral Saints," in *Virtue Ethics*, ed. Roger Crisp and Michael Slote (Oxford: Oxford University Press, 1997), 79, 82.

14. James M. Gustafson and Elmer W. Johnson, "The Corporate Leader and the Ethical Resources of Religion: A Dialogue," in *The Judeo-Christian Vision and the Modern Corporation*, ed. Oliver F. Williams, C.S.C., and John W. Houck (Notre Dame, Ind.: University of Notre Dame Press, 1982), 310. See also MacIntyre, *After Virtue*, 204–5; and Hauerwas and Pinches, *Christians among the Virtues*, ch. 7.

15. E. F. Schumacher, *Good Work* (New York: Harper & Row, 1979), 23–65.

16. See Harvey Leibenstein, *Beyond Economic Man: A New Foundation for Micro-economics* (Cambridge, Mass.: Harvard University Press, 1976); idem, *Inside the Firm: The Inefficiencies of Hierarchy* (Cambridge, Mass.: Harvard University Press, 1987).

17. Michael Piore and Charles F. Sabel, *The Second Industrial Divide: Possibilities for Prosperity* (New York: Basic Books, 1984), 265–66.

18. Alford and Naughton, *Managing as if Faith Mattered*, 77.

19. W. Edwards Deming, *Quality, Productivity, and Competitive Position* (Cambridge: Massachusetts Institute of Technology, Center for Advanced Engineering Study, 1982).

20. Robert K. Massie, Jr., "Prophets to Profit," in *The Calling of the Laity: Verna Dozier's Anthology*, ed. Verna Dozier (Washington, D.C.: Alban Institute, 1988), 18–19. In fairness to the faculty at Harvard Business School, Massie indicates they were interested in imbuing a more morally based, listening style of management. Amitai Etzioni has written a strikingly similar complaint about Harvard Business School student arrogance while visiting there as an instructor in business ethics. See his "My Turn" column entitled "Money, Power, and Fame," in *Newsweek*, September 18, 1989, 10.

21. Linda C. Raeder, "Liberalism and the Common Good: A Hayekian Perspective on Communitarianism," *The Independent Review* 2, no. 4 (Spring 1998): 519–35.

22. Quoted in Daly and Cobb, *For the Common Good*, 139.

23. M. Douglas Meeks, *God the Economist: The Doctrine of God and Political Economy* (Minneapolis: Fortress Press, 1989), 110, 134, 143.

24. Ibid., 135–41.

25. Ibid., 146.

26. Ibid., 170–77.

27. For an account of how the American economy constructed a belief in insatiable needs, see Jeremy Rifkin, *The End of Work: The Decline of the Global Labor Force and the Dawn of the Post-market Era* (New York: G. P. Putnam's Sons, 1995), 19–25.

28. Alford and Naughton, *Managing as if Faith Mattered*, 160–61.

29. See, e.g., David A. Krueger, "The Business Corporation and Productive Justice in the Global Economy," in *The Business Corporation and Productive Justice*, ed. Max L. Stackhouse, Donald W. Shriver, Jr., and Laura Nash (Nashville: Abingdon Press, 1997). Other worthy attempts have been made to modify economic theory to a more godly model. See n. 1 above.

30. For an excellent example, see William Droel, *Full-Time Christians: The Real Challenge from Vatican II* (Mystic, Conn.: Twenty-third Publications, 2002); also *Initiatives in Support of Christians in the World*, a periodical of the National Center for the Laity, and other publications by this group; see also William E. Diehl, *The Monday Connection: A Spirituality of Competence, Affirmation, and Support in the Workplace* (San Francisco: HarperSanFrancisco, 1991); Pete Hammond et al., *The Marketplace Annotated Bibliography: A Christian Guide to Books on Work, Business, & Vocation* (Downers Grove, Ill.: InterVarsity Press, 2002).

31. Aidan Kavanagh, *On Liturgical Theology* (New York: Pueblo, 1984), 87–88.

32. Søren Kierkegaard, *Purity of Heart Is to Will One Thing*, trans. Douglas V. Steere, (New York: Harper & Row, 1984), 173–84.

33. Henry George Liddell and Robert Scott, *A Greek-English Lexicon*, rev. Henry Stuart Jones (Oxford: Clarendon Press, 1966), s.v. *leitourgia*, 1036.

8. TYING THEMES TOGETHER

1. See chapter 2, under "What One Cannot Be: Perfect."

2. Paul Tillich, *Dynamics of Faith* (New York: Harper & Row, 1958), ch. 3.

3. For a fuller discussion, see chapter 2, under "A Worker's Object of Contemplation"; and chapter 7, under "Skill."

4. For a fuller discussion, see chapter 7, under "Skill."

5. See, e.g., James Barr, *Biblical Faith and Natural Theology* (Oxford: Clarendon Press, 1993).

6. E.g., David Tracy, *The Analogical Imagination: Christian Theology and the Culture of Pluralism* (New York: Crossroad, 1981).

7. *Consonance* is a term coined and used in the literature of science and religion. It refers to instances where a religious belief is compatible (but not necessarily in exact agreement) with some aspect of a scientific theory. For example, the "big bang" might be thought consonant with *creatio ex nihilo*.

8. See the discussion of natural theology in chapter 5, under "An Apology for Natural Theology."

9. For a full treatment of this topic, see chapter 3, under "The Kingdom of God."

10. One of the best books I have found in this area of discussion is Thomas L. Shaffer's *Faith and the Professions* (Provo: Brigham Young University, 1987).

11. A fuller discussion can be found in chapter 3, under "The Public and the Private" and "Corporate Superpersonal Structures and the christus victor Atonement."

12. The periodical *Initiatives* is uniquely the best publication with this attitude. Its special contribution is a close and ongoing listing of the efforts churches are making toward secular lay occupations. It is published by the National Center for the Laity, P.O. Box 291102, Chicago, IL 60629.

13. A fuller discussion can be found in chapter 3, under "The Kingdom of God."

14. A fuller discussion can be found in chapter 1, under "The Impact of Women on Work."

15. Richard Swinburne's recent work reviews the traditional arguments for the existence of God, but argues that a Baysean argument will lead to a reasonable belief in God's existence (*The Existence of God* [Oxford: Oxford University Press, 1979]).

16. This term and the general ecosystem argument comes from Stuart Kauffman's *At Home in the Universe: The Search for Laws of Self-Organization and Complexity* (Oxford: Oxford University Press, 1995), ch. 10. Kauffman frequently invokes an "invisible hand" in the way ecosystems evolve and seek stability, but he views complexity as a self-organizing phenomenon. It is my belief that the "invisible hand" connotes a divine creative synergism.

17. A fuller discussion can be found in chapter 5.

18. Examples come mostly from *Scientific American* 287, no. 6 (December 2002): 54–83.

19. A fuller discussion can be found in chapter 4.

20. A fuller discussion can be found in chapter 6.

21. A fuller discussion can be found in chapter 7.

22. See chapter 7, under "Godly Work."

23. See, e.g., their compendium by Pete Hammond, R. Paul Stevens, and Todd Svanoe, *The Market Place Annotated Bibliography: A Christian Guide to Books on Work, Business, and Vocation* (Downers Grove, Ill.: InterVarsity Press, 2002).

24. This vision is especially well expressed by William Droel in *Full-Time Christians: The Real Challenge from Vatican II* (Mystic, Conn.: Twenty-third Publications, 2002). The theme gets a deeper theological expression in Paul Lakeland's *The Liberation of the Laity: In Search of an Accountable Church* (New York: Continuum, 2002).

Index